MW01518285

Another Generation of Fundamental Considerations in Language Assessment

Gary J. Ockey · Brent A. Green
Editors

Another Generation of Fundamental Considerations in Language Assessment

A Festschrift in Honor of Lyle F. Bachman

 Springer

Editors
Gary J. Ockey
Iowa State University
Ames, IA, USA

Brent A. Green
Brigham Young University–Hawaii
Laie, HI, USA

ISBN 978-981-15-8951-5   ISBN 978-981-15-8952-2   (eBook)
https://doi.org/10.1007/978-981-15-8952-2

This Springer imprint is published by the registered company Springer Nature Singapore Pte Ltd.
The registered company address is: 152 Beach Road, #21-01/04 Gateway East, Singapore 189721, Singapore

Forward: "It's Been a Great Ride!"

It is a pleasure for me to write the *Forward* to this Festschrift honoring Lyle F. Bachman, who has been my colleague and co-author since 1971 when our early academic career paths crossed in Bangkok, Thailand. Because Lyle's academic career spans 50 years and spreads over a variety of domains, trying to do justice to the breadth and importance of his professional contributions is quite a challenge. Nevertheless, it is one I am happy to accept.

In this *Forward*, I will first provide a brief overview of Lyle's career path. I follow this overview with a summary of the scope and impact of his scholarship. Finally, I provide a historical commentary on Lyle as an academic visionary by describing how his work has influenced me and the field of language testing.

Lyle's Career Path

Lyle's university studies did not initially lead him in the direction of language testing. Lyle received his A.B. and M.A. degrees in *English*, and his Ph.D. degree in *English Language* from Indiana University in 1965, 1969, and 1971, respectively. His early teaching career began as a high school English as a Second Language teacher in the Peace Corps in the Republic of the Philippines. After completing his service in the Peace Corps, he returned to Indiana to work on his Ph.D. Although he began his doctoral studies in American literature, he fairly quickly gravitated to medieval English literature, and from there to linguistics and English linguistics. However, his teaching experience in the Philippines had kindled an interest in second language learning, and he conducted his dissertation research in Thailand studying the acquisition of English as a second language by Thai elementary and secondary school students. While in graduate school he also taught freshman literature and introduction to the English language. He then took his first academic position at the University of Hawai'i at Manoa, where he taught introduction to language, modern English syntax, Old English, and sophomore literature.

Lyle has said on more than one occasion that he was more or less "dropped" into the field of language testing. In 1971, he accepted a position as "Project Specialist in Psycholinguistics" with The Ford Foundation in Bangkok, Thailand, where he worked on research and development projects for 5 years. His first assignment was to oversee the development and administration of language tests for placement and achievement at the Central Institute of English Language. (It was during this time that he and I first met and began what became a nearly 40-year-long collaboration in research and writing.) Lyle's on-the-job learning about language testing led him to the library and to the discovery of works on language testing by Robert Lado and John B. Carroll, two scholars whose work in contrastive linguistics and psycholinguistics had informed his dissertation research. Lyle has said that he was fortunate to have been able to work on research projects with Carroll, and to have had an ongoing scholarly exchange with him over the years. He credits a great deal of the conceptualization in his book, *Fundamental Considerations in Language Testing* (Bachman, 1990), to his interactions with Carroll. While in Thailand, he was also co-director of a 5-year longitudinal R&D project to implement an individualized language learning curriculum for Thai elementary school children. In order to conduct the ongoing monitoring and evaluation of this project, he learned how to use statistics, including multiple linear regression and factor analysis.

From 1976 to 1979, Lyle directed the University of Illinois TEFL Internship Program, in Tehran, Iran, where he supervised the graduate internship program, taught MA-level courses, supervised the development and implementation of an ESP reading syllabus and teaching materials, and oversaw budgeting and planning for the program. When he completed his assignment in Iran, he took a full-time position at the University of Ilinois at Urbana-Champaign (UIUC) before moving on to assume the academic position he held at the University of California, Los Angeles (UCLA) until his retirement in 2012. While a professor at UCLA, he served as Chair of the Department of Applied Linguistics for several years. He also held interim positions at The Chinese University of Hong Kong, Jiaxing University in Jiaxang, China, and the Akademie für Lehrerfortbildung und Personalführung in Dillingen, Germany.

An Overview of Lyle's Scholarship and Professional Achievements

Lyle's scholarly work includes 41 journal articles and reviews, 32 chapters in books, 13 books, 15 research instruments and reports, and 139 presentations at conferences and meetings. The scope of his work spans several disciplines, including second language acquisition, language test validation, tests of communicative competence, theories of language performance, school-based language ability assessment, web-based language assessment, justifying the development and use of language assessments, and conceptual frameworks for developing and using classroom-based assessments. He supervised over 30 Ph.D. students (and numerous M.A. students) in language testing while at UIUC and UCLA. In addition, Lyle has directly influenced a wide variety of institutions through the 64 consultancies that he accepted in academic, educational, professional, and public domains in the United States and around the world. Lyle also served as Co-editor (with Charles Alderson) of *Language Testing* for 5 years, and as co-editor (with Charles Alderson) of the *Cambridge Language Assessment Series*.

Lyle has received 18 different honors and awards from educational institutions, government agencies, and professional/scholarly associations, which testify to the impact of his work and the esteem with which he is held in our profession. These major awards span more than 45 years and include two Mildenberger Prizes (Modern Language Association of America), one in 1990 for *Fundamental Considerations in Language Testing* and one in 1996 for *Language Testing in Practice* (with A. Palmer). In 2010, he and his co-author (A. Palmer) received the ILTA-SAGE award for the best book published in language testing. Lyle has also served as President of two major professional organizations—the American Association of Appflied Linguists (AAAL) and the International Language Testing Association (ILTA). Both associations recognized him with their highest award for scholarship and service, ILTA with the Lifetime Achievement Award in 2004 and AAAL in 2010 with the Distinguished Scholarship and Service Award.

Lyle's Vision for Language Testing

When I look back over the field of language testing for the last 60 years, a number of major contributions stand out for me. When I consider these contributions individually, I see that many of them involve Lyle and his vision for the field of language testing, including his contributions to LTRC, the nature of language ability, the structure of assessment tasks, qualities of useful language tests, components of language use, the Assessment Use Argument, (AUA), assessment justification, and software for the design and development of language tests.

The Beginning of the Language Testing Research Colloquium (LTRC)

Lyle helped launch LTRC in 1979 and kept it going for many years by chairing and co-chairing 10 LTRC meetings. He also played a pivotal role in guiding LTRC from an independent annual colloquium as it transitioned to become the annual meeting for ILTA. The history of LTRC and ILTA and the role that Lyle played in these institutions have already been well documented (https://www.iltaonline.com/page/History).

From the very beginning of LTRC, Lyle and the other founders believed that it should play both an academic and a social role. Lyle has often said that in fulfilling its academic role, it would be a place where senior scholars in language testing could identify the major theoretical and practical concerns of the field and then engage in rigorous discussions and debates relative to these concerns. Lyle often reminded us that LTRC was also a venue for encouraging and welcoming new scholars to the field, and this was long before there was a cadre of graduate students in language testing attending LTRC. In fulfilling its social role, LTRC also encouraged and welcomed the informal exchange of ideas and provided an occasion for scholars to have fun with and enjoy others who had the same passion for language testing. Considerable information has been compiled about the social dimension of LTRC (https://www.iltaonline.com/page/History).

The Nature of Language Ability

One of the main theoretical issues facing language testers in the 1970s was whether language ability was a unitary trait or partially divisible traits. Oller and Hinofotis (Oller, 1976; Oller & Hinofotis, 1980) were making strong claims about and providing research support for the Unitary Trait theory, while other researchers had equally strong beliefs about the divisibility of the language ability trait. This distinction between the unitary and divisible trait views of language ability was important not only to researchers interested in theories of language ability but also to language testers trying to develop tests consistent with theoretical frameworks. Which framework should they follow?

Working with members of the early LTRC's, Lyle designed two major studies. The first aimed to answer the question of the viability of a unitary trait theory of language ability. The results of this first study, which Lyle and I conducted together (Bachman & Palmer, 1981), answered the research question by showing that a unitary theory of language ability did not provide a model that fit the data in the study.

These results led to a second study to investigate the construct validity of a variety of tests constructed specifically based on a language ability framework (communicative competence) proposed by Canale and Swain (1980). This theoretical framework made the implicit claim that tests of different components of communicative competence measured different abilities. The results of this study, which Lyle and I again conducted together (Bachman & Palmer, 1982), indicated that the model that best explained the trait structure of the data included a general factor and two specific trait factors: grammatical/pragmatic competence and sociolinguistic competence. The results also showed the relative influence of language ability and test method factors on the scores of tests used in the study. As a result of these two studies, the unitary trait hypothesis was largely dismissed by the language testing field. The last 40 years of research have only further confirmed that Lyle was right—language ability is multidimensional.

The Structure of Assessment Tasks

In his 1990 book, *Fundamental Considerations in Language Testing*, Lyle built upon Carroll's (1968) and Clark's (1972) taxonomies of factors affecting performance on language tests to create a framework of test method facets (characteristics). This framework provided a structure for describing the characteristics of the methods used to elicit performance on language test tasks, and that thus could be used both by researchers and by test designers and users. When I first saw Lyle's framework, it struck me that language testers now had a tool as useful for language testers as are widely used standard frameworks for describing the characteristics of speech sounds for phoneticians and teachers of pronunciation.

Qualities of Useful Language Tests

The period preceding *Language Testing in Practice* (Bachman & Palmer, 1996) saw a proliferation of proposed qualities of language test usefulness, which at one time numbered at least 30, including 25 different types of validity—an unusable number by any measure. Bachman and Palmer's seven carefully defined qualities formed a teachable and learnable basis for the evaluation of test usefulness of language and helped inform the qualities of outcomes of claims in his later Assessment Use Argument (see below).

Components of Language Use

To make a case for the generalizability of performance on a language assessment to performance in non-testing situations, one needs to be able to compare the characteristics of language use when performing *language assessment tasks* to the characteristics of *real-world language use tasks* in the target language use domain of test takers. Doing so requires a way to characterize the components of language *use* that go beyond the areas of language *knowledge* (organizational/pragmatic and sociolinguistic) frequently used by language testers when developing language tests. Bachman's Components of Language Use (Bachman 1990; Bachman & Palmer, 1996, 2010) provides just such a framework. Moreover, Bachman's framework awakens students' appreciation of non-language-specific components of language use while avoiding overwhelming them with complexity. For example, it uses terms such as "topical knowledge," "personal attributes," "goal setting," and "planning" that students can easily relate to from their personal experience with language use.

The Assessment Use Argument

Lyle introduced his Assessment Use Argument (AUA) at LTRC in 2004 on the occasion of his LTRC lifetime achievement award lecture. Here is how Lyle presented his case for an Assessment Use Argument:

> By articulating an assessment use argument, test developers and test users alike can arrive at a much clearer and more transparent conceptualization of decisions and inferences they intend to make on the basis of an assessment, of the ways in which these uses and inferences need to be justified, and the kinds of evidence they need to collect in order to support the intended uses and inferences. An assessment use argument can thus not only guide the design and development of assessments, but it can also lead to a much more focused, efficient program for collecting the most critical evidence (backing) in support of the inferences and uses for which the assessment is intended (Bachman, 2004, p. 32).

Lyle's initial AUA proposal was based on Stephen Toulmin's (2003) argument structure consisting of claims, warrants, backing, and rebuttals. More importantly, Lyle proposed an overall argument structure that consisted of four linked, stacked argument structures: Use/Decisions, Interpretations, Results, and Performance on Assessment Tasks. Lyle's innovative combining of Toulmin argument structures by stacking them sequentially one upon another provided the basis for Assessment Justification, which ultimately evolved into a fully developed structure for justifying language assessment design, development, and use.

When Lyle and I wrote our first book, *Language Testing in Practice* (Bachman & Palmer, 1996), we described the usefulness of language tests in terms of relatively traditional qualities, such as reliability, construct validity, and authenticity. As useful as these qualities were in and of themselves, we did not provide a structure that showed how the qualities built upon and were related to one another.

When Lyle described the structure of his Assessment Use Argument for the first time at LTRC in Temecula, CA, I finally saw how the qualities were related to one another categorically and sequentially and how they "added up" to test usefulness. Lyle's AUA was so easy to understand and made so much sense that I said to myself, "I can't believe what I've just seen. This changes everything!" Although I have had the privilege of being present at a number of "game-changing" professional presentations in the last 55 years, nothing had ever struck me with the impact of Lyle's AUA. From that moment on, I have believed that test developers, test users, and students of language testing would forever look at the usefulness of language tests in a very different way and that the process of justification would actually make sense to them. (I confess that I have often been confused by justification systems I have encountered on the way to encountering Lyle's AUA.) I feel the same way about the importance of Lyle's AUA today in 2020 as I first felt at LTRC in Temecula in 2004.

Justification

I can present Lyle's contribution to justification best if I briefly describe the path Lyle and I took when we wrote our second book, *Language Assessment in Practice* (LAIP) (Bachman & Palmer, 2010). We knew that our first book, LTIP, needed revising and decided to do so and, in the process, add a chapter on justification. We ground away through the revision for probably 2 years, but the book as a whole seemed to lack a sense of direction. Then one day, Lyle said, "Why don't we start over, beginning with justification." I said, "sure," knowing that we'd be letting go of much of 2 years work in doing so. As has always been the case, Lyle considered getting it right more important than saving time.

Starting with justification meant far more than moving chapters around. After all, we had dealt with pieces of justification to some extent in our previous book, *Language Testing in Practice,* in the chapter on the logical evaluation of usefulness. However, in our new book, justification became a single structure that *from the outset* guided the many choices/decisions made in designing and using language tests. So, for example, if a student asked us why we defined a construct in a certain way, instead of hunting through the qualities of usefulness, a chapter on defining constructs, another chapter on logical evaluation of usefulness, and then using all of this material to justify our construct definition, we could point to the relevant warrant of the Assessment Use Argument and say, "This explains why." When we design language tests, these "why" questions are continuous and wide-ranging, and starting with justification provides a place to answer all of these "why" questions and, in the process, systematically guide the design, development, and use of the tests. So, Lyle was right. We needed to start with justification.

Our process resulted in a comprehensive framework for assessment design, development, and use, comprising processes, products, and justification. This framework (Bachman & Palmer, 2010) provided a structure that could enable test developers to justify and document the process of assessment development that would meet the needs of their particular assessment use situations, such as making interpretations about the effectiveness of instruction, rather than necessarily relying upon tests developed by others for different situations, such as for making college admission decisions.

The Contribution of Software

In writing *Language Assessment in Practice*, Lyle and I had to figure out how all of the components of the test development process fit together, and we did the best we could to describe this fit in the linear, fixed format that printed text imposes. However, using the information presented in our book in a frequently iterative, non-linear way was quite different from reading about it, and some students, and maybe other readers as well, either got lost in the process or found the print format too complicated to use.

Lyle was very aware of the difficulty of using the material in book format to actually guide the process of test design and development, and one day he tossed off the comment, "I'll bet software would make this a lot easier." After 6 years of hard work, this software has finally been developed (Palmer & Dixon, 2017). The use of this software more than confirms the wisdom of Lyle's initial suggestion. It provides test developers with templates needed to document the process of test design, development, and use while also managing the many hundreds of links among parts of the documents that a test developer or a student learning how to design language tests now does not have to keep track of. The response to the software has been very positive; in fact, students in Palmer's Introduction to L2 Test Design absolutely love it (Palmer, Dixon, & Christison, 2018).

Conclusion

This Festschrift is a fitting tribute to Lyle's contributions to the profession of language testing because the chapters are written by his former graduate students. In a metaphorical sense, the authors of the chapters are including you in Lyle's professional journey because the way in which they view language testing reflects not only Lyle's overall influence but also the stages in Lyle's career in which they studied under him. In fact, when his students meet socially, they often characterize their experiences with Lyle in terms of when they studied with him, for example, the "construct years," the "qualities years," or the "AUA years." Lyle has always considered working with graduate students to be a privilege, so to see the work of his graduate students in this Festschrift will please him enormously. It is a fitting tribute to the energy he put into his mentoring.

Personally, I have considered working with Lyle to be an enormous opportunity, but even more than that. Recently, when we were reflecting on our long collaboration and friendship, Lyle said, "It's been a great ride!" And, I agree; it most certainly has.

Adrian S. Palmer
University of Utah, Salt Lake City, USA

References

Bachman, L. F. (1990). *Fundamental considerations in language testing.* Oxford, England: Oxford University Press.

Bachman, L. F. (2004). Building and supporting a case for test utilization. ILTA Lifetime Achievement Award Lecture, 26th Annual Language Testing Research Colloquium, Temecula, California, March 28, 2004.

Bachman, L. F. & Palmer, A. S. (1981). The construct validation of the FSI oral interview. *Language Learning, 31*(1), 67–86.

Bachman, L. F. & Palmer, A. S. (1982). The construct validation of some components of communicative proficiency. *TESOL Quarterly 16*(4), 449–65.

Bachman, L. F. & Palmer, A. S. (1996). *Language testing in practice*. Oxford, England: Oxford University Press.

Bachman, L. & Palmer, A. (2010). *Language assessment in practice*. Oxford, England: Oxford University Press.

Canale, M., & Swain, M. (1980). Theoretical bases of communicative approaches to second language teaching and testing. *Applied Linguistics 1* (1), 47.

Carrol, J. B. (1968). The psychology of language testing. In A. Davies (Ed.) *Language testing symposium. A psycholinguistic perspective* (pp. 46–69). London: Oxford University Press.

Clark, J. L. D. (1972). *Foreign language testing: Theory and practice*. Philadelphia, PA: Center for Curriculum Development, Inc.

Oller, J. W. (1976). Evidence of a general language proficiency factor: An expectancy grammar. *Die Neuren Sprachen, 7*(6), 165–74.

Oller, J. W., & Hinofotis, F. B. (1980). Two mutually exclusive hypotheses about second language ability: Indivisible and partly divisible competence. In J. W. Oller & K. Perkins (Eds). *Research in language testing* (pp.13–23). Rowley, MA: Newbury House.

Palmer, A., & Dixon, D. H. (2017). *Test-ifize: Software for language assessment design, development, and use*. Published on Microsoft Office 365 https://pdenterprises.sharepoint.com/sites/AUA/Assessment%20Use%20Argument/Forms/AllItems.aspx.

Palmer, A., Dixon, D. H., & Christison, M. A. (2018). Discovery learning and the contribution of software to the teaching of language test design and development. Paper presented for the Language Learning Roundtable, 40th Annual Language Testing Research Colloquium (LTRC), July 2, 2018. Auckland, New Zealand.

Toulmin, S. E. (2003). *The uses of argument* (updated ed.). Cambridge, England: Cambridge University Press.

Foreword: Some Reflections on Mentoring Ph.D. Students

When I first heard about plans that were being made for holding a conference in my honor, I was truly overwhelmed. I was honored to think that my former students wanted to do this. At the same time, I was a little skeptical about whether it would actually happen, given all of the busy schedules, and the distances involved for people to attend. Then, in June 2016, at the Language Testing Research Colloquium in Palermo, Barbara and I hosted a UCLA get-together, and we started some concrete planning for a conference in Salt Lake City. The former students who were there asked me what I'd like to hear at the conference. I said, "This conference isn't about me, it's about you. I don't want to listen to a bunch of "Lyle" stories and reminiscences. That's in the past. If you really want to honor me, I want to hear what you're doing, about your current research interests, your projects, your plans, work-in-progress, completed research, whatever you are currently passionate about." The presentations that were given at that conference were more than I could have hoped for. Equally so with the papers that are included in this collection.

Introduction

Since the presentations at the Salt Lake City conference and the papers in this collection arose from the fact that you all were mentored by me, and that this was an okay experience, I thought I would share with you my own evolution as a mentor, and how I arrived at where I was when I was working with all of you. I will begin with my own experience as a Ph.D. student. Then I will talk about my early experiences as a Ph.D. advisor at the University of Illinois. Next I will discuss my experience advising Ph.D. students at UCLA, and how my approach to mentoring evolved over the years there. Then, I will discuss some of the lessons I learned about mentoring Ph.D. students. Finally, I will offer some concluding thoughts about my experience and about mentoring Ph.D. students.

My Own Experience as a Ph.D. Student

As most of my former students know, I did my Ph.D. at Indiana University in the Department of English. My first intellectual loves were philosophy and medieval English literature, but I had a gifted teacher in a course on the history of the English language, who kindled an interest in the language itself. As a result, in addition to courses in English literature, I took courses in linguistics: historical linguistics, Indo-European linguistics, phonetics, phonology, and syntax. So by the time I was ready to start a dissertation, I was in a quandary as to which direction to go—literature or linguistics. I was pretty sure I didn't want to spend a year in the bowels of the university library perusing arcane minutiae of literary criticism (I'd spent a summer as a research assistant digging out publication dates of W. D. Howell's writings for the critical edition of his work), nor did I fancy conducting linguistic fieldwork describing a dying Scottish dialect on some remote island in the North Sea, which was "the dream gig" of one of my professors. And even though I had been encouraged by another of my professors to use transformational grammar to untangle the meaning of Shakespearean sonnets, I was not convinced that this was a meaningful approach to literature. From my experience teaching English as a foreign language in the Philippines as a Peace Corps Volunteer, I had gotten interested in second language acquisition (SLA), which was still, in late 1960s, a nascent field. So I applied for and received a grant to spend a year doing my Ph.D. research in Thailand studying the acquisition of English by Thai school children.

My graduate advisor, whose primary area of research was English syntax, agreed to continue working with me, despite the fact that he knew very little about SLA. Furthermore, as a result of my decision to conduct my research overseas, I found myself working essentially on my own in Thailand, receiving very little feedback from my advisor. I would finish a chapter and send it off to him, and I would never hear anything from him. (These were the days when people still corresponded by aerogrammes and post, difficult as this is to imagine nowadays.) So I'd send him the next chapter, and the same thing—nothing from him. By the end of the 10 months for which I was funded, I'd finished three chapters and sent them off to my advisor. I had collected all of my data, and had transcribed all of the spoken protocols I had collected. When I returned to Indiana the next summer to finish analyzing my data and writing up the results, I asked my advisor, "Why didn't you ever give me any feedback while I was in Thailand?" He replied, "I wanted you to keep writing. I wasn't there to guide you, and I was afraid that if I sent your chapters back with lots of comments and suggestions, you'd stop writing new material." Which, at the time, I thought made good sense, but which later, after years of mentoring experience, I realized was probably a rationalization. So, as a Ph.D. student, I worked basically on my own with very little feedback from my advisor. Although I did finish my dissertation under these conditions, I did not feel that this was the most effective way for a Ph.D. advisor to mentor students.

My Early Experience as a Ph.D. Advisor at Illinois

After finishing my Ph.D. I spent several years overseas, during which time I began to specialize in language testing. I took a position as Assistant Professor in the Division of English as a Second language (later renamed the Division of English as an International Language, DEIL) at the University of Illinois, Champaign-Urbana (UIUC). I first served as Director of a UIUC Curriculum Research and Development project at the University of Tehran. Subsequently, I moved to Urbana-Champaign, where I served as a member of the UIUC faculty. DEIL didn't have its own Ph.D. program, so I initially served on dissertation committees in other departments, primarily Educational Psychology and the Applied Linguistics section of the Linguistics Department. After working with Ph.D. students as a committee member for 2 or 3 years, I started directing dissertations, but could not serve officially as committee chair. During this time I basically worked with students in other departments. Most dissertations were in areas other than language testing, e.g., program evaluation, second language reading, and bilingual education. A few were in language testing, looking at "integrative" language tests, e.g., cloze and dictation, or applications of item response theory. Basically, I was working one-on-one with individual students as a dissertation director.

Although I was gaining experience in mentoring Ph.D. students, it was a different kind of experience while I was at Illinois, a personal experience, that had a greater influence on my evolution as a mentor. In the neighborhood where I lived, I had two neighbors, both of whom were in the physical sciences at UIUC. One was a professor of chemistry and the other was a Ph.D. student in physics. We frequently discussed the differences between our disciplines in how graduate students were mentored. In the social sciences, humanities, and education, the model was essentially individual students working with individual professors. In the physical sciences, however, the model was very different, with groups of students in working groups, or laboratories, all working collaboratively on research projects under the direction of one or more professors.

UCLA

In 1988, I received an offer I could not refuse to join the faculty of the Department of Applied Linguistics at the University of California, Los Angeles (UCLA). One of my main reasons, other than the weather, of course, for moving to UCLA was to be able to work with my own Ph.D. students. At UCLA, my evolution as a mentor occurred in three phases: (1) my early years at UCLA, (2) the years immediately following a leave of absence in Hong Kong, and (3) the establishment of the Language Assessment Laboratory (LASSLAB).

Phase 1: Early Years at UCLA

When I arrived at UCLA, there was one student in language testing who had already started the program with a professor who subsequently decided to leave UCLA. During my first year, I taught three seminars and one survey course in the area of language testing. The seminars were attended largely by students who were still deciding what area of applied linguistics they wanted to focus on, and wanted to find out something about language testing and, of course, to check out the new professor on the block. Some of these students did, indeed, choose language testing after taking some courses with me. Later, a few more students joined the program specifically to work in language testing. However, there were relatively few students in language testing, all basically working individually with me, but informally interacting with each other.

Phase 2: After My Return from Hong Kong

I took a leave of absence from UCLA for 2 years to teach at the Chinese University of Hong Kong (CUHK). Serving as a chair professor at CUHK and working with colleagues in other universities and in the Department of Education was a broadening experience. However, I had no opportunity to work with Ph.D. students, and so was eager to return to UCLA at the end of my contract with CUHK. When I returned to UCLA, there were still two students in language testing from before I went to Hong Kong, and two new students who had been admitted while I was there. However, reflecting on my own experience as a Ph.D. student with virtually no mentoring, and my experience at both Illinois and UCLA as an isolated mentor working with individual students, I realized I would not be happy to continue mentoring students just one-on-one, as this provided no structure for students to learn from each other.

I wanted to find a more effective way to mentor Ph.D. students, so I read the research literature on the nature of expertise, and how this develops as learners evolve from novices to experts. I also read extensively about the effectiveness of collaborative learning. I remembered my neighbors in Illinois, the chemistry professor and the physics student, and looked to the physical sciences as a model: a working group, or laboratory, with students and professors working collaboratively and interactively on research projects and on their own research.

Phase 3: LASSLAB

In order to implement my idea for establishing a working group, or laboratory, I admitted several new students the year after I returned from Hong Kong. These plus the continuing students formed the "critical mass" needed to establish a working group, or laboratory, which I called the "Language Assessment Laboratory" (LASSLAB). The basic concept that informed LASSLAB was twofold:

- *collaborative learning*: students would work together on joint research projects, would discuss assignments and projects for their classes, or their own individual research;

- *developing expertise*: more advanced students (near-experts) would mentor beginning students (novices) in the content relevant to their research. Students would develop knowledge and skills together, and would develop expertise in mentoring by mentoring.

Thus, LASSLAB consisted of a continuum of Ph.D. and M.A. students, with the students who had been in the program longer and had more expertise mentoring the newer students. LASSLAB group activities included:

- regular team meetings as part of project development;
- regular group meetings to discuss students' individual research and to rehearse conference presentations;
- group planning of topics for advanced seminars;
- mentoring of new students by more advanced students, either one-on-one or in groups, typically concerning material related to specific courses they were taking;
- one-on-one mentoring of individual students with me.

What I Learned about Mentoring Ph.D. Students

What did I learn about mentoring from all of these experiences over the years? The most important lesson is that one approach to mentoring does not fit all. Each Ph.D. student is unique in his or her background, interests, configuration of knowledge and skills, and needs. Irrespective of their background and prior preparation, Ph.D. students all have times of self-doubt, uncertainty, and sometimes anxiety. At these times, they need your support. Likewise, Ph.D. students all have moments, and sometimes long stretches, of brilliance and energy, when it's best to let them run with their ideas, with minimal support and monitoring.

I also developed some guiding principles.

- Always let your students know that they have your support and your respect.
- Always let your students know that you care not only about their research, but also about them as individuals, as human beings.
- Humbly recognize and freely acknowledge that as your students develop from novice to expert, they become more knowledgeable than you are in the area of research they are investigating. As this happens, you become their student, their mentee.

Conclusion

I have been truly blessed to have been able to work with students like all of you. With bright, motivated students who have a clear view of what they want to do, it is hard to go wrong with mentoring. As you grew from novices to experts, I became a learner, which enriched my own professional knowledge and expertise. Working with all of you as students and seeing you now as colleagues—accomplished scholar/researchers—has enriched my life immensely. The student–mentor relationship is for a lifetime, and I thank you all for being my students, my colleagues, and my friends.

Lyle F. Bachman
Professor Emeritus
University of California, Los Angeles, USA

Acknowledgements

Editing this book has been our pleasure. It has given us an opportunity to honor Professor Bachman and show him a bit of appreciation for all that he did while we were formally his students and for his continued support over the years. He also read and gave feedback on many parts of the book. Our biggest acknowledgement goes to him. Thank you for everything you have done to positively impact the writings in this book and our professional lives. We also got to renew and strengthen relationships with our University of California, Los Angeles classmates, who contributed to this book. In addition to writing a chapter for the book, each read multiple chapters and provided feedback on our and others' papers. We appreciate your efforts in making this project happen. Adrian (Buzz) Palmer was also very instrumental in making this book happen. He worked on the *Forward* for the book relentlessly, trying to do justice to Lyle's contribution to the field of language assessment. As has been the case over the decades, Buzz deflected credit away from himself in writing the *Forward*. Lyle and both of us had to push hard for him to even take a little of the credit for what he and Lyle accomplished over the years. Thanks Buzz! You deserve a lot of credit for the success of this book as well as the co-authored work between you and Lyle that is heavily cited in this book. We also wish to recognize Roz Hirch, a graduate student at Iowa State University. She helped us chase down reviews, revised papers, etc., and she helped in assembling the book and keeping the project on track. Without her efforts in keeping us focused, this book would likely still be a pipedream. Thank you Roz! Finally, we wish to acknowledge the editors at Springer. They were very supportive throughout the entire process.

Contents

Chapter 1
Introduction

Brent A. Green and Gary J. Ockey

Professor Bachman has been one of the leading second language assessment experts in the field for decades. His seminal book, *Fundamental Considerations in Language Testing* (1990), played a major role in helping second language testing become its own discipline. His subsequent signature books: *Language Testing in Practice* (1996), *Language Assessment in Practice* (2010), and his most recent, *Language Assessment for Practicing Teachers* (2018) have had, and will continue to have, a profound impact on the theory and practice of language testing. He trained a number of language assessment researchers in his years at the University of Illinois, Urbana Champaign and the University of California, Los Angeles. Many of these students have gone on to become leaders in the field, in both testing companies and institutes of higher education. Some are book authors, journal editors, and/or have played important roles in developing high stakes language assessments for various contexts and regions of the world. The purpose of this Festschrift is to share some of the work of this group who were trained by Lyle and to honor him through their work.

On June 1 and 2, 2017, 21 of Lyle's former students, close friends, and family members (Lyle's wife, Barbara and his daughter, Tina) gathered in Salt Lake City, Utah, USA for a conference convened to honor Lyle. The title of the conference, *Fundamental Considerations in Language Testing*, seems fitting to honor a man who had spent most of his academic career focusing on language testing fundamentals (see Fundamental Consideration in Language Testing, 2017). A total of 21 presentations were given over those 2 days including one from Lyle about mentoring students, and an introduction to the life and work of Lyle given by his close lifelong friend and colleague, Adrian Palmer. The conference was filled with amazing papers,

B. A. Green (✉) · G. J. Ockey
Brigham Young University–Hawaii, Laie, HI, USA
e-mail: brent.green@byuh.edu

G. J. Ockey
Iowa State University, Ames, IA, USA
e-mail: gockey@iastate.edu

© Springer Nature Singapore Pte Ltd. 2020
G. J. Ockey and B. A. Green (eds.), *Another Generation of Fundamental Considerations in Language Assessment*, https://doi.org/10.1007/978-981-15-8952-2_1

compelling conversations, dinners in rustic mountain locations, and opportunities to reunite with friends and classmates. On the last day during lunch, the discussion of compiling the conference papers into a Festschrift to share some of the excellent scholarly work that we had enjoyed and to honor Lyle was commenced. The work presented in this volume is the fruition of that discussion. It includes Adrian's introduction, Lyle's presentation on mentoring, and 12 papers which pay homage to Lyle, his mentoring, and his work by sharing some of the innovative research that he inspired his former students to conduct.

In this edited volume, the aim is to provide a transparent discussion of some of the current issues in second language assessment. Included are both theoretical papers on current issues and practical research examples investigating some of these issues. The part that runs through all of the papers relates to constructs that language assessment researchers aim to measure. As many in the language testing world know, Lyle was the consummate construct man. Throughout his time as our mentor, he made certain that his students understood the importance of constructs in language assessment. It was an important aspect of our training, and we all got it. In fact, in one conference presentation in the early 2000s, one of his graduate students said the following during her presentation, "Of course, I am Lyle's student, so I am going to define the constructs." At another conference in the early 2000s, we observed Lyle respond to a paper which seemed to have lost its "construct" bearings. In fact, there were no constructs being defined in this body of work. In his prepared response, he wondered aloud, while alluding to a popular song in the 1960s, "where had all the constructs gone." Replacing "flowers" with "constructs" was the point Lyle was keen on making, and the message has been clear to language testing researchers at that time and ever since.

In 2010, Bachman and Palmer stated the following about constructs:

> …we can consider a construct to be the specific definition of an ability that provides the basis for a given assessment or assessment task and for interpreting scores derived from this task. The construct definition for a particular assessment situation becomes the basis for the kinds of interpretations we can make for the assessment performance. In designing, developing, and using language assessments, we can define the construct from a number of perspectives, including everything from the content of a particular part of a language course to a needs analysis of the components of language ability that may be required to perform language use tasks in a target language use domain, to a theoretical model of language ability. (p. 43)

Throughout his storied career in language assessment, Lyle has been a strong promoter of construct definitions and the key role those definitions play in the ways language tests are designed, interpreted, and used to make decisions about test takers.

For our text, construct is reflected in three parts: assessment of evolving language ability constructs, validity and validation of language assessments, and understanding internal structures of language assessments. Given the emphasis Lyle has placed on constructs throughout his academic career, it seems fitting that we would organize this book along these core construct parts.

As with most edited books, the chapters can be read in any order. None are dependent on any other. The chapters follow a similar structure with the aim of making the book transparent and coherent. The conceptual chapters begin with an introduction, which shows how they are related to Bachman's work. The introduction is followed by Constructs; Historical Perspectives; Critical Issues; and Conclusions, Implications, and Future Directions sections. The empirical chapters follow a traditional research paper approach with an Introduction which connects the work to Bachman's, followed by a Literature Review, and Methods, Results, and Discussion sections, and finishing with a Conclusions, Implications, and Future Directions section. The reader may notice that many of the chapters focus on the speaking skill. This is because the speaking construct is rapidly evolving in applied linguistics (Galaczi & Taylor, 2018; Ockey & Wagner, 2018) and is being very actively examined through language assessment research. What follows is a brief description of the chapters in each of the core parts.

Part One, *Assessment of evolving language ability constructs*, contains four papers. It opens with a paper by Gary Ockey and Roz Hirch, *A step toward the assessment of English as a Lingua Franca*, which addresses concerns raised about defining and assessing ELF constructs. This conceptual paper describes the need for L2 English tests to consider English as a lingua franca (ELF) in their development. Based on their analysis of an oral communication placement test at a large Midwestern University, the authors argue that the lack of agreement on ELF principles has to be mitigated before frameworks of ELF analysis can be used to determine the degree to which EFL can be assessed in language tests.

In the second paper, *Revisiting the role of content in language assessment constructs*, Lorena Llosa examines a major assessment conundrum: the role of content in language assessment and construct definitions. She revisits Bachman's model of communicative competence and the role of content within the model and how these have influenced assessment in three language education contexts: language for specific purposes (LSP), US K-12 English learner education, and content and language integrated learning (CLIL). The author highlights the latest conceptualizations of the role content plays in their assessment constructs.

In the third paper, Paul Gruba explores the construct of multimodal listening. In his paper, *What does language testing have to offer to multimodal listening?*, he addresses the issues of multimodal listening constructs and how they may inform listening assessments. The answer for Gruba, as he carefully argues in his paper, is to foster a stronger relationship between listening assessment and multimodal studies. He relies on the recent work of Bachman and Damböck (2018) as a model which can inform thinking about multimodal listening assessments for the classroom teacher.

The final paper of this section, *Learner perceptions of construct-centered feedback on oral proficiency*, by Jonathan Schmidgall, focuses on the role feedback, based on specific construct definitions, plays in oral proficiency. He reports on the results of a small-scale study of learners' perceptions of construct-centered feedback in international teaching assistants' oral proficiency assessment. He concludes that construct-centered approaches to feedback may be used by teachers to complement other approaches to feedback and argues that since oral proficiency assessments typically elicit performances that may serve as the basis for an evaluation of proficiency, they can be used as the basis for more elaborate, learning-oriented feedback.

Part Two, *Validity and validation of language assessments*, contains four papers. Antony Kunnan's paper, *A case for an ethics-based approach to evaluate language assessments*, which starts off this section describes the shortcomings of the two prominent approaches to language assessment evaluation: *standards-* and *argument-* based approaches. Kunnan then recommends an ethics-based approach as a way to articulate what he terms as a "justifiable research agenda for the evaluation of language assessments."

In the second paper, *Alignment as a fundamental validity issue in standards-based K-12 English language proficiency assessments*, Mikyung Wolf discusses how Bachman and Palmer's (2010) Assessment Use Argument framework helps us integrate an expanded view of K-12 target language use domain alignment by reinforcing consideration of the consequences of assessment uses in validity. Wolfe also presents a needed review of a range of pressing areas of research on alignment evaluation for K-12 ELP assessments.

In the third paper, *Validating a holistic rubric for scoring short answer reading questions*, Sara Cushing and Rurik Tywoniw present a study which investigates the validity of a practical scoring procedure for short answer (sentence length) reading comprehension questions. The use of a holistic rubric for sets of responses rather than scoring individual responses on a university-based English proficiency test is examined. Their results seem to confirm that holistic section-based scores are only predicted by fidelity ratings and this provides evidence in support of the scoring inference of the validity argument.

The final paper in this section by Ikkyu Choi titled, *The curse of explanation: Model selection in language testing research*, examines statistical modeling conundrums in language testing research. In his paper, he explores issues which arise when research attempts to approximate and study a true model which is the underlying system that is responsible for generating data. Specifically, he introduces and illustrates three issues: (1) uncertainty due to model selection in statistical inference, (2) successful approximations of data with an incorrect model, and (3) existence of substantively different models whose statistical counterparts are highly comparable. Referring back to guidelines in Bachman's research use argument framework (2006, 2009), Choi calls for explicitly acknowledging and justifying model selection processes in language assessment research.

In the final part of our text, *Understanding internal structures of language assessments*, four empirical studies examine a variety of test constructs and their internal structures. Additionally, three of the four papers use generalizability theory and multivariate generalizability theory in their analyses. The first paper, *Developing summary content scoring criteria for university L2 writing instruction in Japan*, by Yasuyo Sawaki, examines the functioning of two types of summary content scoring methods: content point scores and a holistic summary content rating scale, otherwise referred to as an integration scale. The subjects were Japanese L1 students at a Japanese university writing academic texts in English. Sawaki's results suggested a satisfactory level of score dependability of the integration rating scale for the intended uses, supporting the rating consistency warrant for the assessment record claim in Bachman and Palmer's (2010) assessment use argument (AUA) framework.

Sawaki also discovered that summary content scores based on both scoring methods were distinct from a language quality score. Based on this finding she suggests that employing either one with the language quality rating would enhance the representation of the summary writing construct and thus support the meaningfulness warrant for the test score interpretation claim in the AUA.

In the second paper, *Consistency of computer-automated scoring keys across authors and authoring teams*, Nathan Carr examines the extent to which scoring keys written by different authors and different teams of authors are comparable. Using multivariate generalizability studies to compare the differences revealed that single-author scoring keys can be insufficiently reliable or dependable for high-stakes decisions. Carr recommends using authoring teams to draft the key as a solution to the dependability issues. His research also identified scoring key issues which need to be attended to when training key authors.

In the third paper, *Distinguishing language ability from the context in an EFL speaking test*, Hongwen Cai provides empirical evidence for understanding the relationship between language ability and context in task-based language assessments. Using the results from over 23,000 subjects on an EFL speaking test in China which consists of three tasks—retelling, topic-based talk, and discussion—Cai found the contribution of language ability and contextual factors to test scores could be separately assessed, and that task performance is a multidimensional construct involving both language ability and topical knowledge. In his conclusion, he stresses the need for clear definitions of both constructs in language testing practice.

The final paper by Sunyoung Shin, titled, *The effects of proficiency differences in pairs on Korean learners' speaking performance*, focuses on the effects of the test task type, which he breaks down into individual and paired speaking tasks on the scores obtained in two groups of learners of Korean (heritage learners and non-heritage learners). The results of Shin's study show that both heritage and non-heritage learners performed similarly across different test tasks regardless of the backgrounds of their partners (heritage or non-heritage). Further analysis indicated that pairing heritage learners or high oral proficiency with non-heritage learners of lower ability produced higher oral proficiency scores in the paired tasks. Shin concludes that these findings better illuminate the relationships between test constructs and contextual features in paired oral assessment.

It is our hope that reading these summaries will encourage readers to further explore the full papers presented in this book. By way of conclusion, we take you back to the closing day of our conference in Salt Lake City in early June 2017. On that last day, we gave Lyle a few gifts as an expression of our appreciation for his mentorship. One of the gifts was a lidded polished cherry hardwood bowl that I (Brent) had made from a branch of a tree that grew on the property near Salt Lake City where I was raised. The tree had born fruit for many years and then grew old and eventually died. The branch from the tree was then mounted on a wood lathe and carved into a bowl. The inside was left rough, but the outside of the bowl was sanded for many hours with varying degrees of sandpaper coarseness until it began to shine. After hours of polishing, a basic finish of linseed oil mixed with wax was all that was needed to illuminate its beautiful color, accentuate its intricate wood grain, and retain its shine. For each one of Lyle's students over the years, this bowl is symbolic of who we were and what we were to become under his supervision and tutelage. Many of us came to Lyle rough and unpolished, much like the inside of our gifted cherry wood bowl, but through many hours of tutorship, mentoring, and even a little bit of tough love, he polished and refined us. The works in this volume are an indication of the degree to which we have been polished. And for this, we will always be grateful. Thank you, Lyle!

References

Bachman, L. F. (1990). *Fundamental considerations in language testing.* Oxford, England: Oxford University Press.
Bachman, L. F. (2006). Generalizability: A journey into the nature of empirical research in applied linguistics. In M. Chalhoub-Deville, C. A. Chapelle, & P. Duff (Eds.), *Inference and generalizability in applied linguistics: Multiple perspectives* (pp. 165–207). Dordrecht, The Netherlands: John Benjamins.
Bachman, L. F. (2009). Generalizability and research use arguments. In K. Ercikan & W.-M. Roth (Eds.), *Generalizing from educational research* (pp. 127–148). New York, NY: Tayler & Francis.
Bachman, L. F., & Damböck, B. (2018). *Language assessment for classroom teachers.* Oxford: Oxford University Press.
Bachman, L. F., & Palmer, A. S. (1996). *Language testing in practice.* Oxford, England: Oxford University Press.
Bachman, L. F., & Palmer, A. S. (2010). *Language assessment in practice.* Oxford, England: Oxford University Press.
Fundamental Considerations in Language Testing. (2017). Retrieved from https://sites.google.com/view/fcltconference2017/home.
Galaczi, E., & Taylor, L. (2018). Interactional competence: Conceptualisations, operationalisations, and outstanding questions. *Language Assessment Quarterly, 15*(3), 219–236.
Ockey, G. J., & Wagner, E. (2018). *Assessing L2 listening: Moving towards authenticity.* Amsterdam: John Benjamins.

Part I
Assessment of Evolving Language Ability Constructs

Chapter 2
A Step Toward the Assessment of English as a Lingua Franca

Gary J. Ockey and R. Roz Hirch

Abstract This conceptual paper describes the need for L2 English tests to consider English as a lingua franca (ELF) in their development. After discussing what is meant by ELF, it describes an oral communication placement test developed at a large Midwestern University in the United States. The test is then analyzed based on a framework designed to determine the extent to which it can be considered to have adhered to ELF principles. It is argued that for the most part the test does appear to assess ELF. However, it does not completely follow ELF principles, and sometimes, because there is little agreement on ELF principles, it is difficult to determine the extent to which the test actually does assess ELF. It is recommended that researchers in the field come to agreement on what can be considered critical aspects of ELF, which will make it possible for language assessment researchers to better design their assessments to include ELF.

Introduction

Changing demographics and globalization, among other factors, have led to the increasing use of English as a lingua franca (ELF), which we broadly define as a communication context in which at least one user in an English-mediated communication has a different first language (L1) than other users (Canagarajah, 2006; Jenkins, 2009; Mortensen, 2013; Seidlhofer, 2011). Based on this definition, it is becoming more common to find ELF than non-ELF contexts. It follows that oral assessments designed to determine the degree to which a test taker has the necessary oral proficiency to function in a given context should be designed to assess ELF. Because the ELF context has become so common, there has been growing criticism directed at the language assessment community for not targeting ELF when designing L2 English

G. J. Ockey · R. R. Hirch (✉)
Iowa State University, Ames, Iowa, USA
e-mail: rhirch@iastate.edu

G. J. Ockey
e-mail: gockey@iastate.edu

© Springer Nature Singapore Pte Ltd. 2020
G. J. Ockey and B. A. Green (eds.), *Another Generation of Fundamental Considerations in Language Assessment*, https://doi.org/10.1007/978-981-15-8952-2_2

assessments (e.g., Jenkins, 2016; Canagarajah, 2006; Leung & Lewkowicz, 2017; McNamara, 2018). These criticisms may not be completely accurate, however, since some L2 assessments already take into account many ELF concerns. In fact, a move within the language testing community to consider the ideas underlying ELF can be traced at least back to when Bachman argued that L2 assessments should assess communicative language ability (Bachman & Clark, 1987; Bachman, 1990). The assessment of communicative language ability removed the focus from assessing a rule-governed linguistic system devoid of context to using the language successfully within a given context and for a particular purpose. While neither Bachman nor others in the language assessment field discussed the concept of ELF at the time, this move toward communicative language testing was a critical step toward future ELF testing, as many language assessments have increasingly morphed into assessments that integrate aspects of ELF, whether intentionally or not. An example of a test with many ELF features is in current use at Iowa State University (ISU). ISU's oral communication placement test was designed with ELF as a guiding principle; however, this proved to be a challenge, in part because there is little agreement on what ELF is and almost no practical guidance on how ELF could be used to inform L2 test design. This chapter was inspired by the challenges of designing an ELF university placement test. It begins with a discussion of how ELF has been defined. Next, it describes the design of ISU's oral communication placement test. This is followed by a discussion of the extent to which ISU's oral communication placement test can be considered an ELF test. The paper concludes with implications and future directions for ELF and assessment researchers and developers who aim to develop ELF assessments.

Constructs and Historical Perspective

English as a Lingua Franca

English as a lingua franca (ELF) is, in many ways, related to two other concepts in English as a second language: World Englishes (WE) and English as an International Language (EIL). The three are frequently mentioned together and share many attributes; indeed, ELF is sometimes seen as growing out of WE. All three reference Kachru's (1992) concentric circles to varying degrees. However, there are distinctions. In WE, communication occurs based on local conventions, so the focus is on shared linguistic components (Canagarajah, 2006; Leung, Lewkowicz, & Jenkins, 2016). EIL is also concerned about local use of English, but rather than being about linguistic features, it focuses on the needs of users (Brown, 2014). ELF, on the other hand, focuses on negotiating communication between speakers of different L1s. This section will explore the different phases of ELF which has led to its current definition, as well as setting out the definition for ELF that will be used in the rest of this chapter. This will be followed by ELF criticism of language testing and language testers' responses to these criticisms.

What Is English as a Lingua Franca?

Jenkins (2015) identifies three phrases of the evolving definition of ELF. The first began in the 1980s with her own research in pronunciation and mutual intelligibility. Other researchers subsequently focused on additional features such as grammar and lexis and identifying features shared among English speakers from different L1s. Phase 1 closely resembled WE; the break would come in the 2000s. In phase 2, researchers relied less on Kachru's circles, as the circles were criticized for having too great a focus on native identity (Jenkins, 2015). More significantly, researchers dispensed with lists of commonalities, paying greater attention to the ways in which English speakers of different L1s negotiate meaning (Seidlhofer, 2006). Jenkins (2015) also proposes a third phase, which she dubs "English as a multilingual franca"; this phase has many features of the second phase, except that English is given less precedence. In phase 3, English is one of many languages that speakers have at their disposal, and speakers may draw on those other languages to communicate, which essentially becomes a form of translanguaging. While this is an interesting development, we feel the third phase focuses more on communication generally (Guzman-Orth, Lopez, & Tolention, 2019), and would therefore require a test of communication more than a test of English language. For that reason, our definition is drawn from Jenkin's phase 2.

There are two essential points that definitions of ELF in phase 2 have in common: (1) at least one speaker in a communication situation has a different L1 from other speakers, which may be English or another language (e.g., three Chinese L1 speakers and one English L1 speaker) and (2) the speakers choose to use English in the communication context (Canagarajah, 2006; Jenkins, 2009; Mortensen, 2013; Seidlhofer, 2011). Identity is also an important concept. ELF is not a natural language in that no one identifies as an ELF speaker; instead, speakers identify as being a member of their L1 communities. Since native English speakers (NESs) therefore cannot be native ELF speakers, "native English" should not take precedence nor serve as a model for ELF (Davies, 2009; Elder & Davies, 2006; McNamara, 2011).

Criticisms of Tests and of ELF

The use of native English speakers (NESs) as a standard for testing is one of the main criticisms ELF researchers make of current practices in language testing. Using a NES standard assumes that, when a test taker is in real-world English language situations, the person with whom they speak will also be a native English speaker. In fact, given the number of non-native English speakers (NNESs) in the world today, we know that this will likely not be the most frequent situation, even within an English-speaking country (Brown, 2014; Jenkins & Leung, 2017; McNamara, 2011; Newbold, 2015; Ockey & Wagner, 2018). The reliance on the NES standard also suggests that the NNES is in some way deficient or even incapable of achieving the level of an NES (Leung et al., 2016; McNamara, 2011). Another criticism of current language tests expressed by ELF researchers is their focus, which is usually on formal aspects such as lexis and grammar. Instead, tests should focus less on the rules of communication and more on whether speakers are able to mutually understand each other (Brown, 2014; McNamara, 2011). Similarly, ELF practitioners would like to see more emphasis placed on pronunciation and dialects in the testing situation (Jenkins & Leung, 2017; Leung et al., 2016; McNamara, 2011).

While most assessment researchers agree that these are valid criticisms, they also have concerns about ELF and its application to tests. For language testers, one of the greatest complications of incorporating the ideas supported by ELF researchers is that it is difficult to pin down a practical definition for assessment purposes (Elder & Davies, 2006). Often, ELF ideas are focused on political concepts rather than linguistic ones, so assessment practitioners, who rely on construct definitions, can find it difficult to fit ELF principles into a practical testing situation (Davies, 2009; Newbold, 2015). Furthermore, there may be consequences for psychometrics, which generally rely on a stable definition of the construct being tested; considering that ELF is highly context oriented and describes shifting communication situations, many of the psychometric bases of large-scale, standardized tests may need to be reconsidered (Jenkins & Leung, 2017). It is also important to take into account the effects on test takers, many of whom may not be familiar with ELF, or who may for many reasons be unprepared for diverse dialects (Brown, 2014). Finally, as Brown (2014) points out, testing is much more than standardized tests such as TOEFL or IELTS, which are largely the target of ELF researcher criticisms—indeed, the focus of this chapter is on a test type that is commonly administered at universities throughout the world: placement tests. The next section briefly describes the form and content of such a test that is currently in use at Iowa State University and is representative of a type seen at numerous universities. This description is expanded in the third section, which examines the test in relation to an ELF framework to suggest that this placement test may function as a form of ELF assessment.

The English Placement Test of Oral Communication (EPT OC)

General description. The English Placement Test of Oral Communication (EPT OC) is a face-to-face assessment of oral communication ability that aims to determine the extent to which test takers have the academic oral communication skills necessary to be successful at the university. Students who do not obtain a passing score on the test are placed into appropriate English language courses for their level, which are designed to give them the requisite skills to communicate effectively in the university.

Test design and development. The course and test were designed based on a needs analysis of second language English users at the university and the English required for them to be successful in their content courses and in navigating their way through the university. Content and ESL instructors as well as international students provided feedback on the students' English needs at the university as part of the needs analysis. The course and the test were developed simultaneously and shared the same constructs/objectives. The test tasks were selected from the range of activities completed in the course.

Test construct. Aligned with the course objectives, the EPT OC aims to assess the following: Interactional Competence, the ability to respond appropriately in various contexts—for example, to effectively interact with professors, instructors, peers, and other university staff; Fluency, the ability to use the language fluently; Comprehensibility, the ability to produce language comprehensible to English users at the university; Vocabulary/Grammar, the ability to use academic vocabulary and grammar effectively and appropriately (Ockey & Li, 2015).

Test administrators/raters. The test is administered and rated by graduate students and instructors, who teach the Oral Communication courses for test takers who do not pass the EPT OC, as well as other English courses offered at the university. All raters have advanced English language abilities, have taught English language courses, and are working on or possess advanced degrees in the field of applied linguistics. They come from a variety of backgrounds. For example, during the fall 2018 administration, raters had 11 different L1s, were from 11 different countries, and represented diverse cultures as well as subcultures and dialects within these cultures and L1s.

Test takers. The test takers are students who have been accepted to the university but may need further English language support courses as they begin their undergraduate or graduate journey. To limit the resources needed for the test, students who have demonstrated success in an English-medium academic context (e.g., have a bachelor's degree, master's degree, or high school diploma from an English-medium school) or have sufficient scores on a standardized English test (e.g., SAT, ACT, GRE, TOEFL iBT, IELTS, PTE Academic) are exempted from taking the test and the oral communication class. Test takers can choose to not take the test if they prefer to take the oral communication class. If they desire to be exempted from the class and do not satisfy any of the other exemption criteria (Iowa State University English placement test (ISU EPT): https://apling.engl.iastate.edu/english-placement-test), they can choose to take the test. This results in a test taker population from many parts of the world, who received high school or university degrees in non-English-medium universities and have TOEFL iBT scores between 71 and 99 (or their IELTS or PTE Academic equivalent); 71 is the minimum TOEFL iBT score for university acceptance, and exemption from taking the speaking class is given to students who have TOEFL iBT scores of 100 or above.

Procedures and test tasks. The EPT OC is video recorded, takes approximately 20 min, and is composed of three tasks: a scripted one-on-one interview with a test administrator, a retell to two test administrators and a peer test taker, and a paired discussion with the peer test taker. After brief introductions with a test administrator, the scripted interview task is administered. For this task, test takers are asked three questions. First, they are shown a picture and asked to describe it; second, they are asked to respond to a hypothetical question associated with the situation in the picture; and third, they are asked to talk about what they would do in the hypothetical situation posed in the second question. Students are asked to provide 60-second responses to each of the three questions.

For the retell task, test takers listen to a 30-second recording supporting one side of a two-sided issue. The speakers on the recordings are judged to have strengths of accents based on Ockey and French's (2016) Strength of Accent scale, which was designed to make it possible for language assessments to include diverse speech varieties, regardless of the speaker's L1, which would not unfairly influence a test taker's score on a test. Speakers' strengths of accent on the EPT OC are of two types: (1) "The speaker's accent was NOT noticeably different than what I am used to and did NOT require me to concentrate on listening any more than usual; the accent did NOT decrease my understanding." Or (2) "The speaker's accent was noticeably different than what I am used to but did NOT require me to concentrate on listening any more than usual; the accent did NOT decrease my understanding." A speaker's strength of accent is judged by highly proficient L1 and L2 listeners familiar with the local speech variety. After listening to the position, one test taker is asked to retell the speaker's view and reasons for this view in their own words. Students then listen to another 30-second recording from a speaker who expresses the opposing view on the issue and the other test taker is asked to retell that speaker's view.

The third task is a paired discussion task, in which the two test takers are asked to discuss and defend the positions they summarized in the retell task. Test takers are given 4 minutes for their discussion. After the discussion begins, the test administrators listen quietly away from the two test takers engaged in the discussion. Further details about the test and example test tasks can be found at the ISU EPT website: https://apling.engl.iastate.edu/english-placement-test.

The content of the items is based on topics that test takers might encounter at the university. Examples of content for the one-on-one oral interview include explaining how one might deal with: losing a library book; plagiarizing a course paper; cheating on an exam; and working on a group project with an uncooperative group. The prompts encourage test takers to talk about these issues based on their own cultural experiences. Examples of items for the retell and paired discussion include taking a position on topics such as the value of group work; the importance of a part-time job while studying; and the usefulness of online classes.

Evaluation criteria. Test takers' performances are evaluated independently by the two trained raters who administer the test. Ratings are based on a four-point analytic scale, with subscales of pronunciation, interactional competence, fluency, and grammar/vocabulary (see Appendix A for Oral EPT rubric). Test takers are assigned two sets of scores by the test administrator with whom they talked during the one-on-one oral interview, and one by the test administrator who listened to them during the retell and paired discussion tasks.

Raters have the option of requesting a test taker be given another opportunity to take the test if it is felt that the test was in some way unfair (e.g., a test taker's partner dominates the paired discussion task), or that another trained rater evaluates the video recording of the test, if the rater feels biased against assigning a fair rating. Scores are adjusted for rater severity and prompt difficulty with Many-facet Rasch Measurement techniques (Eckes, 2015; McNamara, Knoch, & Fan, 2019). Test takers assigned scores of 3 or higher on the rating scales, after taking into account the standard error of measure of the test, are assigned passing scores. Typically, this means a score of roughly 2.75. This is a weighted score based on doubling the importance of scores for interactional competence and comprehensibility as compared to fluency and grammar/vocabulary (English Placement Test, 2020).

Critical Issues

A framework for designing or analyzing a test based on ELF principles does not exist, but Brown (2014) developed a "criteria for locally defined EIL curriculum development that could equally well apply to testing locally defined EIL" (p. 10). This framework was originally developed for assessment of EIL, which is different from but related to ELF, as described in the introduction above; Brown's framework therefore served as a useful starting point to build an ELF framework because there is a great deal of overlap between the two. It should be noted that Canagarajah (2006) also contains a framework for assessing EIL and influenced the development of the framework presented in this chapter, but it focused on classroom assessment, whereas Brown's framework was about non-classroom tests such as the placement test we evaluate in this chapter. Changes to Brown's framework were made based on differences between EIL and ELF, Canagarajah's (2006) framework, current research on ELF, and ELF researchers' criticisms of English assessments (Table 2.1). Additionally, the framework is divided into two parts, the first being attributes of the test taker that an ELF test should measure (five points) and the second being qualities that the test should have (two points). The aim of this seven-point framework was to provide guidelines that could be used to determine the degree to which an assessment could be considered an ELF test. While there may not be any tests perfectly designed to assess ELF, we contend that some tests do embody many aspects of ELF. To this end, the EPT OC test, described above, was judged according to each of the criteria to see to what extent it can be considered an ELF test. Each point in the framework below begins with a criterion based on ELF principles, followed by a more detailed definition of the term and its relation to ELF. Each point ends with an evaluation of the EPT OC according to that criterion.

Table 2.1 Framework for evaluating the extent to which a test can be considered ELF

Criteria	Description	
English rhetorical sensitivity	How effectively the test evaluates the test taker's ability to…	• Use awareness of linguistic and cultural differences to identify and use the appropriate rhetorical style to communicate effectively with English speakers from cultures other than their own in a variety of contexts
International communicative competence		• Comprehend and be comprehended by advanced speakers of English from any culture
Context sensitivity		• Show respect for and confidence in local varieties of English while exemplifying the capacity to contribute to the international body of information
Motivation		• Communicate in ways that are appropriate for personal or cultural goals
Grammatical appropriacy		• Communicate in a way that is grammatically mutually comprehensible to speakers of English from any culture
Relevance	Qualities of assessment	• Should include materials and activities based on local and international situations that are recognizable and applicable to the students' everyday lives
Fairness		• Should be based on an inclusive model that incorporates NNESs and NESs in every aspect of the assessment

English rhetorical sensitivity. The first of the test taker traits listed, rhetorical sensitivity is required in all language situations (Bachman & Palmer, 1996); learners should always be aware of the genre they are in and respond to the situation appropriately, whether speaking or writing (Canagarajah, 2014). ELF researchers point out that, while native English rhetorical structures are generally well taught, rhetorical structures from other cultures are not always as widely known (Elder & Davies, 2006; Jenkins, 2011). This also means that people from two different L1s may be accustomed to different approaches to rhetoric as well as having knowledge of native English rhetoric. The difference between ELF and other testing situations is that ELF speakers should be able to draw on non-English rhetoric as well as their knowledge of English rhetoric—which may also differ between them—as part of their communication. This description is abstract; a practical application might be a situation such as an argument. English has its own rules for structuring arguments that differ from those of Chinese; learners should be able to draw from both if they choose.

Part of rhetorical sensitivity, as it is presented in ELF literature, are pragmatics and sociolinguistics, which ELF scholars tend to closely associate together. This connection is clear in Canagarajah (2006) when he writes "We have to focus more on proficiency in pragmatics. Sociolinguistic skills of dialect differentiation, code switching, style shifting, interpersonal communication, conversation management, and discourse strategies are important for shuttling between English varieties" (p. 233). An ELF view of pragmatics is one that takes into account cultural differences and the need to negotiate these in the course of any given interaction (Newbold, 2015). One of the interesting consequences of this view of pragmatics is that it has less focus on idiomaticity, since idioms would likely be more of an impediment to communication than most grammar errors (Cogo & Dewey, 2006; Hall, 2014; Kim & Billington, 2016; Newbold, 2015; Prodromou, 2010). Thus, an ELF test would highlight sensitivity to differences in dialect, culture, and identity, while downplaying the use of traditional native-like fluency indicators such as idiom use.

The EPT OC paired discussion task, in which two students, usually with different cultural backgrounds and L1s, discuss a topic, shows this type of rhetorical sensitivity. Students are able to structure their arguments as they like and often need to negotiate meaning based on the structure of each other's arguments because their rhetorical styles may differ. Rhetorical style is not indicated as part of the construct; instead, responding appropriately and effectively negotiating meaning are included in the test construct as part of the interactional competence subscale. At the same time, the raters also have various cultural backgrounds and L1s and make judgements of the test takers' language abilities while having their own culturally influenced approaches to rhetoric. Raters are furthermore instructed not to judge according to an NES standard or expect or require test takers to use idiomatic expressions. Instead, the focus is on how well test takers adapt to the conversation with another L1 speaker. Given these features of the test, it is likely that the EPT OC assesses English rhetorical sensitivity in line with ELF standards.

International communicative competence. An ELF view of communicative competence in speaking can be broken down into three aspects: intelligibility, accommodation to variety, and correction. Intelligibility is what Jenkins (2015) began with in 1980. In ELF research, intelligibility tends to be summarized as how well a person is understood, and is therefore related to the act of speaking (Chopin, 2015; Elder & Davies, 2006; Isaacs & Trofimovich, 2012). Accommodation to variety is the flip side of intelligibility in that it is how well a person can understand other speakers, particularly those with unfamiliar dialects, and thus relates to listening (Canagarajah, 2014; Jenkins & Leung, 2017; Ockey & Wagner, 2018). Correction refers to repairs, but these are not grammatical; they are, instead, communication repairs and are similar to Canale and Swain's (1980) strategic competence (Canagarajah, 2014; Chopin,

2015; Newbold, 2015). Thus, an ELF definition of communicative competence in a speaking context can be viewed as how well the test taker can be understood by the other speaker (intelligibility), how well the test taker can understand a variety of speech types (accommodation), and in cases where one of those breaks down, how well the test taker can make corrections.

Communicative competence is a substantial component of the EPT OC rating scale in all three categories:

Intelligibility. The construct of the test includes the subscale, Comprehensibility, which refers to the degree to which the speech variety of the test taker requires effort to understand, as judged by the raters. The rating scales do not make reference to native-like speech.

Accommodation: How well a person can understand another speaker is part of the EPT OC construct. It manifests itself in the interactional competence rating subscale, which has been shown to require "Active Listening" (Ducasse & Brown, 2009; Galaczi, 2014; May, 2011) since an appropriate response is often based on understanding another speaker. In fact, raters are trained to judge the degree to which it is necessary to accommodate to the needs of a partner. For example, successful accommodating may require slowing one's speech or using more simple vocabulary or sentence structure to communicate with a partner with a different speech variety or proficiency level.

Correction. The ability to correct miscommunication is also part of the EPT OC construct and is indicated in the interactional competence rating subscale. Because test takers speak with both a highly proficient test administrator and a peer who could have rather limited English proficiency, both of whom are likely to speak different English speech varieties, communication break downs are common. The ability to correct these miscommunications is judged by the rater as part of the test construct.

Context sensitivity. Within test use, ELF is concerned with context: where the test is being delivered, who is delivering it, and who is taking it, among other concerns (Brown, 2014; Canagarajah, 2006; Leung et al., 2016). Each context may have its own norms and expectations; some contexts may be more flexible and allow for more negotiation than others. In contexts that allow for more flexibility, too strict an adherence to an NES standard could lead to bias from an ELF perspective (Canagarajah, 2014). For example, delivering a business proposal to a company in an English-speaking country may require stricter adherence to NES standards than a conversation with classmates in a university in an English-speaking country would. In the former case, a large-scale standardized test with formal linguistic features may be appropriate (Chopin, 2015), while the latter situation may be better served by a test that contains more ELF elements (Jenkins & Leung, 2017).

However, most ELF researchers would suggest that ELF is necessary in all assessment situations to varying degrees. Brown (2014) laid out eight language constituencies to consider: the local community where the test will be administered; test takers, which may be from the local community or elsewhere; test content; test proctors; test raters; the community that will be affected by the decision (which may be different from the local community); the purpose of the decision being made with the test; and the people who are making the decisions. When any of these Englishes is different—which would presumably happen in almost all language assessment situations—then there is a potential for unfairness (Brown, 2014). Looking at these eight different constituents might be a useful tool to assist test developers with deciding on the degree to which ELF should be incorporated into a test.

The design of the EPT OC includes placing test takers into different contexts and judging their abilities to navigate these different contexts. The one-on-one individual interview with an examiner is meant to be a formal situation, and test takers are expected to recognize this formality and respond appropriately to it. The paired discussion with a peer test taker is meant to be a somewhat informal situation. In this context, test takers are expected to use less formal language. In neither context is the test taker expected to conform to an NES norm. Rating scales refer to concepts such as effectiveness, appropriateness, and comprehensibility. Using these two tasks makes it possible for test takers to use more standard English, as they would with an instructor, or less standard English, as they would with a group of classmates.

The EPT OC takes into account all eight of the constituents suggested by Brown (2014). Most test takers are from outside of the local community, while the raters/test administrators are mostly from outside the local community but familiar with the local speech variety and culture. They can judge a test taker's oral communication ability based on both an insider and an outsider perspective. This is important since test takers will need to be able to communicate with both of these groups of English users in the university setting. The test content is based on topics and genres commonly encountered at the university that afford students opportunities to talk about their values and cultures.

Motivation. Brown (2014) highlighted two aspects of use: the ways that test takers use English and the way that the test is used. In ELF, considerable attention is given to characteristics of the speakers, especially their first languages and the fact that they are choosing to communicate in English. However, less attention is paid to why they are speaking English—what is the speakers' motivation? And in a testing situation, what are the motivations of the stakeholders? Motivation is important in ELF because it can affect the degree of negotiation that may be needed or expected of the speakers. Motivations can take many forms, either locally, such as for communication with residents who speak a language or for advancement in a company or similar purposes, or globally, such as for business, travel, immigration, or even things like online gaming (Brown, 2014). Another related issue is consideration for the different experiences and the meaning that learning English has for the test takers, which could vary considerably depending on their L1 and their country of origin (McNamara, 2011). Learners are affected by not only the differences or similarities of their L1 to English, but also by the varying experiences their countries have had in contact with English language-speaking countries, and the cultural beliefs and customs of their countries as well (McNamara, 2011). The personal and cultural experiences of the test taker will likely affect their motivation for learning English.

From an assessment researcher's perspective, "motivation" is closely tied to the concept of assessment validity; is the test valid for the use being made of it? In the case of the EPT OC, the immediate motivation for test takers is to be able to take content classes with English as the language of instruction; hence, the test should assess whether learners are able to communicate in an English-medium classroom. A needs assessment was conducted in the development phase that included discussions with various stakeholders regarding classroom communication needs. Additionally, the test is aligned with an English course to ensure that students who do not meet the minimal requirements will still have the opportunity to achieve their learning goals. It should also be noted, however, that learners may have motivations beyond taking content courses in English that are still tied to their success in university. For example, students may want to graduate from an English-medium university to get a better job in their home country or to emigrate to an English-speaking country. The EPT OC cannot be used as an assessment for those purposes, nor would anyone suggest it should; it can only assess learners for the immediate goal of communication within the university and the surrounding community. Large-scale tests are sometimes blind to any of the test taker's motivations, and it is a difficult component to understand—in fact, knowing a test taker's motivation may mean discouraging them from taking a test on ethical grounds if the use of the test is not valid.

Grammatical appropriacy. Grammar is frequently a subconstruct to be measured in most assessment situations; the rubrics for TOEFL's, iELTS's, and the CEFR's speaking tests each have a descriptor band that includes grammatical accuracy, and both iELTS and CEFR mention native speakers at least once in theirs. Because these rubrics are frequently adapted for use in other testing situations such as university placement, test takers' performances are likely to be compared to some standard of native-like grammar (Chopin, 2015). Despite the reliance assessments often have on NES grammar, ELF researchers seem hesitant to do away with grammar entirely, since some form of grammatical knowledge is needed to communicate (Canagarajah, 2014). ELF researchers suggest that grammar should be viewed as something "emergent, not preconstructed. As [speakers] collaborate with each other in attaining their communicative objectives, they construct certain norms that make their interaction possible" (Canagarajah, 2014, p. 770). There are clearly several problems with this description for testing purposes, the first being that this definition is too fluid for defining a construct (Davies, 2009; Newbold, 2015). Furthermore, this idea of grammar as something that may be constructed over time is more appropriate as a long-term classroom goal than an aspect of assessment, which has been observed in other studies (Newbold, 2015; Prodromou, 2010). Canagarajah (2018) suggests that assessors should reject structuralist definitions of grammar by acknowledging that a test taker's grammar need not be perfect by NES standards, but should be sufficient to achieve mutual comprehension. Adopting Canagarajah's (2018) view of grammar, rubrics would require two changes in the grammar category: (1) grammar would play a less significant role in scoring, and may indeed be combined with another category and (2) "grammatical errors" would be defined in the context of the conversation as instances where grammar interfered with comprehension, not as deviations from prescriptivist rules.

The EPT OC includes in its construct grammatical accuracy, but accuracy is not defined based on an NES norm; instead, it is based on the judgement of the diverse population of raters. During rater training sessions, examples of speakers who do not have accurate grammar based on an NES norm but are nonetheless good at communicating are provided as examples of speakers that should be assigned passing scores. Raters are trained to focus on the degree to which what the test taker says is understandable. The use of grammatical structures that lead to breakdowns in communication is judged negatively, while the use of comprehensible grammar forms that do not conform to NES standards is judged much less negatively.

Nevertheless, just as ELF researchers do not have a shared view of how to approach grammar, it is not clear what exactly the role of grammar is and should be for the EPT OC. For example, in the picture description task, a test taker might attempt to describe a picture, which includes two bottles on a table. If the test taker said, "Two bottles are on the table," the sentence would be acceptable from both a grammatical accuracy point of view and an ELF point of view. However, if the test taker said, "Two bottle on table," the discourse would be considered inaccurate from a grammatical accuracy point of view, but probably appropriate from an ELF perspective. The EPT OC does include grammatical accuracy in scoring because instructors of both ESL and content courses base grades on it; excluding it would not align with the real-world needs of the students. However, to also align with ELF standards, the focus is on communication, rather than accuracy. Thus, following ELF standards for rating grammar would result in a rather high overall score (probably passing), but would not result in the maximum point value.

It should be noted that despite this training, it is apparent from observations of and conversations with raters that they do pay attention to NES norms when evaluating grammar structures during the assessment. However, it is also clear that they value comprehensible grammatical forms over incomprehensible ones. In short, raters seem to struggle with how to evaluate grammar beyond its comprehensibility and accuracy when compared to an NES norm.

One further element that should be pointed out is that, although grammar is given its own category (along with vocabulary), the EPT has been designed so that grammar would not be given as much weight as other categories; therefore, it is given half the weighting of interactional competence and comprehensibility in the final EPT OC score. Thus, from an ELF perspective, grammar should not play an overly important role in assessing the test takers.

Relevance. As described above, oral communication tests that involve an element requiring negotiation best fit ELF; this section and the next look at appropriate characteristics of tasks and tests as a whole. While it might be possible to adapt currently administered tests, this may be insufficient; several aspects need to be considered that may change the structure of a test (Elder & Davies, 2006). Testers need to consider the context of the test to identify appropriate types of Englishes (Brown, 2014). For example, in a university placement test, consideration should be given both to the variety of dialects likely to be encountered in the local community and in the university. Local dialects in a rural area will probably be more homogeneous than those in a major metropolis. The test should also have a variety of tasks that are performance-based and interactive, allowing for social negotiation and pragmatic competence relevant to the testing context; discrete items are therefore considered less likely to be useful for ELF assessment (Canagarajah, 2006; Chopin, 2015; Elder & Davies, 2006; Jenkins & Leung, 2017; Newbold, 2015). At the same time, receptive skills should be considered; in the case of speaking, listening will undoubtedly be a component of the task, so different dialects may need to be built into the test (Brown, 2014; Ockey & Wagner, 2018). Finally, the materials used to elicit test taker responses should be relevant to the assessment context (Elder & Davies, 2006; Newbold, 2015). In a university placement situation, this could mean including topics that are not only relevant to students as a whole but also to students at that particular university.

The EPT OC was designed to assess the ability to negotiate meaning and pragmatic competence; the paired discussion task was created with precisely this purpose in mind. Receptive skills are also important on the EPT OC, in all three tasks. Test takers must comprehend other speakers and a recorded input (in the Retell task) to be successful. Finally, the materials for the test were created specifically for the targeted test takers. The prompts were all created (and continue to be created) based on a needs analysis of the types of communication commonly encountered at the university. Furthermore, the topics (as described above) are drawn from situations that students may experience in a university situation or may be related to current and relevant circumstances at the university.

Fairness. One of the subtler ways in which NNESs are judged against NESs is in the use of item writers and raters who are native English speakers. Incorporating NNESs in assessments is not only an issue of fairness, but also the reality of the world today; there are more NNESs in the world than there are NESs, so it is simply practical to include a variety of voices (Davies, 2009; Leung et al., 2016). In the case of item writing, there are many aspects that can be affected, both in the topics that are used and the language of the text (Elder & Davies, 2006). It is not enough to have different accents; the words and phrasing should be authentic to the accent, which requires having writers from the dialects being tested. Similarly, raters should be advanced English speakers from a variety of L1s (including NESs, and also potentially different from the test takers' L1) because ELF requires that a speaker be intelligible, and not only to NESs (Jenkins & Leung, 2017; Leung et al., 2016).

ELF researchers recommend extensive training on non-standard forms, particularly of the rubric elements described above, to break habits of attempting to conform to native standards (Canagarajah, 2006; Davies, 2009; Elder & Davies, 2006). Of course, since studies have found that there is little difference between NES and NNES ratings, it may not be necessary to have NNESs (Brown 2014). A counterargument to this is that other studies have found that there may be qualitative differences—for example, Zhang & Elder (2011) found that, although speech ratings were similar, NESs focused more on the descriptors related to content and ideas, while NNESs focused more on appropriateness and completeness. Thus, while the scores may be similar, the meaning of them may not be; it is possible that the effect of these differences could be more pronounced in an ELF test.

At present, most language tests are required to be taken only by NNESs; the exceptions are some tests for academic English, such as those that place students into academic writing classes. One of the recommendations for an ELF test is that

NESs should also be required to take the test (Canagarajah, 2014; Chopin, 2015; Jenkins & Leung, 2017; Leung et al., 2016; McNamara, 2011; Newbold, 2015). Proponents argue that this is an issue of social justice; when non-native speakers have to take a test that native speakers do not have to take, it can make NNESs feel that they are somehow different or even deficient (Chopin, 2015; McNamara, 2011).

The EPT OC includes NNESs and NESs at every stage of test development, administration, and scoring. Prompts are created by groups of item writers and then go through numerous stages of feedback about the content and the language. The aim is to create prompts that will be of interest and relevance to the test takers with language that is considered appropriate by advanced speakers from various L1 and L2 English speech varieties. After scripts have been written, speakers for the listening input are encouraged to revise what they will say in accordance with their speech variety. Test takers encounter multiple speech varieties on the test, including the oral interviewer, who is an advanced English speaker, two different recorded speakers for the retell task, one male and one female who are both advanced English speakers with different speech varieties, and a peer with a lower level of English proficiency from an L2 speech variety. Given that much of this language is not scripted, a test taker will encounter a variety of Englishes. Raters are advanced English speakers from a variety of L1s; it is highly unlikely that a test taker would be assessed by two raters with the test taker's own speech variety. Moreover, it is highly likely that at least one of the raters and recorded speakers will be an L2 user of English. Raters go through extensive online and face-to-face training, which underscores the need to rate based on effectiveness, clarity, and comprehensibility rather than targeting a native-like norm.

Requirements for taking the oral communication class or passing EPT OC are based on the lack of demonstrating sufficient English proficiency to be likely to be successful at the university. Students who have graduated from an English-medium high school or university are exempted regardless of their L1 or country of origin. Sufficient scores on various English assessments, both ones commonly taken by L1 and L2 English speakers, are also grounds for exemption. Likewise, being a citizen of the country where the university is located is not grounds for exemption. The exemption criteria are designed to reduce the resources needed for testing (by not requiring students to take the test who are very likely to pass it anyway) but ensure reasonable equity in who is exempted from taking it.

Conclusions, Implications, and Future Directions

Given the widespread use of ELF, it is pretty clear that most English tests should be guided at least to some degree by ELF principles. Criticisms by ELF researchers that English tests are not considering ELF issues are no doubt to some extent legitimate. On the other hand, ELF researchers should recognize that many L2 English tests have developed in ways that suggest ELF principles are, whether intentional or not, part of their design. Many of the same forces, such as globalization, increased use of English among non-native speakers, and communicative language teaching that have influenced ELF have also affected language test design.

This paper suggests that ELF tests can not only exist but that to one degree or another already do. For example, the ISU oral communication English placement test has been shown to have many ELF features. However, this paper also makes clear that assessment of ELF may conflict with some language assessment principles. This paper further indicates the need for a clear framework that could be used to determine the extent to which a test can be considered an ELF test and even more importantly, a framework that can guide language assessment test developers who aim to create ELF tests. The adaptation of Brown's (2014) EIL framework used in this paper was at best a rudimentary start to something that could be used for this purpose. Researchers will, no doubt, point out many limitations to this framework, which should help to move research in this area forward. However, before a defensible framework can be fully developed, researchers need to come to a shared agreement about what the critical aspects of ELF are. This will make it possible to better target these aspects in a useful ELF test development framework.

Effort to adopt a clear definition of ELF that could help guide language assessment developers is an important future direction for both ELF and language assessment researchers. Such agreement could lead to the development of an ELF framework that could be used to guide ELF test development and raise awareness of the degree to which English tests in current use already follow many ELF principles. Once this is sorted out, it may be discovered that ELF tests, to one degree or another, already exist. While it is unlikely that Bachman foresaw the future trend toward ELF assessment when he was writing about communicative competence in the 1980s and 1990s (e.g., Bachman, 1990; Bachman & Clark, 1987), it is likely that his vision of communicative language assessments aimed the field toward the assessment of ELF.

Appendix: Iowa State University Oral English Placement Test Rubric

(Also available online at: https://apling.engl.iastate.edu/wp-content/uploads/sites/221/2016/04/EPT-Oral-Communication-scale-updated.pdf)

EPT OC rating scales

		Fluency	Interactional competence	Comprehensibility/ Pronunciation	Grammar/ Vocabulary
		• Speaking rate • Repetition/ self-correction and pauses • Ability to speak naturally (e.g., effective use of fillers and markers)	• Appropriateness of response to a given situation	• Individual sounds/word levels • Stress, linking, rhythm, and intonation • Listener effort to understand	• Accuracy & range of grammatical structures • Accuracy & range of vocabulary
PASS	4	• Speech is **almost always** at an appropriate pace • Speech has **very rare** repetitions, self-corrections, or unnatural pauses • Speech is **almost always** natural (e.g., effective use of fillers and markers)	Response is **almost always** appropriate in any given situation, for example: • Initiating and expanding on own ideas • Connecting own ideas to a partner's ideas • Expanding on a partner's ideas • Making relevant comments • Taking turns appropriately • Asking appropriate questions • (Dis)agreeing politely • Answering questions in an appropriate amount of time	• Speech is **almost always** clear with well-articulated individual sounds and accurately pronounced words • Speech shows good control of stress and intonation; words in an utterance are almost always accurately and effectively blended. • Speech variety does **not** require focused listening and does **not** interfere with comprehension	• Speech **almost always** shows a range of accurate grammatical structures • Speech **almost always** shows a range of accurate use of academic vocabulary
	3	• Speech is **usually** at an appropriate pace • Speech may have **a few** repetitions, self-corrections, or unnatural pauses • Speech is **mostly** natural (e.g., effective use of fillers and markers)	Response is **usually** appropriate in any given situation, for example: • Initiating and expanding on own ideas • Connecting own ideas to a partner's ideas but may not fully expand on a partner's ideas • Making relevant comments • Taking turns appropriately • Asking appropriate questions • (Dis)agreeing politely • Answering questions in a somewhat appropriate amount of time	• Speech is **usually** clear with well-articulated individual sounds and with accurately pronounced words • Stress and intonation patterns **may not be completely accurate**, but this **does not interfere** with communication; words in an utterance are accurately and effectively blended • Speech variety **may** require focused listening, but is completely comprehensible	• Speech **usually** shows a range of accurate grammatical structures • Speech **usually** shows a range of accurate use of academic vocabulary

(continued)

(continued)

		Fluency	Interactional competence	Comprehensibility/ Pronunciation	Grammar/ Vocabulary
NOT PASS	2	• Speech is **generally** at an appropriate pace • Speech **may have some** repetitions, self-corrections, or unnatural pauses • Speech is **generally** natural (e.g., a little misuse of fillers and markers)	Response is **generally** appropriate in any given situation, for example: • Initiating but may not expand on it very well • Speaking without completely connecting own ideas to a partner's ideas • Making relevant comments • Taking turns appropriately • May ask questions that are not completely appropriate • May not (dis)agree completely appropriately/politely • May not answer questions in a completely appropriate amount of time	• A **little** mispronunciation of individual sounds and words might be present and may **slightly interfere** with communication • Stress and intonation patterns may be present and may **slightly interfere** communication; words are accurately and effectively blended in an utterance to some extent • Speech variety **requires** focused listening and may result in **slight lack** of comprehensibility	• Speech **generally** shows a range of grammatical structures, and **accuracy** may not be completely consistent • Speech **generally** shows a range of academic vocabulary. Some **errors** in vocabulary may be present but rarely hinder communication
	1	• Speech is **often too** fast or slow • Speech **may have frequent** repetitions, self-corrections, or unnatural pauses • Speech **may be quite** unnatural (e.g., some misuse of fillers and markers)	Response is **often** not appropriate in any given situation, for example: • Rater may assume a speaker cannot understand questions or what a partner says • May not initiate and develop topics • May not contribute much to the discussion • May respond minimally and irrelevantly to a partner • May not ask appropriate questions • May not (dis)agree politely • May not answer questions in an appropriate amount of time	• Mispronunciation of individual sounds and words may **often interfere** with comprehensibility • Stress and intonation patterns may be missing and may **often** cause difficulty for comprehension; words may not be accurately and effectively blended in an utterance • Speech variety **requires** focused listening and **may substantially** interfere with comprehensibility	• Speech **often** presents a range of grammatical structures; grammatical **errors** may **usually present** • Speech **often** shows a range of academic vocabulary. Some **errors** in vocabulary may be present and **hinder** communication to **some extent**

References

Bachman, L. F. (1990). *Fundamental considerations in language testing.* Oxford: Oxford UP.

Bachman, L. F., & Clark, J. L. (1987). The measurement of foreign/second language proficiency. *The ANNALS of the American Academy of Political and Social Science, 490*(1), 20–33.

Bachman, L. F., & Palmer, A. S. (1996). *Language testing in practice.* Oxford: Oxford University Press.

Brown, J. D. (2014). The future of world Englishes in language testing. *Language Assessment Quarterly, 11*(1), 5–26.

Canagarajah, S. (2006). Changing communicative needs, revised assessment objectives: Testing English as an international language. *Language Assessment Quarterly, 3*(3), 229–242.

Canagarajah, S. (2014). In search of a new paradigm for teaching English as an international language. *TESOL Journal., 5*(4), 767–785.

Canagarajah, S. (2018). The unit and focus of analysis in lingua franca English interactions: In search of a method. *International Journal of Bilingual Education and Bilingualism, 21*(4), 1–20.

Canale, M., & Swain, M. (1980). Theoretical bases of communicative approaches to second language teaching and testing. *Applied Linguistics, 1*(1), 1–47.

Chopin, K. (2015). Reconceptualizing norms for language testing: Assessing English language proficiency from within an ELF framework. In Y. Bayyurt & S, Akcan (Ed.). *Current perspectives on pedagogy for English as a Lingua Franca.* (pp. 193–204). Berlin: De Gruyter Mouton.

Cogo, A., & Dewey, M. (2006). Efficiency in ELF communication: From pragmatic motives to lexico-grammatical innovation. *Nordic Journal of English Studies, 5*(2), 59–93.

Davies, A. (2009). Assessing world Englishes. *Annual Review of Applied Linguistics, 29,* 80–89.

Ducasse, A. M., & Brown, A. (2009). Assessing paired orals: Raters' orientation to interaction. *Language Testing, 26*(3), 423–443.

Eckes, T. (2015). *Introduction to Many-Facet rasch measurement. analyzing and evaluating rater-mediated assessments.* 2nd Revised and Updated Edition. Series: Language Testing and Assessment. Volume 22. Frankfurt am Main: Peter Lang.

Elder, C., & Davies, A. (2006). Assessing English as a lingua franca. *Annual Review of Applied Linguistics, 26,* 282–304.

Galaczi, E. (2014). Interactional competence across proficiency levels: How do learners manage interaction in paired speaking tests? *Applied Linguistics, 35*(5), 553–574.

Guzman-Orth, D., Lopez, A., & Tolention, F. (2019). Exploring the use of dual language assessment tasks to assess young English learners. *Language Assessment Quarterly, 16*(4–5), 447–463.

Hall, C. J. (2014). Moving beyond accuracy: From tests of English to tests of 'Englishing'. *ELT Journal, 68*(4), 376–385.

Iowa State University English Placement Test. (2020). https://apling.engl.iastate.edu/english-placement-test.

Iowa State University English Placement Test Rating Scale. https://apling.engl.iastate.edu/alt-content/uploads/2016/04/EPT-Oral-Communication-scale-updated.pdf.

Isaacs, T., & Trofimovich, P. (2012). Deconstructing comprehensibility: Identifying the linguistic influences on listeners' L2 comprehensibility ratings. *Studies in Second Language Acquisition, 34*(3), 475–505.

Jenkins, J. (2009). *World Englishes* (2nd ed.). London: Routledge.

Jenkins, J. (2011). Accommodating (to) ELF in the international university. *Journal of Pragmatics, 43*(4), 926–936.

Jenkins, J. (2015). Repositioning English and multilingualism in English as a Lingua Franca. *Englishes in Practice, 2*(3), 49–85.

Jenkins, J. (2016). International tests of English: Are they fit for purpose? In H. Liao (Ed.), *Critical reflections on foreign language education: Globalization and local interventions.* Taipei: The Language Training and Testing Center.

Jenkins, J., & Leung, C. (2017). Assessing English as a Lingua Franca. In E. Shohamy, I. G. Or, & S. May (Eds.), *Language testing and assessment* (3rd ed., pp. 103–117). Switzerland: Springer.

Kachru, B. B. (Ed.). (1992). *The other tongue: English across cultures.* Urbana: University of Illinois Press.

Kim, H., & Billington, R. (2016). Pronunciation and comprehension in English as a lingua franca communication: Effect of L1 influence in international aviation communication. *Applied Linguistics, 39*(2), 135–158.

Leung, C., & Lewkowicz, J. (2017). Assessing second/additional language of diverse populations. In E. Shohamy, I. G. Or, & S. May (Eds.), *Language testing and assessment* (3rd ed., pp. 343–358). Switzerland: Springer.

Leung, C., Lewkowicz, J., & Jenkins, J. (2016). English for academic purposes: A need for remodeling. *Englishes in Practice, 3*(3), 55–73.

May, L. (2011). Interactional competence in a paired speaking test: Features salient to raters. *Language Assessment Quarterly, 8*(2), 127–145.

McNamara, T. (2011). Managing learning: Authority and language assessment. *Language Teaching, 44*(4), 500–515.

McNamara, T. (2018). *A challenge for language testing: The assessment of English as a Lingua Franca,* Language Assessment Research Conference, Ames, Iowa, March 21–23.

McNamara, T., Knoch, U., & Fan, J. (2019). *Fairness, justice, and language assessment.* Oxford: Oxford University Press.

Mortensen, J. (2013). Notes on English used as a lingua franca as an object of study. *Journal of English as a Lingua Franca, 2*(1), 25–46.

Newbold, D. (2015). Engaging with ELF in an entrance test for European university students. In Y. Bayyurt & S, Akcan (Ed.). *Current perspectives on pedagogy for English As a Lingua Franca.* (pp. 205–222). Berlin: De Gruyter Mouton.

Ockey, G. J., & French, R. (2016). From one to multiple accents on a test of L2 listening comprehension. *Applied Linguistics, 37*(5), 693–715.

Ockey, G. J., & Li, Z. (2015). New and not so new methods for assessing oral communication. *Language Value, 7*(1), 1–21.

Ockey, G. J., & Wagner, E. (2018). *Assessing L2 listening.* John Benjamins.

Prodromou, L. (2010). *English as a Lingua Franca. A Corpus-based analysis.* London: Continuum.

Seidlhofer, B. (2006). English as a Lingua Franca in the expanding circle: What it isn't. In R. Rubdy & M. Saraceni (Eds.), *English in the world: Global rules, global roles* (pp. 40–50). London: Continuum.

Seidlhofer, B. (2011). *Understanding English as a Lingua Franca.* Oxford: Oxford UP.

Zhang, Y., & Elder, C. (2011). Judgments of oral proficiency by non-native and native English speaking teacher raters: Competing or complementary constructs? *Language Testing., 28*(1), 31–50.

Chapter 3
Revisiting the Role of Content in Language Assessment Constructs

Lorena Llosa

Abstract In 1990, Bachman first introduced his model of communicative language use, which focused not just on an individual's communicative language ability, which he defined as language competence plus strategic competence, but also psychophysiological mechanisms, the language use context, and the language user's knowledge structures. In this paper, I first review Bachman's model, specifically his conceptualization of the role of content (or knowledge structures) in language use and in construct definitions. I then examine how his conceptualizations have been taken up and built on in the language assessment practices of three key contexts in which content and language intersect: language for specific purposes, U.S. K-12 English learner education, and content and language integrated learning. For each context, I highlight examples of the latest conceptualizations of the role content plays in their assessment constructs. I conclude by arguing that, if we are to develop language assessments that yield meaningful interpretations about test takers' ability to use language in specific target language use domains, future research must focus on the role of content in language assessment constructs.

Introduction

Bachman's model of communicative language use (Bachman, 1990) has had a major impact in the field of language assessment specifically, and in applied linguistics more broadly. Bachman's model, which builds on Canale and Swain's (1980) conceptualization of communicative competence, involves not just an individual's communicative language ability, which he defined as language competence plus strategic competence, but also psychophysiological mechanisms, the language use context, and the language user's knowledge structures. At a time when the focus tended to be on grammatical and textual knowledge, this model highlighted the complexity of language use and of language competence itself. This model, updated by Bachman and Palmer (1996), together with Bachman's concept of test method facets (later

L. Llosa (✉)
New York University, New York, United States
e-mail: lorena.llosa@nyu.edu

© Springer Nature Singapore Pte Ltd. 2020   29
G. J. Ockey and B. A. Green (eds.), *Another Generation of Fundamental Considerations in Language Assessment*, https://doi.org/10.1007/978-981-15-8952-2_3

referred to as the task characteristics framework in Bachman & Palmer, 1996) was the foundation of his conceptual framework, which guided his approach to language assessment research and development.

Bachman's model, which has been influential in defining the constructs of many language assessments in use today, has been the subject of much theoretical discussion, particularly in terms of the role context plays in defining language assessment constructs (see Bachman, 2007; Chapelle, 1998; Chalhoub-Deville, 2003). One component of his model that has received relatively less attention is content, which he referred to initially as knowledge structures (Bachman, 1990) and later as topical knowledge (Bachman & Palmer, 1996, 2010). The field of language for specific purposes (LSP) is one exception since, due to its very nature, it has had to grapple with the role of content in language assessment (Douglas, 2000).

I argue that content has become more important in language assessment since Bachman's model was introduced 30 years ago due to a number of changes in the nature of language education and in the field of language assessment. Language education has been moving toward approaches that integrate content and language, many of which, like bilingual education and content-based instruction, are not new. We continue to see them used in schools throughout the world to address the educational needs of students who, due to globalization and immigration, are learning content through a second or additional language. In recent decades, instructional approaches that integrate content and language have expanded further. One example is the content and language integrated learning (CLIL) movement, initially active in Europe and now also in Asia and Latin America. There also has been a rapid increase in the number of English-medium universities located in places where English is a second or foreign language (Coyle, Hood, & Marsh, 2010).

The field of language assessment research has also changed since Bachman's model was introduced. It has expanded beyond the study of high-stakes, summative tests of English proficiency to focus on classroom assessments used for summative and formative purposes. Moreover, since language classrooms are increasingly becoming spaces in which language and content intersect, assessments in these spaces have to account for the role of content.

In this paper, I first review Bachman's model of language use, specifically his conceptualization of the role of content in language use and construct definitions. I then examine how his conceptualizations have been taken up and built on in the language assessment practices of three key contexts in which content and language intersect: LSP, the education of English learners in U.S. K-12, and CLIL. I highlight examples of the latest conceptualizations of the role content plays in each context's assessment constructs. I conclude by arguing that, if we are to develop language assessments that yield meaningful interpretations about test takers' ability to use language in specific target language use (TLU) domains, future research must focus on the role of content in language assessment constructs.

Historical Perspective: The Role of Content in Bachman's Model of Communicative Language Use

One of Bachman's main contributions is his model of communicative language use, first introduced in his book, *Fundamentals Considerations in Language Testing* (1990). His model includes three components—language competence, strategic competence, and psychophysiological mechanisms—that interact with "the language use context and language user's knowledge structures" (p. 84). Content, or "knowledge structures," is defined as "sociocultural knowledge, 'real-world' knowledge." The role of content in the model is only addressed within the definition of strategic competence: "Strategic competence thus provides the means for relating language competencies to features of the context of the situation in which language use takes place and to the language user's knowledge structures" (p. 84).

In their 1996 book, *Language Testing in Practice,* Bachman and Palmer refer to content as "topical knowledge." Topical knowledge plays a role similar to that of knowledge structures in the 1990 model, and, like knowledge structures, represents a broad definition of content, ranging from the topic of a particular reading passage to a specific subject area. In the 1996 model, topical knowledge interacts with language knowledge, the test takers' personal characteristics, and the characteristics of the language use or test task situation and setting through strategic competence and affective schemata. Bachman and Palmer (1996) described this as "an interactional framework of language use" that presents "a view of language use that focuses on the interactions among areas of language ability, topical knowledge, and affective schemata on the one hand, and how these interact with characteristics of the language use setting, or test task, on the other" (p. 78). Bachman and Palmer went on to address the role of topical knowledge in defining the construct for language assessments. They questioned the commonly held belief at the time that topical knowledge is always a source of test bias or invalidity in language assessment and suggested that there are situations where topical knowledge "may, in fact, be part of the construct the test developer wants to measure" (pp. 120–121). They proposed three ways to account for topical knowledge when defining a construct: "(1) define the construct solely in terms of language ability, excluding topical knowledge from the construct definition; (2) include both topical knowledge and language ability in the construct definition, or (3) define topical knowledge and language ability as separate constructs" (p. 121). Bachman and Palmer (2010) offered the same three options, but option 2 was described slightly differently, as "topical knowledge and language ability defined as a single construct" (p. 218).

Options 1 and 3 assume that topical knowledge and language ability can be separated and either included or not as part of an assessment's construct. In option 2, on the other hand, Bachman and Palmer (1996, 2010) conceded the possibility that both topical knowledge and language ability could be a single construct (the phrasing of option 2 in Bachman & Palmer, 2010) or that at the very least they could overlap. Bachman and Palmer (1996) indicated that option 2 should only be applied when test takers have homogeneous topical knowledge (thus minimizing its effect on performance), and they warned about inference: "The test developer or user may mistakenly fail to attribute performance on test tasks to topical knowledge as well as to language ability" (p. 124).

Bachman (2007) acknowledged that, even though his (Bachman, 1990) and Bachman and Palmer's (1996) models of communicative language use and task characteristics framework "recognize and discuss language use in terms of interactions between ability, context, and the discourse that is co-constructed, their two frameworks are essentially descriptive" and do not "solve the issue of how abilities and contexts interact, and the degree to which these may mutually affect each other" (p. 55). I would add that the frameworks do not specify how language ability and *topical knowledge* interact or the degree to which they may mutually affect each other. Understanding this relationship has become increasingly important as the field of language education has shifted toward approaches that integrate content and language, and the field of language assessment has expanded its reach to the classroom context.

Critical Issues: Grappling with the Role of Content in Language Assessment Constructs

In this section, I explore how scholars in three different contexts in which language and content intersect—LSP, U.S. K-12 education, and CLIL—have accounted for the role of content in language use and in language assessment constructs. In all of these contexts, content refers specifically to a profession or a particular discipline or subject area in school. For each context, I highlight examples of their latest conceptualizations of the role of content in their assessment constructs.

Language for Specific Purposes Assessment

The field of LSP has the longest history of grappling with the relationship between language proficiency and content in assessment. An outgrowth of the communicative language movement of the 1970s, LSP addresses teaching and learning at the intersection of language and a specific content area, often a professional field (e.g., German for business, Spanish for tourism, English for health professions). LSP assessments address the need to make decisions about individuals' performance on tasks in a specific academic or professional field. To define the construct of what he calls "specific purpose language ability," Douglas (2000) built on Bachman's (1996) model. He defined it as "the interaction between specific purpose background knowledge and language ability, by means of strategic competence engaged by specific purpose input in the form of test method characteristics" (p. 88). Douglas (2000) argued that "specific purpose background knowledge is a necessary feature of specific purpose language ability and must be taken into account in making inferences on the basis of LSP test performance" (p. 88). This view, however, was not shared by all in the field. For example, Davies (2001) argued that "LSP testing cannot be about testing for subject specific knowledge. It must be about testing the ability to manipulate language functions appropriately in a wide variety of ways" (p. 143).

A special issue in the journal *Language Testing* provides a comprehensive illustration of the tension between these two approaches to defining the construct in LSP assessment. The special issue focuses on the Occupational English Test (OET), a test used to assess the English language skills of overseas-trained health professionals who seek licensure in Australia, New Zealand, and Singapore (Elder, 2016). The OET uses health-related materials or scenarios to assess listening, reading, speaking, and writing. The listening and reading sections are the same for all professions, but the speaking and writing sections differ by occupation. The articles in the special issue describe studies conducted to revise the speaking section of the test, which were motivated by the need to increase its authenticity. The criteria used to score performance on this section include overall communicative effectiveness, fluency, intelligibility, appropriateness of language, and resources of grammar and expression—in other words, criteria that reflect a generalized view of language, consistent with Bachman and Palmer's (1996) option 1 for defining the construct solely in terms of language ability. Many stakeholders (e.g., healthcare professionals), however, did not perceive this approach to be authentic. As Pill (2016) explained, it may be that "the test is not measuring sufficiently those aspects of performance that matter to health professionals in the workplace" (p. 176).

To address this concern, Pill (2016) turned to "indigenous assessment criteria" (Jacoby & McNamara, 1999), that is, assessment criteria derived from the TLU domain. He asked doctors and nurses to provide feedback on test takers' performance on the speaking tasks to help him understand what these health professionals (as opposed to language professionals and educators) value in spoken interactions so he could expand on the more traditional linguistic criteria in their rubric. Based on these professionals' comments, he proposed two new, professionally relevant assessment criteria for the speaking test: clinician engagement and management of interaction.

The next step was to investigate the extent to which the language professionals scoring the assessment could orient to the new criteria. O'Hagan, Pill, & Zhang (2016) explored what happened when seven OET language assessors were trained to apply these new professionally derived criteria when assessing recorded speech samples from previous OET administrations. They found that the new criteria were measuring a slightly different construct of speaking ability, one more consistent with Bachman and Palmer's (1996) option 2 of including both topical knowledge and language ability in the construct definition. The OET, however, is intended to assess only language; healthcare professionals' professional knowledge and skills are assessed by a different test. The studies on the OET speaking section thus raised an important question: Is it possible to separate language from content in an LSP assessment and still have an assessment that yields meaningful interpretations about language use in a specific TLU domain?

Cai and Kunnan (2018) conducted an empirical study to determine whether content and language can in fact be separated in an LSP assessment. Their study investigated the inseparability of content knowledge in an LSP test of nursing English. The test consisted of four texts, each addressing one topic in clinical nursing: gynecological nursing, pediatric nursing, basic nursing, and internal medicine nursing. The goal of the study was to examine whether LSP reading performance could be separated psychometrically from domain-general content knowledge (e.g., nursing) and domain-specific content knowledge (e.g., pediatric nursing). They found that "it is psychometrically possible to separate the portion of domain-specific content knowledge effect from LSP reading score assignment, but this separation is impossible for the portion of domain-general content knowledge contained in the domain-general reading factor" (p. 125). They also called attention to the importance of avoiding a simplistic understanding of content knowledge as an "either-or" paradigm in future research on the separability of content and language.

Knoch and Macqueen (2020) propose an even more nuanced characterization of content and its relation to language use in LSP assessments, specifically those for professional purposes. They suggest that the construct should be determined by sampling from various "codes of relevance" that are part of professional purposes communication. They represent these codes of relevance in the form of four concentric circles (see Fig. 3.1). The interior circle, or the intra-professional register layer, represents the professional register used by a smaller number of users with shared professional knowledge (e.g., doctors who speak to each other in "medicalese"). Language use in this circle is practically inseparable from content knowledge. The next circle is the inter-professional register layer, which represents interactions between individuals with some shared professional knowledge (e.g., a doctor interacting with a nurse or social worker in "cross-disciplinary medicalese"). The next circle, the workplace community repertoire layer, is "a confluence of community varieties with professional register" (p. 63). Interactions in this layer are between those with professional knowledge and lay people (e.g., a doctor communicating with a patient). Finally, the outermost circle represents "the array of varieties used in the broader social context of the target language use domain," including "the standard language/languages of the jurisdiction, minority languages and combinations of languages, e.g. patterns of code switching, as well as lingua francas in use" (p. 63). Knoch and Macqueen argue that this layer is essential because, by attending to it, "policy makers and test developers can see which community varieties could be helpful in contributing to decreased risk of miscommunication in the workplace" (p. 63).

Knoch and Macqueen (2020) explain that decisions about which codes of relevance to sample from when developing a language assessment for professional purposes should be determined through a careful analysis of the professional context and the purpose of the assessment. Their codes of relevance represent the latest conceptualization of language use in LSP and highlight the complexity with which language and content interact in this context.

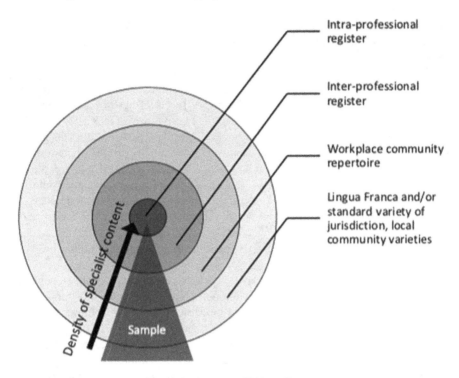

Fig. 3.1 Codes of relevance (Knoch & Macqueen, 2020, p. 61)

Assessment of English Learners in U.S. K-12 Education

Another context that has wrestled with the role of content in language assessment is U.S. K-12 education. Students who are classified as English learners are assessed every year to determine their English language proficiency (ELP) and their content learning (e.g., math, science). As Llosa (2016) explains, content in this context traditionally has been considered a source of construct-irrelevant variance in language assessments, with most assessments adhering to Bachman and Palmer's (1996) option 1—defining the construct solely in terms of language ability. However, it has become clear over time that, to yield valid inferences about students' ability to use English in school, ELP standards and assessments must focus specifically on the types of language used in school, not on general language proficiency (Bailey & Butler, 2003). ELP assessments currently in use are based on ELP standards that link language proficiency to the content areas (language arts, mathematics, science, and social studies). In fact, federal legislation requires that states adopt ELP standards that align with content standards (U.S. Department of Education, 2015). Despite being aligned with content areas, the ELP construct of most of these assessments is operationalized according to the features of academic language at the word, sentence, and discourse level (e.g., see WIDA Consortium, 2012). As Llosa and Grapin (2019) explain, this

operationalization allows ELP assessments to comply with accountability requirements to assess language separate from content and across all content areas at the
same time.

However, despite the fact that ELP assessments focus on academic language
and avoid assessing content, evidence suggests that the separation between the two
may be difficult to achieve, especially at higher levels of performance. Romhild,
Kenyon, and MacGregor (2011) investigated the extent to which ACCESS for ELLs,
an ELP assessment used in 40 U.S. states (WIDA, n.d.), assessed domain-general
linguistic knowledge (i.e., academic language common to various content areas)
versus domain-specific knowledge (i.e., academic language specific to a particular
content area). They found that the test in most forms primarily tapped into the
domain-general factor, but in forms assessing higher levels of English proficiency, the
domain-specific factor was stronger than the domain-general factor. Their study indicates that, even in an assessment specifically designed to assess English language
proficiency, it is difficult to disentangle language from content at higher levels of
English proficiency.

The latest wave of content standards in the U.S. has created an even greater overlap
between language and content. The Common Core State Standards for English
language arts and mathematics (National Governors Association Center for Best
Practices & Council of Chief State School Officers, 2010a, 2010b) and the Next
Generation Science Standards (NGSS Lead States, 2013) emphasize disciplinary
practices. The Next Generation Science Standards, for example, shifted the focus of
science learning from learning discrete facts to engaging in the disciplinary practices
of scientists, such as arguing from evidence and constructing explanations. In this
latest wave of content standards, "engaging in disciplinary practices is not simply
a language skill needed to do the work of the content areas; it *is* the work of the
content areas" (Llosa & Grapin, 2019). When assessing students in science means
assessing their ability to argue from evidence, for example, it becomes even more
difficult to separate language from content. Bachman (2002) had already identified
the challenge of separating content from language in performance assessment tasks
in education and had argued that "performance assessment tasks need to be based
on construct definitions that include both content knowledge and language ability"
(p. 16), in other words, option 2. And yet, high-stakes assessments used for accountability purposes to this day are tasked with separately assessing English learners'
language and content proficiency.

In the classroom, however, the constraints imposed by accountability need not
apply, yet teachers tend to adopt the same definition of ELP in terms of academic
language in the content classroom. Llosa and Grapin (2019) argue that the construct
of academic language at the word, sentence, and discourse level may not be a helpful
way to think about English learners' ability to use language in the content classroom
because it focuses teachers' attention only on *how* students communicate and not
on *what* they communicate. Llosa and Grapin (2019) offer an alternative—a reconceptualization of the ELP construct that leverages the overlap between content and
language for the purpose of supporting English learners in the content classroom.
In this reconceptualization, the overlap between language and content is represented

Fig. 3.2 Reconceptualization of the ELP construct for supporting ELs in the content classroom (Llosa & Grapin, 2019)

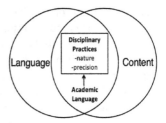

by the disciplinary practices, described in terms of (a) the nature of the disciplinary practices and (b) the precision of the disciplinary meaning communicated through the practices (Grapin, Llosa, Haas, Goggins, & Lee, 2019). As shown in Fig. 3.2, the linguistic features of academic language at the word, sentence, and discourse levels are relevant only to the extent that they contribute to communicating the intended disciplinary meaning through the disciplinary practice.

Llosa and Grapin (2019) argue that, by focusing more narrowly on the language needed to do the work of the content areas, language and content teachers can support English learners' content understanding and also help them develop the aspects of language that are most crucial to engaging in content learning. This reconceptualization of the ELP construct for the content classroom reflects Bachman and Palmer's (2010) option 2, in which "language ability and topical knowledge are defined as a single construct" (p. 218).

Content and Language Integrated Learning

CLIL is an approach to education in which academic content and a second or additional language are taught and learned simultaneously (Coyle, Hood, & Marsh, 2010). In most CLIL contexts, the additional language taught alongside content is English. Over the past several decades, CLIL has expanded from Europe to other parts of the world. It initially was implemented in secondary schools but is now the pedagogical approach used by many English-medium institutions around the world, and it has expanded to elementary education in some countries. An interesting characteristic of the field of CLIL is that, given the variety of contexts in which it is implemented, it is not (yet) subject to mandated, high-stakes assessments, and most of the research in CLIL has focused primarily on the classroom context.

Until recently, the relationship between content and language was not an area of interest in CLIL assessment. As Wilkinson, Zegers, and van Leeuwen (2006) asserted, "the fact that education takes place through a language that is not the students' mother tongue (and, in many cases, not that of the educators either) seems to have little influence on the assessment processes" (p. 30). They noted that the primary approach was to assess students as they would be assessed in a content area course in their first language. Dalton-Puffer (2013) explained that, even though CLIL has "a dual focus on content and language," its implementation has been "driven by the logic of the content-subjects," and attention given to language in these spaces has been limited to vocabulary (p. 219).

More recently, however, significant efforts have been made to conceptualize the nature of content and language integration in CLIL (see Nikula, Dafouz, Moore, & Smit, 2016). Without a mandate to assess content and language separately (like those the LSP and the U.S. K-12 contexts are subject to), CLIL scholars have been able to focus on "how students' language can be addressed in a way which does not separate the language used from the content it expresses" (Llinares, Morton, & Whittaker, 2012, p. 187).

Recognizing that content and language teachers tend to orient to different learning goals, Dalton-Puffer (2013) identified "a zone of convergence between content and language pedagogies" (p. 216). Drawing from theories in education and applied linguistics, she proposed cognitive discourse functions (also referred to as academic language functions) as a transdisciplinary construct that captures integration in CLIL. Based on a review of the literature, Dalton-Puffer proposed seven cognitive discourse functions that subsume most communicative intentions: classify, define, describe, evaluate, explain, explore, and report. She views these cognitive discourse functions as a construct that both applied linguists and content specialists can use to inform research and development on the integration of content and language pedagogies "by making visible how transdisciplinary thought processes are handled in classroom talk" (p. 232). She claimed that, beyond its use as a research heuristic, the cognitive discourse function construct could also "function as a kind of lingua franca that may enable [content and language] educators to communicate across subject boundaries" (p. 242). Her conceptualization of content and language integration could also inform assessment constructs consistent with Bachman and Palmer (2010)'s option 2, defining topical knowledge and language ability as a single construct.

Lamenting the traditional lack of attention to language in many CLIL classrooms, Llinares et al. (2012) proposed a scale that integrates content goals with the language needed to accomplish those goals. They argued that the starting point of instruction and assessment in the CLIL classroom should be the content area. They also argued that only the language needed in that particular content area should be assessed, not general language proficiency. They proposed a content-language integrated scale with a content dimension and a language dimension. In adapting the rubric for a given CLIL classroom, the content goals at each level of the rubric are identified first. Then the language goals are identified, described in terms of the genres (text types) and registers (grammar and vocabulary) through which students will achieve those content goals at each level. The purpose of the language dimension is to bring the language CLIL learners need to use "into the open as an explicit component of the tasks they do" (p. 284). However, Llinares et al. (2012) also argued that language need not be assessed separately from content when using this rubric. They proposed that the assessment be based on the content dimension and that the language dimension be used for formative assessment purposes only. In other words, they argued that a teacher in a CLIL classroom should attend to language only to provide instructional feedback relevant to the achievement of the content goals. They view language "as an enabler, something that is an indispensable component in the achievement of learning goals, but not targeted for separate assessment" (p. 296). This perspective is similar to Llosa and Grapin's (2019) conceptualization of English language proficiency in the U.S. K-12 content classroom and provides another example of Bachman and Palmer's option 2 for defining the construct.

Conclusions, Implications, and Future Directions

Bachman (1990) cautioned that, "for both theory and practice, the challenge is to develop tests that reflect current views of language and language use" (p. 297). Thirty years later, the language education landscape has changed and is increasingly promoting views of language and language use that are integrated with content. This change prompts a reexamination of the role of content in language use and in language assessment construct definitions. Bachman and Palmer (1996, 2010) offered us three options for accounting for content in construct definitions. Until recently, many assessments have opted for options 1 and 3, which presume that language and content can be defined as separate constructs and assessed independently of each other. This approach has been motivated in part by external requirements. As outlined in this chapter, the language assessment literature in LSP and U.S. K-12 education has focused primarily on large-scale assessments used for high-stakes purposes (e.g., licensing or certification in LSP, accountability in U.S. K-12) that specifically require language to be assessed separately from content. In these contexts, Bachman and Palmer's (1996) option 1, defining the construct solely in terms of language ability, has resulted in assessments that did not yield meaningful interpretations about language use in the TLU domain and/or were perceived as inauthentic by stakeholders in that domain. The challenge for these fields has been to find a middle ground. The large-scale ELP assessments in U.S. K-12 and many LSP assessments, such as the OET, assess specialized language; the ELP assessments assess the language of schooling across content areas, whereas the OET assesses language proficiency across a broad range of health professions. These assessments have to be specific enough to serve their purpose but not too specific (e.g., just the language of science or English for doctors), or else they cannot be used for their intended purpose. The consensus is that, in these contexts in which content and language intersect, completely separating language from content in assessment is extremely difficult. Test developers need to figure out how much overlap they are comfortable with for such high-stakes assessments.

Recently, attention to classroom assessment has opened up new possibilities for thinking about the role of content in language assessment constructs. In the classroom, where the goal is to support student learning, there is no requirement to deal with content and language separately. In fact, doing so would be both unrealistic and unnecessary. Several scholars have taken on the challenge of rethinking the language construct in ways that reflect language use in a specific TLU domain and coming up with new constructs that integrate language and content in meaningful ways. In other words, these scholars are exploring what it would look like to truly adopt Bachman and Palmer's (2010) option 2: "Topical knowledge and language knowledge are defined as a single construct." The models proposed by Knoch and McQueen (2020); Llosa and Grapin (2019); Llinares et al. (2012); and Dalton-Puffer (2013) are examples of this effort. In all of these models, the overlap between content and language is leveraged to support students' content and language learning.

Future research could investigate the ways content and language overlap in various contexts. In so doing, future studies would benefit from developing a more nuanced understanding of content, as Cai and Kunnan (2018) point out. Future studies also could attempt to operationalize these integrated constructs of content and language and examine the extent to which assessments based on these constructs actually provide teachers with useful information that supports student learning in the classroom. Specifically, future studies could investigate the extent to which language and content teachers can orient to these new constructs and use them to provide meaningful formative feedback. Another promising direction would be for scholars across these three contexts, which have traditionally operated separately, to come together to explore new ways of thinking about and assessing language at the intersection of language and content. This type of research collaboration will be critical if we are to develop language assessments that yield meaningful interpretations about test takers' ability to use language in specific TLU domains and, as Bachman (1990) advocated, "reflect current views of language and language use" (p. 297).

References

Bachman, L. F. (1990). *Fundamental considerations in language testing*. Oxford, England: Oxford University Press.

Bachman, L. F. (2002). Alternative interpretations of alternative assessments: Some validity issues in educational performance assessments. *Educational Measurement: Issues and Practice, 21*(3), 5–17.

Bachman, L. F. (2007). What is the construct? The dialectic of abilities and context in defining constructs in language assessment. In J. Fox, M. Wesche, D. Bayliss, L. Cheng, C. E. Turner, & C. Doe (Eds.), *Language testing reconsidered* (pp. 41–72). Ottawa: University of Ottawa Press.

Bachman, L. F., & Palmer, A. (1996). *Language testing in practice*. Oxford, England: Oxford University Press.

Bachman, L. F., & Palmer, A. (2010). *Language assessment in practice: Developing language assessments and justifying their use in the real world*. Oxford, England: Oxford University Press.

Bailey, A. L., & Butler, F. A. (2003). *An evidentiary framework for operationalizing academic language for broad application to K-12 education: A design document* (CSE Technical Report No. 611). Los Angeles: University of California, Center for the Study of Evaluation/National Center for Research on Evaluation, Standards, and Student Testing.

Cai, Y., & Kunnan, A. J. (2018). Examining the inseparability of content knowledge from LSP reading ability: An approach combining bifactor-multidimensional item response theory and structural equation modeling. *Language Assessment Quarterly, 15*, 109–129.

Canale, M., & Swain, M. (1980). Theoretical bases of communicative approaches to second language teaching and testing. *Applied Linguistics, 1*(1), 1–47.

Chalhoub-Deville, M. (2003). Second language interaction: Current perspectives and future trends. *Language Testing, 20*(4), 369–383.

Chapelle, C. (1998). Construct definition and validity inquiry in SLA research. In L. F. Bachman & A. D. Cohen (Eds.), *Interfaces between second language acquisition and language testing research* (pp. 32–70). New York: Cambridge University Press.

Coyle, D., Hood, P., & Marsh, D. (2010). *Content and language integrated learning.* Cambridge, England: Cambridge University Press.

Dalton-Puffer, C. (2013). A construct of cognitive discourse functions for conceptualising content-language integration in CLIL and multilingual education. *European Journal of Applied Linguistics, 1*(2), 216–253.

Davies, A. (2001). The logic of testing languages for specific purposes. *Language Testing, 18,* 133–147.

Douglas, D. (2000). *Assessing languages for specific purposes.* Cambridge, England: Cambridge University Press.

Elder, C. (2016). Exploring the limits of authenticity in LSP testing: The case of a specific-purpose language test for health professionals. *Language Testing, 33,* 147–152.

Grapin, S. E., Llosa, L., Haas, A., Goggins, M., & Lee, O. (2019). Precision: Toward a meaning-centered view of language use with English learners in the content areas. *Linguistics and Education, 50,* 71–83.

Jacoby, S., & McNamara, T. (1999). Locating competence. *English for Specific Purposes, 18,* 213–241.

Knoch, U., & Macqueen, S. (2020). *Assessing english for professional purposes.* New York, NY: Routledge.

Llinares, A., Morton, T., & Whittaker, R. (2012). *The roles of language in CLIL.* Cambridge, England: Cambridge University Press.

Llosa, L. (2016). Assessing students' content knowledge and language proficiency. In E. Shohamy & I. Or (Eds.), *Encyclopedia of language and education* (Vol. 7, pp. 3–14). New York: Springer International.

Llosa, L., & Grapin, S. E. (2019, March). *Academic language or disciplinary practices? Reconciling perspectives of language and content educators when assessing English learners' language proficiency in the content classroom.* Paper presented at the Language Testing Research Colloquium (LTRC), Atlanta, GA.

National Governors Association Center for Best Practices & Council of Chief State School Officers. (2010a). *Common Core State Standards for English language arts and literacy in history/social studies, science, and technical subjects.* Washington, DC: Author. Retrieved from http://www.corestandards.org/wp-content/uploads/ELA_Standards1.pdf.

National Governors Association Center for Best Practices & Council of Chief State School Officers. (2010b). *Common Core State Standards for mathematics.* Washington, DC: Author. Retrieved from http://www.corestandards.org/wpcontent/uploads/.

States, N. G. S. S. L. (2013). *Next generation science standards: For states, by states.* Washington, DC: The National Academies Press.

Nikula, T., Dafouz, E., Moore, P., & Smit, U. (Eds.). (2016). *Conceptualizing integration in CLIL and multilingual education.* Bristol, England: Multilingual Matters.

O'Hagan, S., Pill, J., & Zhang, Y. (2016). Extending the scope of speaking assessment criteria in a specific-purpose language test: Operationalizing a health professional perspective. *Language Testing, 33*(2), 175–193.

Pill, J. (2016). Drawing on indigenous criteria for more authentic assessment in a specific-purpose language test: Health professionals interacting with patients. *Language Testing, 33,* 175–193.

Romhild, A., Kenyon, D., & MacGregor, D. (2011). Exploring domain-general and domain-specific linguistic knowledge in the assessment of academic English language proficiency. *Language Assessment Quarterly, 8*(3), 213–228.

U.S. Department of Education. (2015). *Every Student Succeeds Act*. Washington, DC: Author. Retrieved from https://www.gpo.gov/fdsys/pkg/BILLS-114s1177enr/pdf/BILLS-114s1177enr. pdf.

WIDA Consortium. (2012). *Amplification of the English language development standards*. Madison: Board of Regents of the University of Wisconsin System. Retrieved from http://www.wida.us/sta ndards/eld.aspx.

WIDA (n.d.). About WIDA. Retrieved from https://wida.wisc.edu/about.

Wilkinson, R., Zegers, V., & van Leeuwen, C. (2006). *Bridging the assessment gap in English-Medium Higher Education*. Maastricht, Netherlands: Maastricht University Language Centre.

Chapter 4
What Does Language Testing Have to Offer to Multimodal Listening?

Paul Gruba

Abstract In response to a question posed first by Bachman (1991), the aim of this chapter is to discuss what the fields of language assessment and multimodal studies may have to offer each other. Using video-based, or "multimodal," listening as a case study, the chapter argues that the placement of semiotic resources at the core of transdisciplinary SLA (The Douglas Fir Group, 2016) demands greater attention to SFL principles in language assessment. After establishing constructs and reviewing historical precedents, the AUA framework for classroom assessment (Bachman & Damböck, 2018) is proposed as a way to structure the integration of multimodal studies concepts into the testing of semiotic resources. Work by language assessment specialists, particularly in ethical considerations and quantitative methods, may well benefit research in multimodality. The chapter concludes with an agenda for multimodal listening assessment research that points to the fact that language testing has much to offer to this area of increasing importance in classroom assessment.

Introduction

Nearly three decades ago, Bachman (1991) asked: "What does language testing have to offer to researchers and practitioners in other areas of applied linguistics, particularly in language learning and language teaching?" (p. 672). Since that time, digital technologies have not only reshaped contemporary life but also made it clear that many assessment regimes have failed to recognize new ways of learning (Kress, 2003, 2009). As a growing number of educators now see that assessments built on "flat literacies" are neither relevant nor fit-for-purpose (Bali & Mostafa, 2018; Hung, Chiu, & Yeh, 2013; Kern, 2014; Lotherington & Jenson, 2011), it is more important than ever to develop classroom language assessment as it "has emerged as one of the most exciting and challenging areas of our field" (Bachman, 2014, p. 8).

In this chapter, I respond to Bachman (1991) and seek to forge stronger links between classroom language assessment and multimodal studies. I limit my scope to

P. Gruba (✉)
University of Melbourne, Melbourne, Australia
e-mail: p.gruba@unimelb.edu.au

© Springer Nature Singapore Pte Ltd. 2020
G. J. Ockey and B. A. Green (eds.), *Another Generation of Fundamental Considerations in Language Assessment*, https://doi.org/10.1007/978-981-15-8952-2_4

research concerning the role of digital video in second language listening that, for our purposes, can be thought of as "multimodal listening" although such a construct is hardly novel or new. On YouTube alone, people watch over a billion hours of content per day across more than 100 countries in 80 different languages (YouTube, 2020). Second language educators have long made use of audiovisual media in the classroom. In the 1920s, Disney Studios produced films made specifically for language learners (Hendy, 2013) and analog video cassettes were widely used as pedagogical media for language instruction throughout the latter part of the twentieth century (Altman, 1989; Armes, 1988).

Although digital videotext is now a dominant medium of instruction in language teaching and learning (e.g., Herrero & Vanderschelden, 2019), a range of challenges have delayed its uptake in testing. We have yet to resolve, for example, how the presence of visual elements influences listening comprehension (Suvorov, 2015), determine ways to rank the specific level of a videotext (Alghamdi, 2020), or how to create listening tasks that incorporate dynamic visual media (Wagner, 2013). Work to link multimodal listening and assessment, particularly in the classroom, has emerged as a prime area of research and development (Campoy-Cubillo, 2019; Campoy-Cubillo & Querol-Julian, 2015).

Following Kress (2015), this chapter first sets out a series of foundational concepts that underpin multimodal studies with reference to listening assessment. The discussion then moves to illustrating how the work of Bachman and Damböck (2018) may help to frame multimodal listening assessments in the classroom. A third section of the chapter points out what language assessment may offer to multimodal studies, and then concludes with suggestions for further research.

Constructs

As we begin a discussion of constructs, it is useful to place our efforts within a prevailing theory of language (Bachman & Palmer, 2010, pp. 66–78) such as those set out by Valdés, Kibler, and Walqui (2014). In each orientation, assessments align with a particular view of language. Though perhaps dated, early formalist views of language promoted assessment designs that required learners to demonstrate their ability to produce correct grammatical patterns. Cognitive orientations underpin assessment designs that are grounded in the universal stages of second language acquisition; in functional orientations, learners are assessed on their ability to demonstrate the use of language in both meaning and form. The focus on assessment in sociocultural orientations seeks to track the movement of learners from peripheral to more central areas of participation in communities. The link of listening assessment to multimodal studies would require a recognition of both functional and sociocultural views of language in line with Halliday (1978). Accordingly, the role of video as a mode of presentation would be crucial to assessment designs that see context as crucial to the meaning of a given utterance. Seeing who, what, and how a topic was being discussed clearly influences a listeners' understanding and assessment outcome (Wagner, 2013).

Our continued discussion would reveal how the term "multimodal" varies across disciplines (Norris & Maier, 2014). Briefly, in health-related disciplines, multimodal approaches involve the use of differing techniques to treat patients in ways that may involve a combination of pharmaceuticals, radiotherapy, and surgery (Bain, Keren, & Stroud, 2017). In the fields of computer science and information systems, research on multimodality involves the various ways to provide security for computers through, for example, variations in biometric-based physical and cybersecurity systems (Obaidat, Traore, & Woungang, 2019). Among scholars in communication and media theory, the term "multimodal" signals a concern for the use of gestures, gaze, and touch as they relate to the production of meaning across a range of settings (Olteanu, 2019; Wong, 2019).

Closer to language assessment, Kress (2015) discusses the relationship between multimodal studies and applied linguistics, and begins with the point that there is no commonly agreed upon definition of the concept as there is "… a vagueness, a vacillation often … an ambiguity between naming a phenomenon 'out there' in the social-semiotic world, and the name for an 'approach', a theory for research and practice around that phenomenon" (p. 53). Historically, the conceptual framework that underpins the concept of multimodality is found in systemic functional linguistics (SFL) set out by Halliday (1978, 2014) who saw language as a social semiotic that evolves through the use and understanding of multiple resources (Eggins, 2004; Halliday & Webster, 2009). Extensive language curricula and materials, particularly in Australia, have been developed based on SFL concepts (e.g., Butt, Fahey, Feez, Spinks, & Yallop, 2000) and have gained traction in North America (e.g., Byrnes, 2006, 2019; Coffin & Donohue, 2014; Gleason, 2014).

Publications in the area can be found in journals that include *Social Semiotics*, *Text & Talk*, *Discourse, Context & Media*, and *Functional Linguistics*. Pulling together a synthesis of the area, Jewitt, Bezemer, and O'Halloran (2016) situate studies of multimodality within one of three dominant research traditions. As shown in Table 4.1, these traditions revolve around concepts that can be traced to work in systemic functional linguistics (SFL), social semiotics and conversation analysis.

Of the three core theoretical influences shown in Table 4.1, research in multimodality brings questions of meaning-making to the fore. For our present purposes, we can see how SFL sets aside concepts in structural linguistics as they "… can no longer be sufficient to provide satisfactory accounts of the materials to hand and the questions they pose" (Adami & Kress, 2014, p. 231). Language teachers, as Valdés and colleagues (2014) note, are moving away from views that learners be "evaluated primarily in terms of their acquisition of forms, structures, or communicative behaviors thought to be characteristic of educated speakers raised from birth in a monolingual environment" (p. 45). Using SFL as a basis for assessment design, Gleason (2014) suggests that models "based on structuralist assumptions of language as a set of rules and language learning as the acquisition of a correct set of forms is insufficient for responsible and fair language assessment practices in today's world" (p. 667). As shown in Table 4.2, work by Gleason illustrates how the assumptions that

Table 4.1 Situating the concept of multimodality in three dominant perspectives

	Systemic functional linguistics	Social semiotics	Conversational analysis
Aims	Recognition of social functions of forms	Recognition of power and agency	Recognition of social order of interaction
Theory of meaning	Meaning as choice	Motivated sign	Sequentiality
History	European functionalism	SFL, critical linguistics, semiotics	American interactionism, ethnomethodology
Conceptualizations of "means for making meaning"	Semiotic resource, mode	Mode, semiotic resource	(Semiotic) resource
Example representatives	Byrnes (2006) and Gleason (2014)	Kress (2013, 2015) and Mickan and Lopez (2017)	Oben and Brone (2016) and Davitti and Pasquandrea (2017)
Empirical focus	Artifacts, including texts and objects	Artifacts, mostly texts	Researcher-generated video recordings of interaction
Methods	Micro-analysis of selected short segments, corpus analysis, multimodal analytics	Micro-analysis of selected short segments, historical analysis	Micro-analysis of (collections of) selected short segments

Adapted from Jewitt et al. (2016, p. 11)

Table 4.2 SFL and structuralist grammar assumptions

Systemic functional linguistics	Structuralist grammar
Focus on the discourse level	Concern for the sentential level and below
Function and uses of language for interaction	Structure and form of language
Context variation and discourse	General description of language
Language as a resource for making meaning	Language as a set of rules
Extending the ability to use resources for meaning-making in context is the goal of language learning	Language learning is a "conduit" because and understanding of form is unrelated to meaning
Proficient learners are able to demonstrate that they can use resources for making meaning within context	Proficient learners are able to demonstrate they can use structure and form correctly

Adopted from Gleason (2014, p. 668)

underpin SFL and structural grammar differ and may influence assessment designs.

Perhaps most importantly, the work of Gleason (2014) in Table 4.2 forces assessment designers to account for the role of context in any demonstration of language proficiency. Given the long-standing interfaces between SLA and language testing (Bachman & Cohen, 1998), it is important to place the "transdisciplinary framework" of the Douglas Fir Group (2016) at the core of our present discussion. The framework is built on three levels—macro, meso, and micro—to account for the multifaceted nature of language teaching and learning. At the macro, or ideological level, the framework seeks to account for belief systems and associated cultural, political, religious, and economic values. At the meso-level, aspects of sociocultural institutions and communities are set out. Social activity, placed at the micro-level, illuminates how individuals engage with each other in the acquisition process to account for the linguistic, prosodic, interactional, and auditory elements that circulate at and influence meaning. Importantly, The Douglas Fir Group (2016) place the term "semiotic resources," defined as "an open set of ever-evolving multilingual and multimodal possibilities for making meaning," at the heart of micro-level activity (p. 37). With links established between SLA and SFL and multimodal studies, we can now draw on Bachman (1991) and ask another question: How could we build a greater recognition of the role of semiotic resources in classroom listening assessment? As shown in Table 4.3, foundational concepts in SFL may provide the basis for such language assessments.

As can be seen in Table 4.3, SFL posits that language can be understood as a semiotic resource that serves three intertwined functions in human communication. The first, or ideational, metafunction points to the need in our interactions to be able to express ideas. Those ideas can be roughly classified as a result of our experiences or perhaps arise out of a sense of logical thinking. The second, or interpersonal, metafunction informs our use of language to navigate and make sense of the many social aspects that we manage in our communication. The third, or textual, metafunction concerns the use of language to organize and structure our thoughts in a coherent manner. Using these three metafunctions as the basis for our task design, our classroom listening assessment could inform how a recognition of the role of

Table 4.3 SFL metafunctions set within the context of listening assessment

Metafunction	Brief definition	Focal information sought in listening assessment task designs
Ideational • Experiential • Logical	Semiotic resources are deployed to represent experience; experiential meaning encode experiences and logical meanings are used to show relationships	Ability to understand how experiences are expressed, and identify the relationships among concepts and idea
Interpersonal	Semiotic resources are deployed to encode interaction, defend propositions, encode obligation and inclination, and express attitudes	Ability to understand the relationship and attitudes among speakers
Textual	Semiotic resources are deployed to organize our experiential, logical, and interpersonal meanings into a coherent and linear whole message unit	Ability to understand the structure and coherence of a text

Based on Butt et al. (2000, pp. 5–7)

semiotic resources, prominent throughout video-based learning activities, may point to a classroom diagnosis of second and foreign language listening abilities.

To illustrate, imagine that a classroom instructor has adopted a functional (or, more specifically, SFL) orientation to language for an ESL class of refugee students. Her view of language leads her to create assessment tasks that are intended to mimic some of the demands that are encountered by her students. Accordingly, she creates listening exercises based on public service videotexts that, for example, advise people to quit smoking, eat healthy food, or drive safely. Her sets of ideational tasks prompt students to listen for slang words so that they can improve their ability to understand how experiences, such as injury, are expressed and link those to words and concepts that appear in standard dictionaries. A second set of tasks, made to sensitize students to the interpersonal functions of language use, centers on the language that is used by the protagonist of a story to assess an ability to detect the attitudes toward behavior and safety. In her third set of tasks, the teacher creates tasks that focus on textual metafunctions to do with coherence such as signposting; in each set of tasks, an understanding of how both the visual and verbal elements are assessed. Students are first allowed to see, and review, the videotext in its entirety. Visual elements, such as gesture, are made into screenshots and presented alongside multiple-choice questions. Short excerpts of the clip are made to constrain specific aspects of the verbal narrative for presentation on digital devices.

In summary, our alignment to functional orientation provides the foundations of our assessment designs, and we can see how the "construct" of multimodality depends on the theoretical basis to which it is referenced by research or test development. Employing SFL as a theory of language provides three core metafunctions that may be used to frame task development and activities. In the next section, we turn to the historical perspective to show how concepts in listening have been shaped by technology over the years.

Historical Perspectives

It is worth remembering that constructs have a history (Bachman, 1990). Exploration of the history of listening traces the ways that audio-centric definitions of the skill arose out of audio recording technologies and related pedagogies (Hendy, 2013). Years of debate among scholars concluded that listening is now best understood as "the process of receiving, constructing meaning from, and responding to spoken and/or nonverbal messages" (International Listening Association [ILA], 1995, p. 4). Despite the wide agreement, however, scholars have yet to settle on what to do with the "nonverbal" aspects of meaning construction and response (Field, 2019). For those seeking to use "audio + visual" material in listening assessment designs, semiotic resources are divisible and thus "spoken data may be accompanied by visual input" (Rost, 2013, p. 183); when videotext is seen as a "whole message unit," no division of aural and visual elements is possible (Gruba, 2006). For language assessment, the alignment of a construct to a mode of presentation is crucial.

Designs in listening assessment are made possible when text, task, and listener are brought together for the purpose of evaluating comprehension against a set of criteria as a means to determine a level of proficiency (Brindley, 1997). Our present discussion may seek to frame "text" as a proxy for a cluster of semiotic resources. Accordingly, an audio text presents aural resources to determine if the speed of delivery, accent, and complexity of linguistic structures, for example, have an influence on task performance (see, for example, Révész & Brunfaut, 2013; Wagner, 2014). A second way to cluster semiotic resources is to present audio text alongside static visual material; in this way, the researcher would seek to examine how combinations of multimodal elements, for example, may signal how an emphasis on either "content" or "context" may inhibit or facilitate assessment performance (e.g., Ginther, 2002). A third strain of research design presents listeners with videotexts in their original form and then as audio-only files to determine how such variations of semiotic resources may influence listener performance (Batty, 2015). A fourth area presents videotext as a non-divisible semiotic resource and uses eye-tracking technologies, for example, to investigate how dynamic interactions of elements influence comprehension (Suvorov, 2015).

Tasks in listening research are designed to prompt a response that indicates the ability of a listener to understand a specific aspect of the semiotic resource (Révész & Brunfaut, 2013); presented with a resource and a prompt, proficient listeners are seen to be able to direct attentional resources to particular elements and thus demonstrate comprehension (Rost, 2013; Vandergrift & Goh, 2012). Although settled debates in listening point toward a recognition of "nonverbal" elements in defining the skill, we nonetheless continue to struggle to pinpoint their roles in assessment. Inspired by concepts grounded in SFL, the placement of semiotic resources at the core of a prominent SLA framework (The Douglas Fir Group, 2016) now provides a link from multimodal studies to language testing. As we turn our attention to critical issues, the work of Bachman and Damböck (2018) can inform efforts to develop a productive and mutual relationship between the two areas of research.

Critical Issues

Recognizing the Role of Semiotic Resources in Assessment

Potentially, the placement of semiotic resources at the heart of transdisciplinary SLA (The Douglas Fir Group, 2016) will firmly situate the concept at the center of language assessment theory and practice. If such a movement occurs, work in multimodal studies would have much to offer assessment specialists. As set out in Table 4.4, language assessors could draw on multimodal studies to frame concepts, motivate a reexamination of current practices, and foster new and innovative approaches to research.

Table 4.4 What multimodal studies may offer language assessment

Area of concern in assessment	Multimodal studies contributions	Associated references
Conceptual basis to situate semiotic resources, new literacies, and multimodality in assessment practices	Theoretical frameworks account for a "theory of meaning," not only a "theory of language," that can be applied across a range of modalities	Jewitt et al. (2016), Halliday (1978), Kress (2015), van Leeuwen (2005)
Stimulus to (re)examine instrument designs, candidate behaviors, and proficiency criteria	Suggests that new skills and abilities require new ways of thinking about assessment practices	Jewitt (2005), Kress (2009, 2013), Kern and Ohlhus (2017)
New methodologies assessment research	Resources for new tools and frameworks to understand text, task design, and learner	Foster et al. (2017), Hoffmann and Bublitz (2017), Zhuravleva et al. (2016), Klous and Wielaard (2016)

Critically, in our collective journey toward argument-based approaches, any evidence-backed claims that language proficiency depends on the deft use of semiotic resources would demand a strong theoretical basis. Accordingly, a greater recognition of semiotic resources would require further movement away from structuralist to functional orientations of language (Gleason, 2014). In turn, such a conceptual framework would stimulate the development of "assessments that will serve the purposes of learning and instruction" (Bachman, 2014, p. 2) in contemporary pedagogies that make extensive use of multimodal texts. Additionally, as shown in Table 4.4, methods used to conduct multimodal research could spur new developments in language assessment research (e.g., Bhatia, 2018; Zhuravleva, de Bot, & Haug Hilton, 2016).

Language testing, too, has much to offer current work in multimodal studies. With reference to Table 4.5, the adoption of argument-based approaches, now prominent in assessment, can guide complex areas of multimodal research. Similar to applied linguistics, the emerging discipline area draws on a wide range of concepts (Jewitt et al., 2016) that can be challenging to apply to specific domains of practice. To illustrate, recent work by Nguyen and Gruba (2019) that employed systemic functional multimodal discourse analysis (SF-MDA) to examine Australian government video advertisements could be extended through a structured argument. In this case, for example, an argument-based approach could help to identify the specific elements of a semiotic resource that may influence behavior across diverse populations.

Multimodal studies would also benefit from the depth of research in computer-assisted language learning and assessment. To repair what may be a blind spot in the emerging discipline to focus on native language contexts, for example, researchers could draw on more than 20 years of research (Chapelle & Voss, 2016) that relates specifically to the understanding of language among non-native speakers. An increased sensitivity to issues of second language use would foster a wider applicability of results to global contexts.

Table 4.5 What language testing has to offer studies of multimodality in listening

Area	Justification	Associated references
Argument-based approaches; SLA interfaces	Provides a framework for development of proposed multimodal instruments	Bachman and Palmer (2010), Pan 2016)
Computer-based instrument design and use	Existing base of tools to work across global samples	Arispe and Burston (2017), Chapelle and Voss (2016), Ockey (2009), Winke and Isbell (2017)
Ethical considerations	Raises the awareness of the power of assessment practices in contemporary practice	Georgakopoulou (2017)
Training in quantitative methods	Workforce skills among applied linguists to be able to collaborate with data scientists	Bachman (2004)

Ethical considerations, already fundamental to language testing (Bachman, 2014, may come into sharper focus in multimodal studies when assessment issues come into play. Adding to the contested nature of multimodal assessment practices in mainstream education (Kress, 2009), what and who and how to represent the semiotic resources of a culture will add yet another dimension to complex selections of videotext material. The basis of selections may well be informed by the experience of language testing instrument design. Further, multimodal studies researchers may well benefit through increased collaborations with assessment specialists who bring crucial expertise in quantitative methods (Bachman, 2004) that can strengthen multimodal studies. At present, for example, multimodal discourse analysis is built on purpose-built software that requires researchers to apply a series of qualitative coding processes to deconstruct a single videotext. Such work is time- and labor-intensive and, as such, requires significant training yet does not reach the scale of analysis needed to produce the robust sets of materials needed for widescale adoption. As shown in the work in Algahamdi (2020), machine learning techniques will be required for videotext analysis at scale: already trained in advanced statistics, language assessors are well poised to work alongside multimodal studies researchers and software engineers to build the innovative tools needed for advanced studies.

The Construction of Classroom Assessments

Returning to the construction of classroom listening assessments, Table 4.6 attempts to demonstrate the utility of the AUA. Based on Bachman and Damböck (2018), it sets out justifications related to an approach to language, a theory of meaning and intentions of consequence, decisions, interpretation, and assessment.

Table 4.6 Building an argument for multimodal listening assessment

Design category	Associated category of argumentation	Claim for the justification in the use of videotext in listening assessment
Approach to language	Pedagogy	Functional views of language, widely used in the classroom, underpin and align the use of multimodal assessments in a course of language study
Theory of meaning	Defensible	Listening is understood as the comprehension of the dynamic aural and visual elements of multimodal texts
Intended consequences	Beneficial	Teaching and assessment with videotext strengthen the links between its use in the classroom and contemporary life
Intended decisions	Values-sensitive; equitable	Instruction and assessment with videotext promote discussion of the role of critical thinking as a core area of media literacy
Intended interpretation	Relevant; sufficient; meaningful; generalizable; impartial	Students can see the relevance of learning a language through videotext in their classroom activities as well as to their assessment performance and everyday media use
Intended assessment	Consistent	Throughout a course, stages of learner development and curriculum design can be regularly aligned to increasingly complex uses of videotext

Following the concepts set out in Table 4.6, our choice of videotext as a representative semiotic resource for listening assessment first requires alignment to prevailing language theory. Bounded by the four major orientations in language classrooms (Valdés et al., 2014), a functional approach to language learning and teaching could be advised as a way to align teaching practices with multimodal assessments. As Gleason (2014) has argued, structuralist perspectives would not be appropriate in this case and, indeed, mismatches between theoretical perspectives and assessment practice may well undermine otherwise effective pedagogies (Bachman & Dambóck, 2018). Importantly, stakeholders in the process may need to justify defending the concept of "theory of meaning," and not just of "language," as a means to account for the call to consider "semiotic resources" when applying current SLA principles to their designs of classroom assessments.

Bachman and Dambóck (2018) next draw our attention to a series of "intentions" as a key element in the construction of AUA for classroom assessments.

The significance of this element is that it strengthens justification for the use of videotext in listening assessment: it aligns with a prevailing theory of language (Valdés et al., 2014), recognizes the need to understand videotext (Campoy-Cubillo & Querol-Julián, 2015), and stimulates further attention to media literacy training (Lotherington & Jenson, 2011). A well-articulated intention to use semiotic resources such as videotext would, hopefully, also make assessments more relevant to students themselves. A final justification set out in the AUA concerns the need to ensure consistency throughout assessment designs; with reference to Table 4.6, designers would be reminded to align their assessments to stages of language proficiency in tandem with an established curriculum.

In an effort to focus on interpretations or "what and how to assess" in language classrooms, we can think about the qualities of interpretation suggested by Bachman and Damböck (2018). Our initial considerations would concern the relevance, or the appropriateness of the information, of the decision. Discussion concerning relevance with regard to the use of videotext in the assessment task, for example, may well serve to elicit a student's ability to demonstrate coping strategies at times of otherwise failed listening comprehension. To illustrate relevance, consider how gestures would be assessed as an aspect of comprehension in multimodal listening. In this case, the videotext would be needed to portray the semiotic resources that are used (not "just language") throughout conversations. Here, then, the meaningfulness of the interpretation would be increased as the language instructor would have a greater number of points, or aspects of semiotic resources, on which to make a justified decision. Finally, the employment of the AUA would help to enhance generalizability in that the video-based assessment would stimulate developing student competency of not only language but exposure to diverse actors and situations throughout a lifetime of interaction with video-sharing sites.

Conclusions, Implications, and Future Directions

In line with scholars who argue that "language learning is semiotic learning" (The Douglas Fir Group, 2016, p. 27), it now follows that "language assessment is semiotic assessment" in ways that can continue to link our work to SLA. Following Bachman and Damböck (2018), the development of classroom-based assessments shows that we have much to offer to language teachers. Integrated with concepts that underpin multimodal studies, the AUA provides a clear structure that can guide us through much needed research in multimodal listening assessment.

Listening research is built on investigating the interplay of texts, tasks, and listeners (Brindley, 1997). As we develop a research agenda for multimodal listening assessment, we first need to better understand videotext. Work in this area will demand that assessment specialists make greater use of systemic functional multi-modal discourse analysis (SF-MDA), for example, and other related concepts inherent in multimodal studies research (e.g., Jewitt et al., 2016). We will also need to develop measures of videotext complexity similar to those used in reading and writing assessment research (Alghamdi, 2020). Given the vast number of video material that is available (YouTube, 2020), the adoption of machine learning techniques and related large-scale computing processes alone will assist efforts to rank videotext levels to appropriate band scale listening descriptors. A second area of research must focus on task development. Greater exploration of the use of SFL metafunctions to frame the domains of meaning may be productive. Additionally, assessment research that is informed by human–computer interaction (HCI) design principles (Schmitt, 2015) will be required to create computer-based instruments: Should tasks be presented above, below, or aside the videotext? How can repeated viewings of a section of a text, for example, be counted as an element of language proficiency? A third area must focus on multimodal reception analysis to better understand the behaviors and strategies of second language listeners. Advances in eye-tracking technology in listening assessment research (Suvorov, 2015) will continue to integrate emerging concepts with those in multimodal studies.

As Bachman and Damböck (2018) have shown, language testing offers those working in multimodal studies with a solid, defensible, and useful means of thinking about the use of language; in turn, it can inform efforts to create multimodal pedagogical designs, and, importantly, further strengthen work in contemporary language curricula that must respond to the increasing demands of new technologies and literacies (Kress, 2009; Lotherington & Jenson, 2011; Valdés et al., 2014). Using the AUA framework and knowledge gleaned from SFL, language teachers would be better able to place semiotic resources at the heart of their assessments. Though better aligned to transdisciplinary SLA (The Douglas Fir Group, 2016), the complexity of such placement will require the deeper integration of multimodal studies. Research in multimodal listening assessment, in particular, could benefit from greater attention to videotext analysis, task construction, and listener strategies. Well into the future, we can respond to Bachman (1991) with a secure understanding that language testing has much to offer to an ever-changing world of language teaching and beyond.

Acknowledgements During my writing of this chapter, Gunther Kress passed away in June 2019. I would like to deeply recognize his significant contribution to multimodal studies.

References

Adami, E., & Kress, G. (2014). Introduction: Multimodality, meaning making, and the issue of "text". *Text & Talk, 34*(3), 231–237. https://doi.org/10.1515/text-2014-0007.

Alghamdi, E. (in preparation, 2020). Towards explanatory and predictive computational models of second language videotext difficulty. Unpublished PhD thesis, University of Melbourne.

Altman, R. (1989). *The video connection: Integrating video in language teaching.* Boston: Houghton Mifflin.

Armes, R. (1988). *On video.* London: Routledge.

Arispe, K., & Burston, J. (2017). Making it personal: Performance-based assessments, ubiquitous technology, and advanced learners. *Language Learning & Technology, 21*(3), 44–58.

Bachman, L. F. (1990). Constructing measures and measuring constructs. In B. Harley, P. Allen, J. Cummins, & M. Swain (Eds.), *The development of second language proficiency* (pp. 26–38). Cambridge: Cambridge University Press.

Bachman, L. (1991). What does language testing have to offer? *TESOL Quarterly, 25*(4), 671–701.

Bachman, L. (2004). *Statistical analyses for language assessment.* Cambridge: Cambridge University Press.

Bachman, L. F. (2014). Ongoing challenges in language assessment (Chapter 94). In A. J. Kunnan (Ed.), *The companion to language assessment.* New York: Wiley.

Bachman, L. F., & Damböck, B. (2018). *Language assessment for classroom teachers.* Oxford: Oxford University Press.

Bachman, L. F., & Cohen, A. D. (1998). *Interfaces between second language acquisition and language testing research*: Cambridge University Press.

Bachman, L. F., & Palmer, A. (2010). *Language assessment in practice: Developing language assessments and justifying their use in the real world.* Oxford: Oxford University Press.

Bain, L., Keren, N. I., & Stroud, C. (2017). *Developing multimodal therapies for brain disorders: Proceedings of a workshop.* Washington, DC: The National Academies Press.

Bali, M., & Mostafa, H. (2018). Listen carefully and you will hear: Using creative multimodal assignments to promote student expression. In J. C. Lee & S. Khadka (Eds.), *Designing and implementing multimodal curricula and programs* (pp. 227–242). New York: Routledge.

Batty, A. O. (2015). A comparison of video- and audio-mediated listening tests with many-facet Rasch modeling and differential distractor functioning. *Language Testing, 32*(1), 3–20. https://doi.org/10.1177/0265532214531254.

Bhatia, A. (2018). Interdiscursive performance in digital professions: The case of YouTube tutorials. *Journal of Pragmatics, 124,* 106–120. https://doi.org/10.1016/j.pragma.2017.11.001.

Brindley, G. (1997). Investigating second language listening ability: Listening skills and item difficulty. In G. Brindley & G. Wigglesworth (Eds.), *Access: Issues in language test design and delivery* (pp. 65–85). Sydney: NCELTR.

Butt, D., Fahey, R., Feez, S., Spinks, S., & Yallop, C. (2000). *Using functional grammar: An explorer's guide.* Sydney: NCLETR.

Byrnes, H. (2006). *Advanced language learning: The contribution of Halliday and Vygotsky.* London; New York: Continuum.

Byrnes, H. (2019). Meeting the challenge of instructed language development: Reflections on systemic-functional contributions. In S. Neumann, R. Wegener, J. Fest, P. Niemietz, & N. Hützen (Eds.), *Challenging boundaries in linguistics: Systemic functional perspectives* (pp. 457–491). Frankfurt am Main: Peter Lang.

Campoy-Cubillo, M. C. (2019). Functional diversity and the multimodal listening construct. *European Journal of Special Needs Education, 34*(2), 204–219. https://doi.org/10.1080/08856257.2019.1581402.

Campoy-Cubillo, M. C., & Querol-Julián, M. (2015). Assessing multimodal listening. In B. Crawford & I. Fortanet-Gómez (Eds.), *Multimodal analysis in academic settings: From research to teaching* (pp. 193–212). London/ New York: Routledge.

Chapelle, C., & Voss, E. (2016). 20 years of technology and language assessment in Language Learning & Technology. *Language Learning & Technology, 20*(2), 116–128.

Coffin, C., & Donohue, J. (2014). A language as social semiotic-based approach to teaching and learning in higher education. *Language Learning*, 64-S, 11–38.

Davitti, E., & Pasquandrea, S. (2017). Embodied participation: What multimodal analysis can tell us about interpreter-mediated encounters in pedagogical settings. *Journal of Pragmatics, 107,* 105–128. https://doi.org/10.1016/j.pragma.2016.04.008.

Douglas Fir Group, T. (2016). A transdisciplinary framework for SLA in a multilingual world. *The Modern Language Journal, 100,* 19–47.

Eggins, S. (2004). *An introduction to systemic functional linguistics* (2nd ed.). New York: Continuum.

Field, J. (2019). Second language listening: Current ideas, current issues. In J. W. Schwieter & A. Benati (Eds.), *The Cambridge handbook of language learning* (pp. 283–319). Cambridge: Cambridge University Press.

Foster, I., Ghani, R., Jarmin, R. S., Kreuter, F., & Lane, J. (Eds.). (2017). *Big data and social science: A practical guide to methods and tools*. Boca Raton, FL: CRC Press.

Georgakopoulou, A. (2017). 'Whose context collapse?': Ethical clashes in the study of language and social media in context. *Applied Linguistics Review, 8*(2/3), 169. https://doi.org/10.1515/applirev-2016-1034.

Ginther, A. (2002). Context and content visuals and performance on listening comprehension stimuli. *Language Testing, 19*(2), 133–167. https://doi.org/10.1191/0265532202lt225oa.

Gleason, J. (2014). Meaning-based scoring: A systemic-functional linguistics model for automated test tasks. *Hispania, 97*(4), 666–688.

Gruba, P. (2006). Playing the videotext: A media literacy perspective on video-mediated l2 listening. *Language Learning and Technology, 10*(2), 77–92.

Halliday, M. A. K. (1978). *Language as social semiotic: The social interpretation of language and meaning*. London: Edward Arnold.

Halliday, M. A. K., revised by Matthiessen, C. M. I. M. (2014). *Halliday's introduction to functional grammar*. New York: Routledge/Taylor & Francis.

Halliday, M. A. K., & Webster, J. (Eds.). (2009). *Continuum companion to systemic functional linguistics*. London: Continuum.

Hendy, D. (2013). *Noise: A human history of sound and listening*. New York: Ecco.

Herrero, C., & Vanderschelden, I. (Eds.). (2019). *Using film and media in the language classroom: Reflections on research-led teaching*. Bristol: Multilingual Matters.

Hoffmann, C. R., & Bublitz, W. (2017). *Pragmatics of social media*. Berlin: Boston; De Gruyter Mouton.

Hung, H.-T., Chiu, Y.-C. J., & Yeh, H.-C. (2013). Multimodal assessment of and for learning: A theory-driven design rubric. *British Journal of Educational Technology, 44*(3), 400–409. https://doi.org/10.1111/j.1467-8535.2012.01337.x.

International Listening Association (ILA). (1995, April). AILA definition of listening. *The Listening Post, 53*, 1, 4–5.

Jewitt, C. (2005). Multimodality, "reading", and "writing" for the 21st century. *Discourse: Studies in the Cultural Politics of Education, 26*(3),315–331. https://doi.org/10.1080/01596300500200011.

Jewitt, C., Bezemer, J., & O'Halloran, K. (2016). *Introducing multimodality*. New York: Routledge.

Kern, R. (2014). *Language, literacy, and technology*. Cambridge: Cambridge University Press.

Kern, F., & Ohlhus, S. (2017). Fluency and the integration of semiotic resources in interactional learning processes. *Classroom Discourse, 8*(2), 139–155.

Klous, S., & Wielaard, N. (2016). *We are Big Data: The future of the information society*. Paris: Atlantis Press.

Kress, G. (2003). *Literacy in the new media age*. New York: Routledge.

Kress, G. (2009). Assessment in the perspective of a social semiotic theory of multimodal teaching and learning. In C. Wyatt-Smith & J. J. Cumming (Eds.), *Educational assessment in the 21st century: Connecting theory and practice* (pp. 19–41). New York: Springer.

Kress, G. (2013). Recognizing learning: A perspective from a social semiotic theory of multi-modality. In I. Saint-Georges & J.-J. Weber (Eds.), *Multilingualism and multimodality: Current challenges for educational studies* (pp. 119–140). Rotterdam: Sense.

Kress, G. (2015). Semiotic work: Applied Linguistics and a social semiotic account of multi-modality. *AILA Review, 28*(1), 49–71. https://doi.org/10.1075/aila.28.03kre.

Lotherington, H., & Jenson, J. (2011). Teaching multimodal and digital literacy in second language settings: New literacies, new basics, new pedagogies. *Annual Review of Applied Linguistics, 31*, 226–248.

Mickan, P., & Lopez, E. (Eds.). (2017). *Text-based research and teaching: A social semiotic perspective of language in use*. Basingstoke, UK: Palgrave Macmillan.

Nguyen, H. V., & Gruba, P. (2019). Construction of risk in government advertising: A case study of Operation Sovereign Borders video advertisement. . *Discourse, Context & Media, 30*. https://doi.org/10.1016/j.dcm.2019.04.004.

Norris, S., & Maier, C. D. (Eds.). (2014). *Interactions, images and texts: A reader in multimodality.* Boston/Berlin: De Gruyter.

Obaidat, M. S., Traore, I., & Woungang, I. (Eds.). (2019). *Biometric-based physical and cybersecurity systems.* Cham: Springer.

Oben, B., & Brone, G. (2016). Explaining interactive alignment: A multimodal and multifactorial account. *Journal of Pragmatics, 104,* 32–51. https://doi.org/10.1016/j.pragma.2016.07.002.

Ockey, G. J. (2009). Developments and challenges in the use of computer-based testing for assessing second language ability. *The Modern Language Journal, 93,* 836–847. https://doi.org/10.1111/j.1540-4781.2009.00976.x.

Olteanu, A. (2019). *Multiculturalism as multimodal communication: A semiotic perspective.* Cham: Springer.

Pan, M. (2016). *Nonverbal delivery in speaking assessment: From an argument to a rating scale formulation and validation.* Singapore: Springer.

Révész, A., & Brunfaut, T. (2013). Text characteristics of task input and difficulty in second language listening comprehension. *Studies in Second Language Acquisition, 35*(1), 31–65.

Rost, M. (2013). Assessing listening ability (Chapter 7). *Listening in language learning* (pp. 175–221). New York: Routledge.

Schmitt, C. (2015). Embodied meaning in audio-visuals: First steps towards a notion of mode. In J. Wildfeuer (Ed.), *Building bridges for multimodal research: International perspectives on theories and practices in multimodal analysis* (pp. 309–325). Frankfurt am Main: Peter Lang.

Suvorov, R. (2015). The use of eye tracking in research on video-based second language (L2) listening assessment: A comparison of context videos and content videos. *Language Testing, 32*(4), 463–483. https://doi.org/10.1177/0265532214562099.

Valdés, G., Kibler, A., & Walqui, A. (2014). Changes in the expertise of ESL professionals: Knowledge and action in an era of new standards. Available: http://www.tesol.org/docs/default-source/papers-and-briefs/professional-paper-26-march-2014.pdf.

van Leeuwen, T. (2005). *Introducing social semiotics.* London, New York: Routledge.

Vandergrift, L., & Goh, C. C. M. (2012). *Teaching and learning second language listening: Metacognition in action*: Routledge, Taylor & Francis Group.

Wagner, E. (2013). An investigation of how the channel of input and access to test questions affect L2 listening test performance. *Language Assessment Quarterly, 10*(2), 178–195.

Wagner, E. (2014). Using unscripted spoken texts in the teaching of second language listening. *TESOL Journal, 5*(2), 288–311.

Winke P.M. & Isbell D.R. (2017). Computer-assisted language assessment. In: Thorne S., May S. (eds) *Language, Education and Technology. Encyclopedia of Language and Education (3rd ed.).* Springer, Cham. https://doi.org/10.1007/978-3-319-02328-1_25-2.

Wong, M. (2019). *Multimodal communication: A social semiotic approach to text and image in print and digital media.* Cham: Springer International.

YouTube (2020). *YouTube for press.* Available: youtube.com/about/press/.

Zhuravleva, A., de Bot, K., & Haug Hilton, N. (2016). Using social media to measure language use. *Journal of Multilingual and Multicultural Development, 37*(6), 601–614.

Chapter 5
Learner Perceptions of Construct-Centered Feedback on Oral Proficiency

Jonathan Schmidgall

Abstract Oral proficiency assessments typically elicit performances that may serve as the basis for an evaluation of proficiency but may also be used as the basis for more elaborate, learning-oriented feedback that can be useful to learners and teachers. In this chapter, I discuss how descriptive comments from raters may be used to provide detailed feedback using a construct-centered approach: explicitly aligned with a relevant conceptualization of oral proficiency and reflecting different levels and dimensions of performance. I report the results of a small-scale study of learners' perceptions of construct-centered feedback in the context of high-stakes oral proficiency assessment for international teaching assistants, and conclude with a discussion of how the construct-centered approach to feedback may be used by teachers to complement other approaches to feedback.

Introduction

In this chapter, I focus on two issues that are major parts in Lyle Bachman's work: the centrality and nature of the construct, and the consequences of test use (e.g., Bachman, 2007, 2013). Bachman's work has consistently emphasized the importance of construct definition and the central role of the construct in test development and validation (e.g., Bachman, 1990, 1991, 2000, 2007, 2014; Bachman & Palmer, 1981, 1996, 2010). In his treatise on the history of approaches to construct definition in language assessment, Bachman (2007) differentiates two traditional focuses (ability/trait, and task/content) which gave rise to a third (interactionalist). The ability/trait focus emphasizes underlying language ability (or components thereof) while the task/content focus emphasizes contextual aspects of language performance (e.g., performance on specific tasks). The interactionalist focus, which can be further parsed into strong, moderate, and minimalist stances, combines both traditional focuses by emphasizing ability-in-context. One's approach to defining the construct is critical because it has implications for assessment design and score interpretations,

J. Schmidgall (✉)
Educational Testing Service, Princeton, NJ, USA
e-mail: jschmidgall@ets.org

and consequently, the use and impact of assessments (Bachman & Palmer, 2010). For example, for the use of an assessment to have a positive impact on teaching and learning, the construct should be defined and operationalized (i.e., implemented into scoring rubric and processes and task design) in a manner that promotes the good instructional practice and effective learning (Bachman & Palmer, 2010). In this study, I draw upon an interaction-focused approach to construct definition that emphasizes the language skills and abilities needed for a particular target language use domain, and a consideration of the consequences of test use for teaching and learning—specifically, through the use of test-based, construct-centered feedback.

Literature Review

Typically, researchers have explored the use and effectiveness of feedback on oral proficiency in second language learning by examining classroom-based interaction between teachers and students. This research includes meta-analyses (e.g., Brown, 2014) which characterize the linguistic dimension of performance (e.g., pronunciation, vocabulary, grammar) and effectiveness of different types of feedback (e.g., prompts, reformulations), typically analyzed at the utterance level. The nature of this feedback is usually immediate (vs. delayed) and focused on a particular linguistic dimension such as the past tense (Ellis, Loewen, & Erlam, 2009; Kartchava & Ammar, 2014), the pronunciation or word-initial /r/in English (Saito, 2015), or article errors (Sheen, 2008).

A distinct and complementary approach to feedback may be characterized as "construct-centered." This approach is complementary in that it also focuses on dimensions of linguistic performance (e.g., pronunciation) and may be used in conjunction with more immediate, interactive feedback. These dimensions of linguistic performance are reflected in the overall construct definition for the assessment which specifies the knowledge, skills, and abilities to be assessed. This approach is distinct in that it also aims to promote students' understanding of their proficiency across different levels, extending from the concrete and observable (i.e., utterances) to the generalized (i.e., functional proficiency). In other words, the focus is not just on the abilities defined in the construct definition, but how they are operationalized in scoring rubrics that elaborate levels of ability or achievement, and in scoring rules that specify how much weight each aspect of performance is given to produce the total score, the overall indication of ability or achievement. This paper describes how construct-centered feedback is a logical extension of language assessments designed to produce a positive impact on teaching and learning and elaborates a case study of its use with a particular population of students. The overarching goal is to explain how this approach may be used by teachers whose students could be expected to benefit from more construct-centered feedback.

Oral Proficiency Assessment and Construct-Centered Feedback

Oral proficiency assessments are typically construct-centered, performance-based, and have become increasingly capable of producing a variety of feedback that can be useful to inform teaching and learning. Assessments are construct-centered in the sense that they are typically based on theoretical models or conceptual frameworks of language knowledge or ability, such as communicative language ability (e.g., Bachman & Palmer, 2010) or complexity-accuracy-fluency (Skehan, 1998). When an assessment is used for more specific purposes, such as measuring oral proficiency in a particular language use domain, the definition of the construct may be further refined in order to focus on the areas of knowledge or ability most relevant for communicative effectiveness in that domain (Douglas, 2000).

The potential impact of assessment on teaching and learning, often referred to as *washback*, has concerned researchers and practitioners in language teaching and assessment for decades. Language assessment can impact language students and teachers in a variety of ways by influencing the language knowledge and skills that teachers emphasize in the classroom, and the types of practice activities used for self-study outside of the classroom (Alderson & Wall, 1993). Washback can be positive if the use of a test helps motivate learners or focuses instruction on relevant and appropriate language knowledge and skills; when testing narrows the curriculum or promotes practice activities that do not benefit learners beyond the test, washback can be negative. Researchers in language assessment have argued that evidence about the washback of a language test on teaching and learning should be incorporated into an evaluation of a test's usefulness (Bachman & Palmer, 1996; Messick, 1996). Washback as a phenomenon is a crucial link between testing, teaching, and learning, and the insistence that language tests should produce positive washback encourages a closer connection between instruction and assessment (Adair-Hauck, Glisan, Koda, Swender, & Sandrock, 2005).

The increasing awareness of washback has spurred the development of assessments that are better aligned to appropriate models of language use and with the needs of teachers and learners. One way in which a language test may have a positive impact on teaching and learning is through the provision of more elaborate feedback (Shohamy, 2001). Typically, language tests used for important decisions quantify performance with scores, but some approaches to testing encourage the provision of specific feedback that can be used by teachers and learners to guide additional study. One alternative approach to assessment, *cognitive diagnostic assessment* (CDA), aims to diagnostically evaluate and monitor particular language skills (Jang, 2008). In CDA, results may provide teachers with information to help plan remedial activities for their students. Other researchers have argued that the principles behind developing *authentic assessments* lead to feedback that supports teaching and learning. Adair-Hauck, Glisan, Koda, Swender, and Sandrock (2005) describe the development of the Integrated Performance Assessment (IPA) and its initial impact on teachers and learners. One feature of the IPA is its use of authentic tasks—or tasks that closely correspond to those used in the real world (Hoekje & Linnell, 1994)—and the development of an analytic scoring rubric that includes multiple modes (e.g., interpretive, interpersonal) and subconstructs (e.g., comprehensibility, language control). Adair-Hauck et al (2005) found that the use of more authentic tasks and relevant scoring rubrics led to a positive impact on teaching. The researchers cited teacher comments that the IPA reaffirmed effective teaching techniques, taught teachers how to clearly assess students, and provided a useful format for classroom activities. Andrade and Du (2005) also found that when presented with feedback in the form of scores and relevant information from a scoring rubric, learners were primarily interested in the latter. Information contained in a scoring rubric may be supplemented with *can-do* statements, or summaries of the expected real-world abilities of test takers at a particular score level. North and Schneider (1998) argued that providing such real-world can-do statements is more helpful than using scoring rubric descriptors that typically need to be interpreted relative to other levels of performance.

Corrective feedback targeted toward pronunciation, vocabulary, grammar, and discourse features has been found to improve oral proficiency (Brown, 2014; Li, 2010; Lyster & Saito, 2010; Russell & Spada, 2006). Corrected feedback is typically targeted toward a specific linguistic dimension or component of a speaker's performance, such as pronunciation. Feedback with respect to a particular dimension can also be decomposed into a variety of subcategories. For example, pronunciation-related feedback can be characterized by *segmental* and *suprasegmental* errors (Isaacs, 2014). Segmental features pertain to phonetic characteristics such as the production of individual consonants and vowels, or combinations of phonemes such as consonant clusters and diphthongs (combinations of vowels). Suprasegmental features include aspects of pronunciation that occur beyond the phonemic level that relate to fluency and prosody, including pausing, intonation, and stress. The finer-grained segmental and suprasegmental features may be the level at which learners and teachers require feedback (e.g., specific phoneme distinctions that are problematic, such as /r/-/l/) but many assessments may be unable to target this level of fine-grained analysis due to the nature of their design or the resources required to produce this type of feedback.

Construct

UCLA's Test of Oral Proficiency (TOP) is an assessment that is used to provide test takers with specific, individualized feedback that is aligned with remedial ESL instructional goals (Avineri, Londe, Hardacre, Carris, So, & Majidpour, 2011). The TOP evaluates the oral English ability of international graduate students who intend to become teaching assistants (TAs) in the context of two instructional tasks: a syllabus presentation and mini-lesson. During each task, the student (test taker) presents material to two trained undergraduate participants and is scored by two trained raters based on a scoring rubric that includes separate scales for pronunciation, vocabulary and grammar, rhetorical organization, and question handling. A total score (scaled from 0–10) is produced after assigning a higher weight to pronunciation scores (1.5) and averaging all rater scores across tasks. If rater scores differ by half a scaled score (0.5) or more, a third rater scores the performance based on a video recording. In cases where this adjudication is required, the total score is based on the two most similar rater scores. Based on the total score, an evaluation decision is made that determines whether the test taker is qualified for teaching assistant positions. Three evaluation decision categories are possible based on total scores: *Pass* (approval to teach undergraduates; total score 7.1 or above), *Provisional Pass* (approval to teach with remedial instruction; total score 6.4–7.0), and *Fail* (not given approval; total score 6.3 and below).

Construct-Centered Feedback

Although the primary use of the assessment is to evaluate students' oral proficiency in order to make a decision about whether they can assume instructional duties, its secondary use is to provide detailed feedback. When students are notified of their score and the evaluative decision that accompanies it (i.e., *Pass*, *Provisional Pass*, *Fail*), they are encouraged to schedule a post-test feedback session with a test coordinator. Typically, around 15% of test takers elect to schedule the post-test feedback session. During this 20–30-minute session, the test coordinator provides specific, detailed feedback that begins with a description of the scoring process and the individual rater scores assigned to each facet of the test taker's performance (TOP subscale by task). In addition, the test coordinator compiles and summarizes rater comments regarding the student's performance with respect to each TOP scale, and reviews the video-recorded test performance to ensure the feedback is accurate and comprehensive. The student is given the opportunity to review the video-recorded performance with the coordinator as well, and receives a feedback form containing detailed information (e.g., particular phoneme distinctions that were problematic) that can be used to guide future learning, regardless of the student's TOP total score level.

   The form includes feedback at various levels of generalization and four dimensions of oral proficiency (see Appendix A). At the highest level of generalization, students receive feedback on their overall oral proficiency (i.e., their total score) as it relates to pre-determined levels of functional proficiency (i.e., the corresponding evaluation of *Pass*, *Provisional Pass*, *Fail*). At a more detailed level, students are given rater scores for each task and scale. Rater scores are interpreted by viewing descriptors in the scoring rubric, an analytic scale that includes separate scores for pronunciation, vocabulary and grammar, rhetorical organization, and question handling. As shown in the left column in the middle of Appendix A, each scale contains subcategories used by the coordinator to identify aspects of each subskill that may need attention. Specific illustrative examples related to relevant subcategories are provided on the right column, which focuses feedback on the utterance level. As feedback is given at increasingly specific levels, it is increasingly focused on one of the four aspects of performance (pronunciation, vocabulary and grammar, rhetorical organization, question handling). Throughout, it is construct-centered in the sense that it reflects an explicit view of how oral proficiency has been defined in this context (i.e., the four scales and their subcategories) as well as the relative contribution of each dimension of performance to functional effectiveness (i.e., the relative weight of each scale, and evaluative decisions based on total scores). The feedback session concludes with a discussion of potential next steps for the student, which may include recommending specific oral skills courses at the university (see the lower left corner of Appendix A).

Appendix A provides an illustration of what the feedback form might look like for a particular student. In the upper right corner, identifying information (student name, test/performance date) and the total score are displayed. Individual rater scores are listed in the table in the upper left corner. Each column of this table corresponds to one of the four TOP scales: pronunciation (P), vocabulary and grammar (V/G), rhetorical organization (RO), and question handling (QH). There are two rows in the table, corresponding to the TOP's two scored tasks (Task 2, Task 3). There are two scores in each cell of the table, one for each rater (Rater 1, Rater 2). Scores for each scale range from 0 to 4. Thus, in the example shown in Appendix A, the test taker received a score of "2" from Rater 1 and "2" from Rater 2 on the pronunciation scale for Task 2, a score of "3" from Rater 1 and "3" from Rater 2 on the vocabulary and grammar scale, and so forth.

The feedback session format enables the TOP coordinator to focus the student's attention on how oral proficiency to TA has been defined by providing all of the individual rater scores for each scale or component of oral proficiency, describing how rater scores are transformed into a total score (pronunciation is more heavily weighted than other subscales; scores are equally weighted across raters and tasks) and relating scores to rubric descriptors. Providing all of the individual rater scores also helps ensure that the scoring process is transparent to test takers. When the coordinator explains how rater scores across tasks and subscales are weighted and averaged to produce a scaled score, the degree to which different aspects of the test taker's performance contributed to the overall evaluation is clarified. Finally, by explicitly focusing a test taker's attention on the rubric descriptors that correspond to their score level on a particular subscale, the coordinator tries to clarify what it means to be proficient with respect to each scale (e.g., pronunciation), and where the student's performance was located on each scale.

After providing this higher level feedback across all four dimensions of performance, the coordinator focuses on the more detailed levels of feedback that take up most of the space on the feedback form. For the pronunciation and vocabulary/grammar scales, feedback is typically focused on errors or features of speech that impacted a speaker's comprehensibility. For the rhetorical organization and question handling scales, feedback is typically more general and includes a mix of positive and critical observations. Raters are encouraged to try to identify features of speech that appear to be systematic from those that do not, and to differentiate errors that have a more substantial impact on comprehensibility (e.g., pronunciation of key words) from those that do not.

The major categories of errors or issues associated with each scale are shown on the left side of the counseling feedback form in Appendix A. For the pronunciation subscale, types of errors include *phoneme distinctions, multiple sounds, deletion, insertion/epenthesis*, and so forth. After examining rater comments and viewing a video recording of the student's performance (if necessary), the coordinator uses his or her expertise to identify errors that were more commonly observed in the performance by marking the relevant categories. Thus, in the example shown in Appendix A, the student's performance with respect to pronunciation was characterized by problems with phoneme distinctions, deletion, and word stress. On the right side of the feedback form, illustrative examples from the student's performance are provided. The student in Appendix A appeared to have difficulty with several consonant-based phoneme distinctions, including /θ/-/s/, /l/-/n/, and /s/-/z/. The student appears to have repeatedly made this type of error when using the key word "theory," as the coordinator wanted to draw particular attention to it by circling it on the feedback form. After this finer-grained feedback with respect to the pronunciation scale, the counselor moves on to discuss the major types of issues and examples associated with the other scales. This discussion takes up the bulk of the feedback session.

After receiving specific, targeted feedback regarding the linguistic features of their performance with respect to each subscale, students discuss potential next steps with the coordinator and may receive a follow-up course recommendation. A list of relevant oral skills courses is provided in the lower left corner of the feedback form, and the coordinator identifies courses that may be appropriate based on feedback and discussion. In Appendix A, the suggested courses were primarily designed to improve pronunciation skills. Thus, students are expected to leave the feedback session with:

- a thorough understanding of how the oral skills necessary to TA have been defined;
- how their performance was evaluated overall with respect to this conceptualization of proficiency and university standards (most general level of feedback);
- their strengths and weaknesses with respect to the dimensions of performance that inform the overall evaluation (diagnostic feedback for the four scales);
- specific categories and illustrative examples from each dimension of their performance which may be used to focus learning (most detailed level of feedback);
- recommendations for courses that may address their learning needs.

The construct-centered approach to feedback across levels and dimensions of performance is intended to provide information that can be used by students and teachers to guide follow-up study. As an initial step toward evaluating the effectiveness of this feedback, semi-structured interviews with students were conducted in order to investigate the following research questions:

(1) What are students' expectations regarding the feedback they will receive from their performance on TOP tasks?
(2) What aspects of the construct-centered feedback do students find most useful?

Method

Participants

Sixteen TOP test takers volunteered to participate in this study prior to their feedback session. The average total score of participants in the study was 6.7 (*SD* =
0.6), which corresponds to the evaluation category *Provisional Pass*. Overall, 3 of 16
test takers received scores classified as *Fail*, 10 classified as *Provisional Pass*, and
3 classified as *Pass* according to the decision rules used by the assessment (UCLA
Center for the Advancement of Teaching, 2020). Most of the participants (n = 14)
were male. The native languages (L1) of participants included Mandarin Chinese
(n = 13), Greek, Hindi, and Vietnamese. This reflects the relevant population of
learners at the university, where the L1 of the largest group of potential international teaching assistants is Mandarin Chinese. Participants primarily belonged to
one of three academic departments: Electrical Engineering, Computer Science, and
Statistics. This also reflects the relevant population, as the two departments with
the highest number of international graduate students were Computer Science and
Electrical Engineering.

Procedure

All feedback sessions began and ended with a semi-structured interview in order to
better understand their expectations (before feedback) and their perceptions of the
usefulness of the different types of feedback (after feedback). Before the feedback
session, participants responded to questions about whether they had received feedback regarding their oral language use in the past, and if so, were asked to describe
the nature of that feedback. Participants also indicated the type of feedback they were
interested in obtaining during the feedback session.

   The researcher then systematically presented the feedback contained in the feedback form, as described in section "Construct". First, the researcher provided a brief
overview of the scoring rubric, highlighting the four scales (pronunciation, vocabulary and grammar, rhetorical organization, question handling) and how proficiency-
level descriptors were used to differentiate levels of performance for each scale.
Rater scores for each task and scale were then presented, as well as the total score
which could be interpreted as an indicator of overall proficiency and readiness to TA.
Next, the researcher reviewed the more descriptive, diagnostic information provided
by raters that was associated with each of the four scales, including the categories
which were flagged (e.g., phoneme distinctions and syllable deletion for the pronunciation scale) and specific illustrative examples (e.g., /s/-/z/in "basic"). Finally, the
researcher suggested oral skills courses at the university that may be particularly
beneficial to the participant given the feedback that had been reviewed (e.g., *Stress
and Intonation*). Throughout the feedback session, participants were encouraged to
ask questions.

After the feedback session, participants were asked if any of the information they received was surprising, and if so, which information and in what manner it was surprising. This broad question was intended to elicit perceptions of the appropriateness of the feedback, the clarity of the feedback, and the specificity of the feedback. Participants were also asked to identify the feedback that was most useful to them, how they planned to use it, and whether they were currently enrolled or planning to enroll in an oral skills course. Individual responses were audio-recorded, and notes were taken by the author throughout the interviews. After each interview, the author transcribed and then coded participants' responses to each question.

Analysis

For each interview question, responses were aggregated in a spreadsheet. For Yes/No questions, the number of responses corresponded to the number of participants; for open-ended questions, participants were allowed to provide multiple responses. Responses to open-ended questions were coded by the author in order to identify major parts or categories for the open-ended responses. A second researcher applied the coding scheme to open-ended responses in order to ensure a degree of consistency of coding, and any discrepancies were resolved through discussion between coders. For some questions, subcategories of codes were identified to further summarize test taker responses. Although the size of subgroups prevented mean comparisons, responses were compared across test takers' TOP decision categories (i.e., *Fail*, *Provisional Pass*, *Pass*) in order to identify potential differences in how feedback was projected to be utilized across TOP score levels.

Results

When asked whether they had previously received feedback on oral language use, most participants (11 of 16) indicated they had not, either from ESL/EFL courses or assessments they had previously taken. Participants indicated that they expected feedback to be useful to guide individual study (10 of 16), help identify appropriate oral skills coursework (4 of 16), and provide information on their overall oral proficiency (3 of 16). Among the ten participants who intended to use feedback to guide individual study, five were specifically interested in improving their pronunciation, three were primarily interested in improving their overall oral proficiency, and one was interested in feedback on grammar. Thus, most participants scheduled feedback sessions with the expectation that they would receive specific, targeted feedback that could be used to direct individual study.

After the counseling session in which the feedback form was presented and explained in detail, participants were asked whether any information in it surprised them. Most participants (13 of 16) responded that the feedback was not surprising in the sense that it seemed appropriate and was clear (e.g., "I think it's all really clear," "It all makes sense," "I expected pronunciation problems," "It seems reasonable"). Only four participants found aspects of the feedback surprising. Among those participants, two were surprised by some of the vocabulary and grammar errors they had made and attributed the errors to performance anxiety rather than a need to further develop these aspects of their linguistic knowledge. The other two participants were surprised by aspects of scoring: one believed that errors that had been attributed to vocabulary and grammar were more likely pronunciation errors, and the other had expected that his pronunciation skills would have been given a different score based on his understanding of the scoring rubric and proficiency-level descriptors.

Next, participants were asked to indicate which information on the feedback form they believed was most useful. Six participants indicated that all of the feedback they had received, including total and individual scale scores, was valuable. Other participants focused on the perceived usefulness of one scale in particular. Overwhelmingly, participants suggested that the feedback they had received regarding their pronunciation was most useful (12 of 16). Among those who found pronunciation feedback most useful, three were most interested in the feedback they received about word stress, three-valued feedback regarding phoneme distinctions, two mentioned syllable deletion, and one pointed to the feedback he received regarding the pronunciation of specific key words in his presentation. In addition, two participants indicated that feedback related to vocabulary and grammar was most useful. One of these participants had recently arrived in the United States from China and concluded based on his feedback that he needed to familiarize himself further with key words and collocations in the TLU domain of teaching assistant (TA) language use.

Participants were asked again how they intended to use the feedback they received and whether they planned to share the feedback with anyone. Eight participants expected to use the information to guide their study in an oral skills course; most of these courses focused on pronunciation. Generally, these students indicated that they planned to share their feedback with an ESL instructor who they expected would help them prepare a course of study to target specific pronunciation errors. Six participants planned to use the feedback to guide individual study in conjunction with language learning textbooks or material available online. These participants often noted that their busy academic schedules would prevent them from enrolling in an oral skills course. Five participants planned to use the feedback primarily to select an appropriate oral skills course. One participant indicated that he would use the feedback to study with a language conversation partner.

Discussion

The results of the semi-structured interviews suggest that most of the participants had received little or no individualized feedback on their oral language use prior to the feedback session and that the session was perceived to provide useful information that could guide future learning activities. Participants also suggested that they would use the feedback to help select appropriate remedial oral skills coursework and to guide their study within their chosen course. Among the features of oral language use evaluated by the TOP, pronunciation was consistently mentioned as the area in which a majority of participants were interested in receiving and subsequently valued detailed feedback, followed by vocabulary and grammar. Among students who valued feedback on their pronunciation, information about errors related to word stress and phoneme distinctions were considered to be most useful.

There are several additional reasons why feedback on pronunciation may be comparatively more valued by test takers. Since pronunciation is given the most weight in determining the TOP scaled scores, it is difficult to attain a *Pass* without a higher pronunciation rating (i.e., 3 or 4), which could explain interest in feedback on pronunciation among test takers who did not receive a passing score. The nature of the pronunciation feedback itself—explicitly differentiating segmental and supraseg-mental errors—is also comparatively well-defined and elaborate, and thus offers a potentially rich source of feedback. Raters are also aware of the importance placed on pronunciation for producing scaled scores and maybe motivated to justify their pronunciation ratings through more elaborate documentation (and thus, feedback). This facet of test design may thus serve to reinforce the comparative usefulness of pronunciation feedback.

Participants' motivation for receiving feedback and intended use of it differed. Some students viewed their current pronunciation skills as a potential barrier to excelling as a TA or academic speaker. Others were more broadly focused on attaining or exceeding the level of functional proficiency corresponding to the *Pass* decision category, regardless of how that could be attained. Some students indicated that their course and work schedules would make it impossible to enroll in remedial oral skills courses, but still believed that the feedback would be useful to identify and prioritize features of oral language use in individualized study. These findings indicate that construct-centered feedback was valued by test takers who intend to use it to guide learning. Thus, these results provide evidence to support the claim that the use of the TOP is beneficial to test takers, a key stakeholder group.

The provision of feedback to test takers through the feedback form may also benefit ESL instructors. Five of the participants in this study were currently enrolled in a remedial ESL oral skills course, and nine indicated that they planned on enrolling in the future. Most ESL Oral Skills courses at the university focus on features of pronunciation that correspond to those categorically identified on the TOP feedback form. Celce-Murcia, Brinton, and Goodwin (2010) encourage ESL instructors to begin with a diagnostic evaluation of learner needs to orient a pronunciation syllabus; given the demands on a teacher's time and class size, evaluating the needs of an entire classroom of learners may not be feasible. While ESL instructors were not formally interviewed for this study, several instructors commended the clarity and relevance of the feedback provided by the TOP in relation to instructional goals.

Despite some positive findings, several features of this study limit the generaliza-tions that can be drawn from it. As indicated earlier, the size of the group of partici-pants interviewed was small, limiting the generalizability of the findings. In addition, students indicated their perceptions of the value of feedback and their intended use of feedback but it is not certain that they will actually use the feedback as indicated. Follow-up interviews with students and ESL instructors would enhance the findings reported in this study by investigating if and how the feedback is actually used. Even if students indicate that feedback is valuable (and follow-up research indicates that it is utilized), an appropriate metric for evaluating the impact of feedback on learning needs to be more clearly specified and examined. While this study provides evidence to suggest that students find construct-centered feedback useful and relevant for making decisions about ESL course enrollment—one of its intended uses—it is not clear if and how it impacts subsequent learning. Some students intended to use the feedback to improve their overall functional proficiency (i.e., as indicated by their total score). Other students were primarily concerned about improving their pronunciation skills in particular. While the feedback offered was intended to facilitate these different learning goals, it may be more effective at supporting some goals over others.

The construct-centered approach to feedback described in this paper has strengths and weaknesses which may complement feedback given to learners that arises out of interaction in the classroom. This approach is fully individualized, and thus requires one-on-one interaction with students. It uses artifacts (e.g., task/activity descriptions, scoring rubrics, feedback forms) that could be adapted for self- or peer-assessment, but scoring rubrics and feedback forms will require a threshold level of expertise in order to use effectively. The feedback provided by this approach is not as immediate as feedback that arises from interaction but intends to promote more explicit, integrated reflection on different levels and dimensions of performance. Finally, construct-centered feedback would need to be carefully considered, planned, and implemented. Its potential benefits for learners would need to be weighed against the additional burden it places on teachers' time and resources, particularly for larger classrooms.

The first step in planning and implementing a construct-centered approach to feedback on oral proficiency is to determine if and how it could be best used to support learning goals. For example, Celce-Murcia, Brinton, and Goodwin (2010) encourage ESL instructors to begin with a diagnostic evaluation of student needs to orient a pronunciation syllabus; given the demands on a teacher's time and class size, evaluating the needs of an entire classroom of learners may not be feasible. If students are enrolled in a language course for specific purposes (e.g., academic, workplace), this approach may help orient them toward functional proficiency as it is conceived in their context. In such cases, a construct-centered approach seems particularly well aligned with learning goals.

If a teacher believes this approach could potentially benefit students, the next step would be to identify an assessment whose construct (i.e., conceptualization of oral proficiency) is well aligned with the teacher's needs. For teachers of international graduate students at North American universities, their local ITA assessment has likely been developed to target the dimensions of oral proficiency and communicative tasks that are valued locally. In general, the potential usefulness of the construct-centered approach will depend on how closely the assessment aligns with the learning context with respect to how oral proficiency is conceptualized and specified via its communicative tasks and scoring rubrics. If students are learning English for the purpose of working in aviation, construct-centered feedback based on a model of academic speaking proficiency may have more limited impact.

After determining the relevance of an assessment's construct to his or her teaching context and determining how it could be best used, teachers would need to obtain the artifacts necessary to produce feedback across levels and dimensions. This may be much easier than it sounds. Many oral proficiency assessments publish their scoring rubrics online or in print, and provide free sample tests or task descriptions that illustrate the communicative tasks students are expected to perform. Teachers will also need to have an understanding of the scoring procedure—how to compute a total score based on ratings—but this information is typically communicated by test developers as well. It will be difficult for a teacher to acquire the level of familiarity with the scoring process that is attained by trained raters, but the intended use of these artifacts is different than a high-stakes testing situation. The teacher's goal would be to attain an understanding of how to interpret performance across different levels of feedback and communicate it to students; it should ultimately be used to make instructional decisions, not high-stakes evaluations that some assessments are designed to support.

Conclusions, Implications, and Future Directions

Ultimately, the construct-centered approach to feedback is a natural extension of the increased concern with the washback of assessment on teaching and learning and may help complement the more immediate, interaction-based feedback that is common in oral proficiency instructional contexts. While research on its effectiveness in the language classroom—and the practicality of its use—is still developing, it also reflects the intent of test developers to better meet the needs of teachers and learners. This approach to feedback also has the potential to strengthen the language assessment literacy of classroom teachers by emphasizing critical features of assessment design and use (e.g., construct definition and operationalization) in a manner that is consistent with recent, comprehensive efforts (e.g., Bachman & Damböck, 2018).

Overall, this study provides some additional support for the notion that the use of language assessments can have a positive impact on test takers, one of the ongoing challenges for assessment (Bachman, 2014) and an important issue for evaluating for the beneficence of the consequences of test use (Bachman & Palmer, 2010). One way in which language assessments can provide positive washback (i.e., benefit teaching and learning) is to provide specific, detailed feedback on performance. By building a mechanism to provide this feedback into its design, the TOP enables motivated test takers to receive useful feedback on aspects of oral language use that might otherwise be difficult to obtain. TOP-based feedback also includes an explicit link to instructional remediation (via course recommendations), which encourages the possibility of closer collaboration between instruction and assessment to help students achieve their learning goals.

Appendix A

A Sample Feedback Form

Test of Oral Proficiency (TOP) Feedback

Task	P	V/G	RO	QH
2	2, 2	3, 3	3, 3	3, 3
3	2, 2	3, 2	3, 4	3, 3

Name: *Sample*
Date: *Sample*
Score: ___6.7___

Pronunciation (P):

- ☑ phoneme distinctions (consonants, vowels)
- ☑ multiple sounds (consonant clusters, dipthongs)
- ☑ deletion (syllable, final consonant, etc)
- ☐ insertion, epenthesis
- ☑ word stress
- ☐ linking
- ☐ intonation
- ☐ pacing, rhythm

- ☐ other: _____

Vocabulary & Grammar (V/G):

- ☐ verb conjugation, verb tense
- ☐ syntactic category
- ☐ case (possessive)
- ☐ word choice
- ☑ prepositions
- ☑ articles
- ☑ plurals
- ☐ other: _____

Rhetorical Organization (RO):

- ☐ problems with overall structure
- ☐ problems with transitional language
- ☐ other: _____

Question Handling (QH):

- ☐ comprehension problems
- ☑ overly simplistic answers
- ☐ relevance/appropriateness of answer

Suggested Courses:

- ☑ 38A Stress & Intonation
- ☑ 38B Sound System (Phonemes)
- ☐ 39B Classroom Discourse
- ☐ 39C Presentation and Discussion

P: Consonants:

$/\theta/-/s/$: theory, thirty, both, with
$/l/-/n/$: number, analyze
$/s/-/z/$: basic

Vowels:
$/i/-/I/$: quiz, sheet, consider
$/\varepsilon/-/æ/$: set, confess, get

Deletion: eco(no)mics, e(v)ery,
                   active(ly), technic(al)

Word stress: computer, economist,
                     cumulative, illustrate,
                     specification

V/G:

→ now I'm gong to talk (say) something about

⌐ Each quiz is due on Monday (at) 8 pm
▶ How intelligent individuals interact (with) one another
└ Confess of their crime, on Friday in the first week

⌐ as you can see on (the) syllabus,
└ you can bring (a) card with formulas

▶ payoff(s), combination(s), most of the quiz(zes)

RO:

Task 2: Provided a brief intro (Welcome to…)
              Used transitions to go from item to item
                        (now I'm going to; Then…)
Task 3: Provided a brief intro
              Used transitions at micro level (so far)
              Used transitions at macro level; rhetorical?

QH:

No evidence of comprehension problems

Some responses are simplistic, not elaborate

Additional Comments:

References

Adair-Hauck, B., Glisan, E. W., Koda, K., Swender, E. B., & Sandrock, P. (2005). The integrated performance assessment (IPA): Connecting assessment to instruction and learning. *Foreign Language Annals, 39*(3), 359–382.

Alderson, C., & Wall, D. (1993). Does washback exist? *Applied Linguistics, 14*(2), 115–129.

Andrade, H., & Du, Y. (2005). Student perspectives on rubric-referenced assessment. *Practical Assessment, Research & Evaluation, 10*(3). Available: https://scholarworks.umass.edu/pare/vol10/iss1/3/.

Avineri, N., Londe, Z., Hardacre, B., Carris, L., So, Y., & Majidpour, M. (2011). Language assessment as a system: Best practices, stakeholders, models, and testimonials. *Issues in Applied Linguistics, 18*(2), 251–265.

Bachman, L. F. (1990). *Fundamental considerations in language testing*. Oxford, England: Oxford University Press.

Bachman, L. F. (1991). What does language testing have to offer? *TESOL Quarterly, 25*(4), 671–704.

Bachman, L. F. (2000). Modern language testing at the turn of the century: Assuring that what we count counts. *Language Testing, 17*(1), 1–42.

Bachman, L. F. (2007). What is the construct? The dialectic of abilities and context in defining constructs in language assessment. In J. Fox, M. Wesche, & D. Bayless (Eds.), *Language testing reconsidered* (pp. 41–72). Ottawa, Canada: University of Ottawa Press.

Bachman, L. F. (2013). How is educational measurement supposed to deal with test use? *Measurement, 11*(1–2), 19–23.

Bachman, L. F. (2014). Ongoing challenges for language assessment. In A. Kunnan (Ed.), *The companion to language assessment* (pp. 1586–1603). West Sussex, UK: Wiley.

Bachman, L. F., & Damböck, B. E. (2018). *Language assessment for classroom teachers*. New York, NY: Oxford University Press.

Bachman, L. F., & Palmer, A. S. (1981). The construct validation of the FSI oral interview. *Language Learning, 31*(1), 67–86.

Bachman, L. F., & Palmer, A. S. (1996). *Language testing in practice: Designing and developing useful language tests*. Oxford, England: Oxford University Press.

Bachman, L. F., & Palmer, A. S. (2010). *Language assessment in practice: Developing language assessments and justifying their use in the real world*. Oxford, England: Oxford University Press.

Brown, D. (2014). The type and linguistic foci of oral corrective feedback in the L2 classroom: A meta-analysis. *Language Teaching Research*. Published online 24 December 2014.

Celce-Murcia, M., Brinton, D. M., & Goodwin, J. M. (2010). *Teaching pronunciation: A reference for teachers of English to speakers of other languages* (2nd ed.). New York, NY: Cambridge University Press.

Douglas, D. (2000). *Assessing language for specific purposes*. Cambridge, UK: Cambridge University Press.

Ellis, R., Loewen, S., & Erlam, R. (2009). Implicit and explicit corrective feedback and the acquisition of L2 grammar. In R. Ellis, S. Loewen, C. Elder, R. Erlam, J. Philip, & H. Reinders (Eds.), *Implicit and Explicit Knowledge in Second Language Learning, Testing and Teaching*. Bristol, UK: Multilingual Matters.

Hoekje, B., & Linnell, K. (1994). "Authenticity" in language testing: Evaluating spoken language tests for international teaching assistants. *TESOL Quarterly, 28*(1), 103–126.

Isaacs, T. (2014). Assessing pronunciation. In A. J. Kunnan (Ed.), *The companion to language assessment* (pp. 140–155). Hoboken, NJ: Wiley-Blackwell.

Jang, E. E. (2008). A framework for cognitive diagnostic assessment. In C. A. Chapelle, Y.-R. Chung, & J. Xu (Eds.), *Towards adaptive CALL: Natural language processing for diagnostic language assessment* (pp. 117–131). Ames, IA: Iowa State University.

Kartchava, E., & Ammar, A. (2014). The noticeability and effectiveness of corrective feedback in relation to target type. *Language Teaching Research, 18*(4), 428–452.

Li, S. (2010). The effectiveness of corrective feedback in SLA: A meta-analysis. *Language Learning,* *60*(2), 309–365.

Lyster, R., & Saito, K. (2010). Oral feedback in classroom SLA: A meta-analysis. *Studies in Second Language Acquisition, 32,* 265–302.

Messick, S. (1996). Validity and washback in language testing. *Language Testing, 13,* 241–256.

North, B., & Schneider, G. (1998). Scaling descriptors for language proficiency scales. *Language Testing, 15*(2), 217–263.

Russell, J., & Spada, N. (2006). The effectiveness of corrective feedback for the acquisition of L2 grammar: A meta-analysis of the research. In J. Norris & L. Ortega (Eds.), *Synthesizing research on language learning and teaching* (pp. 133–164). Amsterdam: John Benjamins.

Saito, K. (2015). Variables affecting the effects of recasts on L2 pronunciation development. *Language Teaching Research, 19*(3), 276–300.

Sheen, Y. (2008). Recasts, language anxiety, modified output, and L2 learning. *Language Learning,* *58*(4), 835–874.

Shohamy, E. (2001). *The power of tests.* London, UK: Pearson Education Limited.

Skehan, P. (1998). *A cognitive approach to language learning.* Oxford, UK: Oxford University Press.

UCLA Center for the Advancement of Teaching (2020, January 21). *TOP scoring.* Retrieved from https://www.teaching.ucla.edu/top/scoring.

Part II
Validity and Validation of Language Assessments

Chapter 6
A Case for an Ethics-Based Approach to Evaluate Language Assessments

Antony John Kunnan

Abstract Two dominant approaches are typically used in the evaluation of language assessments. The oldest and still most popular way is to use the *Standards*-based approach. These standards (mainly a list of test qualities such as validity and reliability, and of late, consequences and fairness) have been developed from the best practices at assessment institutions. A more recent approach that has come to the forefront has been the Argument-based approach. This approach has generally used Toulmin's manner of structuring arguments with assessment claims, warrants, backing, and rebuttals. This chapter, partially based on Kunnan (2018), critically appraises these two approaches and Bachman's contributions based on these approaches to language assessments. It is then argued that the approaches have a fundamental weakness as they lack an articulated philosophical foundation to firm them up. In order to remedy this situation, an Ethics-based approach is then offered as a way to articulate a justifiable research agenda for the evaluation of language assessments.

Introduction

The dominant twentieth-century approach to the evaluation of language assessments was the *Standards*-based approach. The *Standards* most evaluators referred to are the American Psychological Association (APA), American Educational Research Association (AERA), National Council on Measurement in Education (NCME) *Standards* (1999, 2014). These standards (mainly a list of test qualities such as validity and reliability, and of late, consequences and fairness) were developed from the best practices at assessment institutions and had loose connections to theories of educational and psychological measurement. The "Test Usefulness" concept proposed by Bachman and Palmer (1996) was a popular example of the *Standards* approach. In the early part of the twenty-first century, Bachman (2005) proposed an Argument-based approach using Toulmin's way of structuring arguments with claims, warrants, backing, and rebuttals. This approach provided a framework for evaluating language assessments.

A. J. Kunnan (✉)
Duolingo, Inc., Pittsburgh, United States
e-mail: akunnan@gmail.com

© Springer Nature Singapore Pte Ltd. 2020
G. J. Ockey and B. A. Green (eds.), *Another Generation of Fundamental Considerations in Language Assessment*, https://doi.org/10.1007/978-981-15-8952-2_6

Bachman and Palmer's (2010) "Assessment Use Argument" (AUA) is an example of this approach.

While both of these approaches provide ways for researchers to conduct evaluations, they have a weakness, and that is, they generally lack an articulated philosophical grounding. In other words, in the *Standards* approach, why the listed standards are important and not others, and in the *Argument* approach, what aspects are to be included as claims and warrants lacks philosophical grounding. To remedy this situation, I am proposing an *Ethics*-based approach to assessment evaluation. The framework that implements the approach harnesses the dual concepts of fair assessments and just institutions leading to the *Principle of Fairness* and *Principle of Justice*, respectively.

Constructs and Historical Perspective

The Standards-Based Approach

Concept and Examples. The standards-based approach for the evaluation of educational and psychological assessment has a history of over 65 years. This approach to assessment evaluation has attempted to articulate general and specific qualities in assessment development, administration, scoring, and decision-making. These qualities reflect the good practices among assessment developers and score users and have come to be known as standard practice or standards. The first US institution that took a clear interest in assessment evaluation was the APA (American Psychological Association), in Washington, DC. It issued Technical Recommendations for Psychological Tests and Diagnostic Technique (in AERA et al. 1954). A year later, two committees representing AERA and NCME issued a second document titled Technical Recommendations for Achievement Tests. These documents focused on test development and the kinds of information test developers and publishers were to provide to test users, such as test manuals. In 1966, a third document titled the *Standards for Educational and Psychological Testing* (*Standards*, hereafter) was published jointly by AERA, APA, and NCME (AERA et al. 1966). This movement influenced test development and research for many decades. Lado (1961), mirroring the *Standards*, wrote about test evaluation in terms of validity (face validity, validity by content, validation of the conditions required to answer test items, and empirical validation, namely, concurrent and criterion-based validation) and reliability. Later, Davies (1968) presented a scheme for determining validity, listing five types: face, content, construct, predictive, and concurrent. The 1974 *Standards* (AERA et al. 1974) showed the interrelatedness of three different aspects of validity (content, criterion-related, and construct validities). The 1985 *Standards* (AERA et al. 1985) were revised and included Messick's (1989) unified and expanded conceptual framework of validity that included facets of validity of test score interpretation in terms of values and social consequences of tests and testing. The 1999 *Standards*

(AERA et al. 1999) went further and included a chapter titled, "Fairness in testing and test use" for the first time. The authors stated that the "concern for fairness in testing is pervasive, and the treatment accorded the topic here cannot do justice to the complex issues involved. A full consideration of fairness would explore the many functions of testing in relation to its many goals, including the broad goal of achieving equality of opportunity in our society" (p. 73).

In the 2014 *Standards*, (AERA et al. 2014) in Part I: "Foundations," the chapter on "Fairness in testing" was listed as a foundational chapter along with chapters on "Validity" and "Reliability/Precision and errors in measurement." In Part II: "Operations," chapters were devoted to test design, development, scores and scales, administration, and scoring procedures, rights, and responsibilities of test takers and test users. Part III: "Testing applications" offers guidelines for psychological and educational testing and assessment, workplace testing and credentialing, and tests for program evaluation.

Here are a few examples from the 2014 *Standards*:

Validity: *Standard 1.0*
                                 Clear articulation of each intended test score interpre-
                                 tation for a specified use should be set forth, and appro-
                                 priate validity evidence in support of each intended
                                 interpretation should be provided (p. 23).
Reliability/Precision: *Standard 2.0*
                                 Appropriate evidence of reliability/precision should be
                                 provided for the interpretation for each intended score
                                 use (p. 42).
Fairness.   *Standard 3.0*
                                 All steps in the testing process, including test design,
                                 validation, development, administration, and scoring
                                 procedures, should be designed in such a manner as to
                                 minimize construct-irrelevant variance and to promote
                                 valid score interpretations for the intended uses for all
                                 examinees in the intended population (p. 63).
                                 Standard 3.2
                                 Test developers are responsible for developing tests
                                 that measure the intended construct and for minimizing
                                 the potential for tests' being affected by construct-
                                 irrelevant characteristics, such as linguistic, commu-
                                 nicative, cognitive, cultural, physical, or other charac-
                                 teristics (p. 64).

Standard 3.4
Test takers should receive comparable treatment during
the test administration and scoring process (p. 65).

Program evaluation, policy   *Standard 13.4*
studies, and accountability: Evidence of validity, reliability, and fairness for each
purpose for which a test is used in a program evalua-
tion, policy study, or accountability system should be
collected and made available (p. 210).

The authors stated, "fairness is a fundamental validity issue and requires attention throughout all stages of test development and use" (p. 49). They articulated four
general views of fairness: (1) fairness in treatment during the testing process, (2) fairness as lack of measurement bias, (3) fairness in access to the construct as measured,
and (4) fairness as validity of individual test score interpretations for the intended
use. They also identified threats to fair and valid interpretations of test scores: test
content, test context, test response, opportunity to learn, and test accommodations
(adaptations, modifications, and score reporting from accommodated and modified
tests).

These standards have been used to provide guidance to assessment developers,
researchers, and for accountability, enforcement and in court cases. Important
decisions about test takers and institutional programs are made around the world
where these standards have been adopted. Various organizations, such as Educational Testing Practices, Princeton, the International Language Testing Association,
the Association of Language Testers in Europe, and the European Association of
Language Testers' Association adopted the *Standards* for their own purposes and
contexts.

Application of the Standards-Based Approach. Bachman and Palmer's (1996)
Qualities of Test Usefulness was the most popular application of the *Standards*
approach as it translated the somewhat cumbersome *Standards* and the difficult-
to-operationalize Messick (1989) approach for language assessment. They argued,
"the most important consideration in designing and developing a language test is
the use for which it is intended, so that the most important quality of a test is its
usefulness" (p. 17). They expressed their notion thus: "Usefulness = Reliability +
Construct Validity + Authenticity + Interactiveness + Impact + Practicality" (p. 18).
This representation of test usefulness, they asserted, "can be described as a function
of several different qualities, all of which contribute in unique but interrelated ways
to the overall usefulness of a given test" (p. 18). However, Bachman and Palmer
signaled the end of test usefulness as an approach to evaluating the quality of an
assessment when they introduced the case for building a justification for test use
(Bachman, 2005) and subsequently for the Assessment Use Argument (Bachman
and Palmer, 2010). Stoynoff and Chapelle's (2005) collection of 20 test reviews and
three additional chapters titled "Using the test manual to learn more about the test,"
"Evaluating the usefulness of tests," "Deciding to develop a test," and Bachman and
Palmer's (1996) *Qualities of Test Usefulness* signaled the wide influence of the Test

Qualities approach. The reviews had the following structure: Test information, Test Purpose, Test Methods, and Justifying Test Use.

Several authors also used the general *Standards* approach in their reviews of English language proficiency tests. The Alderson, Krahnke, and Stansfield (1987) collection had 47 reviews of some well-known tests such as the Australian Second Language Proficiency Ratings, Cambridge First Certificate in English, and Certificate of Proficiency in English, Pearson English, the Michigan Test of English Language Proficiency, The Test of English as a Foreign Language, Test of Spoken English and the Test of Written English. The main part of the review was the section in which the reviewer provided a description and the format of the test, some comments on validity (mainly content and criterion validity), reliability, scoring, and limitations. The *Mental Measurements Yearbook* (MMY) has had collections of reviews for 75 years; in the 19th edition in 2014, 283 tests were reviewed of which 25 tests were related to language. The structure provided by MMY editors was as follows: purpose, features, test development, reliability, and validity.

In summary, researchers used the *Standards* or Bachman and Palmer's (1996) *Qualities of Test Usefulness* in their evaluations of language assessments. In the words of Plake and Wise (2014), the *Standards* "promote(d) the sound and ethical use of tests and to provide a basis for evaluating the quality of testing practices. The *Standards* …provide(d) criteria for evaluating tests, testing practices, and the effects of test use. The *Standards* also provide(d) information to test developers, publishers, and users about key elements in a testing program that should inform the development, selection, and use of tests" (p. 4).

Critique of the Standards-Based Approach. There are three main criticisms of this approach. First, the *Standards* are listed under various headings with no overarching philosophical grounding. For example, the *Standards* list fairness as an important Standard with many annotations. But they do not provide a philosophical grounding of why fairness should be a critical consideration for assessment developers, score users, and decision-makers. Thus, the motivation to include fairness as an essential component of assessment development and evaluation is missing. Second, justifying assessments in terms of "industry standards" seems more of a legalistic way of responding to audits for a licensing arrangement but much less appropriate as a means of convincing test takers, score users, and policy makers that an assessment and assessment practice are beneficial to the community. Third, as the *Standards* are provided in the form of lists, it is not unlikely that assessment agencies could provide a list of standards that they have complied with in order to claim that their assessment is fair, valid, or reliable. Finally, while working within the establishment of assessment agencies, the Standards approach is concerned with how assessments and assessment practice meet standards rather than examining how assessments and assessment practice relate to test takers and their community.

The Argument-Based Approach

Concept and Examples. For the last two decades, the Argument-based approach to
the evaluation of assessments has become popular. Although this approach is popular
today, Cronbach (1988) argued for validation as a persuasive argument many decades
ago:

> Validation of test or test use is evaluation…What House (1977) has called 'the logic of evalu-
> ation argument' applies, and I invite you to think of 'validity argument' rather than 'validity
> research'…Validation speaks to a diverse and potentially critical audience; therefore, the
> argument must link concepts, evidence, social consequences, and values… (pp. 4–5)

The main argumentation model used in this approach is Toulmin's (1958)
pioneering model in which he states that for an argument to succeed, it needs justification for its conclusion or claim. And, in order to achieve this, he proposed a
layout containing six interrelated components for analyzing arguments; the first three
(claim, grounds or fact, and warrant) are considered essential and the remaining three
(backing, rebuttal, and qualifier) may be needed in some arguments.

For example, a *Claim* could be "Large scale assessment A is consistent or reliable";
a *Ground* could be "All large scale assessments ought to be consistent or reliable";
a *Warrant* could be "Large scale assessment A's consistency or reliability can be
inferred from research consistency or reliability research using test taker performance
data"; a *Backing* could be "Based on research studies of consistency or reliability of
Assessment A, we have support that large scale assessment A is consistent or reliable";
a *Rebuttal* could be "Large scale assessment A is not consistent or reliable"; and a
Qualifier could be: "Large scale assessment A is probably or partially or somewhat
consistent or reliable."

Kane (1992) applied Toulmin's (1958) argumentation model to language assessment. His approach to validation included the following steps:

(1) State an interpretive argument laying out the network of inferences that go
    from test scores to conclusions to be drawn and decisions to be based on these
    conclusions State an interpretive argument laying out the network of inferences
    that go from test scores to conclusions to be drawn and decisions to be based
    on these conclusions
(2) State the validity argument assembling all available evidence relevant to the
    inferences and assumptions in the interpretive argument
(3) Evaluate the problematic assumptions of the argument in detail
(4) Reformulate the interpretive and validity arguments, if necessary, and repeat step
    three until all inferences in the interpretive argument are considered plausible,
    or the interpretive argument is rejected (p. 330).

Kane (2012) further argued that the validation of a proposed interpretive argument
can be separated into two stages: the development stage (i.e., the test development
stage) and the appraisal stage (i.e., the evaluation stage).

- Stage 1: The Development Stage: Creating the test and the Interpretive Argument.
  In this stage, Kane (2012) expects test developers to have detailed interpretive

arguments for four major inferences: scoring, generalization, extrapolation, and decision.

- Stage 2: Appraisal Stage: Challenging the Interpretive Argument. In this Stage, these inferences are to be appraised.

Bachman and Palmer (2010) proposed an application to language assessment termed *Assessment Use Argument* (AUA). They stated that AUA is a component in the process of assessment justification and serves two essential purposes: (1) It guides the development and use of a given language assessment and provides the basis for quality control throughout the entire process of assessment development; and (2) It provides the basis for test developers and decision-makers to be held accountable to those who will be affected by the use of the assessment and the decisions that are made (p. 95). Using the Toulmin model of argumentation, Bachman and Palmer (2010) put forward four a priori claims and associated warrants that need to be included in the AUA:

Claim 1: Consequences are beneficial
Claim 2: Decisions made are values sensitive and equitable
Claim 3: Interpretations are meaningful, impartial, generalizable, relevant, and sufficient
Claim 4: Assessment records are consistent (p. 104).

Application of the Argument-Based Approach. Chapelle, Enright, and Jamieson (2008) applied the validity argument approach by expanding on the three-bridge validity argument (evaluation, generalization, and extrapolation) to include domain description, explanation, and utilization in their evaluation of the TOEFL. Llosa (2008) applied Bachman and Palmer's AUA approach by articulating the claims, warrants, rebuttals, and backing needed to justify the link between teachers' scores, a Standards-based classroom assessment used to make high-stakes decisions, and the interpretations made about students' language ability. She concluded that the AUA provided "a coherent framework that allows for a comprehensive examination of all warrants and potential rebuttals in order to justify interpretations and decisions to stakeholders" (p. 40). Wang et al. (2012) reviewed the new *Pearson Test of English Academic* using Bachman and Palmer's (2010) AUA framework. Two claims that Wang et al. (2012) focused on include impartiality and equitability: Claim 1: Impartiality Warrant and Claim 2: Equitability Warrant.

Critique of the Argument-Based Approach. There are three main concerns regarding Kane's (2012) approach. First, while this approach offers an innovative way of evaluating an assessment, in terms of the two stages, development and appraisal, there is no articulated philosophical basis for the claims that must be articulated and appraised. Second, the chain of inferences begins with scoring and goes all the way to decision, but much in test development takes place before the scoring stage, such as specifying the test purpose, surveying tasks in the target language use domain, selecting source material and content, the writing of tasks development, and finally beyond decision-making into consequences of an assessment. These processes need to be part of the interpretive argument as the data from these processes need to be part of the appraisal stage so that a comprehensive evaluation of an assessment can be undertaken. Third, there is a likely problem of conflict of interest (and the related concept of confirmationist bias), as according to Kane, test developers could make their interpretive argument/claim during or after test development. Their interpretive argument/claim would naturally include appropriate arguments for the inferences that the test developer may value but may ignore or downgrade ones that they may not choose to include. For example, test developers may choose to include claims that they would like confirmed and not to include claims that they would not like to be evaluated, and therefore, in the appraisal stage, the test will be appraised without these matters related to fairness of the assessment. Thus, an appraisal of an assessment conducted only in terms of the interpretive argument developed by a test developer is too internal and can potentially lead to a conflict of interest and biased evaluation of an assessment.

In contrast to Kane (2012), Bachman and Palmer's (2010) AUA approach can be said to have underlying philosophical principles, although unarticulated explicitly, that can be traced to a duty-based ethics for Claim 1 (beneficial consequences) and Claim 2 (sensitive and equitable values). Second, the AUA is wider in scope: from consequences to assessment scores. However, Bachman and Palmer (2010) in their diagramming did not include test content, although this is included in their design and operationalization stages of assessment development. This missing element is critical as test content could influence much that comes later. For example, if test content is biased against a certain group of test takers, the rest of the validation argument could be invalid and meaningless, so, leaving it out of the argument construction process would weaken the evaluation. Finally, although Bachman and Palmer include beneficial consequences and sensitive and equitable values, there is no philosophical grounding for this. Thus, it seems that Argument-based approaches generally seemed to be focused on framing claims and warrants rather than on fair assessments and just institutions and how assessments relate to test takers and their community.

Alternative Perspective

An Ethics-Based Approach

Concept and Examples. An alternative approach to evaluating the quality of language assessments is an Ethics-based approach which draws on the perspective from the world of moral philosophy, in which an ethic or ethical knowledge can be used to morally justify individual and institution practices. This support can empower both approaches in helping with general questions related to assessment and assessment practice: For example, these moral questions can be asked:

(1) Does every test taker have the right to a fair assessment? Is this rule inviolable? Are rights of test takers to a fair assessment universal or only applicable in states

that provide equal rights? Is it adequate that most test takers are assessed fairly while a few are not?

(2)   What responsibilities does a test developer or test score user have? Would it be appropriate to use a cost–benefit analysis to evaluate whether assessments should be improved or not? If harm is done to test takers, does such harm need to be compensated?

(3)   Would the rights of test takers to a fair assessment be supported in authoritarian states that do not provide for equal rights? Would institutions in such states feel less compelled to provide a fair assessment?

(4)   Should assessment developers and users be required to offer public justification or reasoning? Should they present their justifications for assessments backed by research findings in appropriate forums? Should an assessment be beneficial to the society in which it is used? Should assessment developers and users be required to offer public justification or reasoning? Should they present their justifications for assessments backed by research findings in appropriate forums? Should an assessment be beneficial to the society in which it is used?

(5)   Should assessment institutions be just in their approach?

Secular philosophers from centuries ago including Socrates, Plato, and Aristotle have searched for the meaning of justice. The main proponents, however, who addressed these matters were Enlightenment philosophers such as Locke, Hume, Bentham, Mill, and Sidgwick. These philosophers were called utilitarians and their general moral theory holds that the rightness or wrongness of an action is determined by the balance of good over evil that is produced by that action. Thus, rightness of actions (by individual and institution) should be judged by their consequences (caused by the actions). This important aspect of utilitarianism is termed consequentialist thinking in which outcomes of an event are used as tools to evaluate an institution. Another doctrine of utilitarianism is the Greatest Happiness Principle; it promotes the notion that the highest principle of morality is the greatest happiness for the greatest number of people: to maximize utility and to balance pleasure over pain. As a result, the utility principle would trump individual rights.

Implementing utilitarianism in the field of assessment could mean that decisions about an assessment may be made solely on utility and consequences. For example, if an assessment brought in a great deal of revenue as a result of large numbers of test takers taking an assessment, the assessment could be considered successful. In addition, if the consequences of the assessment were positive for a large majority, then the assessment could be considered beneficial to the community. However, maximizing happiness or minimizing unhappiness can result in sacrificing fairness and justice. For example, suppose an assessment was biased against a group of test takers, and to improve the current version or to develop a new assessment would entail a great deal of expenditure. This expense, if carried out, then would result in everyone paying more for the assessment and causing harm to all. One forced choice could be that the assessment be continued the way it is without any improvement. Strict utilitarians, in this case, would argue that these are bad choices and the less harmful of the two options would need to be chosen. Such utilitarians would hold that even if an assessment is biased against a group and fairness and justice may have to be sacrificed, we will have to just live with the assessment without any improvement. It would maximize happiness and minimize unhappiness.

Another way of thinking of ethics emerged with deontological (duty-based) ethics pioneered by the works of Immanuel Kant (1724–1804). Kant argued that to act in the morally right way, people must act from duty, and unlike utilitarianism, it was not the consequences of actions that made actions right or wrong but the motives of the person who carried out the action. His assertion was that there is a single moral obligation called the Categorical Imperative derived from duty and that people are naturally endowed with the ability and obligation toward the right reason and acting. The Categorical Imperative can be considered an unconditional obligation.

In addition, William Ross (1877–1971) offered seven prima facie duties that need to be considered when deciding which duty should be acted upon. Three of them relevant for this discussion were the Duty of beneficence (to help other people to increase their pleasure, improve their character, etc.), the Duty of non-maleficence (to avoid harming other people), and the Duty of justice (to ensure people get what they deserve).

Rawls (1971) treatise "A Theory of Justice" formulated a theory and principles of fairness and justice in which he argued that fairness is foundational and central to justice and therefore it is prior to justice. To quote from Sen's (2009) summary of Rawls's work: In the Rawlsian theory of "justice as fairness", *the idea of fairness relates to persons* (how to be fair between them), whereas the Rawlsian principles of justice are applied to *institutions* (how to identify "just institutions") (p. 72).

Adopting many ideas from these philosophers, I proposed two Principles of Fairness and Principles of Justice:

Principle 1—The Principle of Fairness: An assessment ought to be fair to all test takers, that is, there is a presumption of treating every test taker with equal respect.

Principle 2—The Principle of Justice: An assessment institution ought to be just, bring about benefits in society, promote positive values, and advance justice through public justification and reasoning.

These principles, based mainly on deontological thinking, could guide the evaluation of language assessment professionals to include the concepts and applications of fairness and justice. This focus also alters the dominant view of examining assessments and assessment practice (as seen through the focus on validation and reliability studies) to how assessments relate to test takers and their community (beneficial consequences).

A research agenda based on a combination of the standards and argument approaches.

In his recent application, Kunnan (2018) incorporated the *Standards* approach and the *Argument* approach but extended the approach with an ethical basis for evaluation of language assessments. This is achieved by modifying Toulmin's diagram to accommodate the ethical principles that drive the articulation of claims. Figure 6.1 shows how this is accomplished.

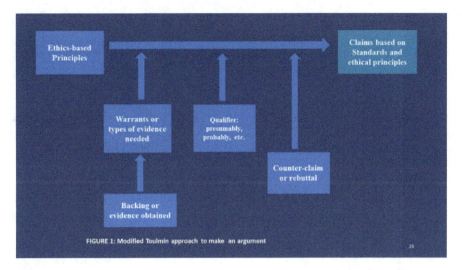

Fig. 6.1 Modified Toulmin approach to evaluate an assessment

A research agenda articulated in terms of the Principle of Fairness and the Principle of Justice is outlined below. The Principle of Fairness refers to the fairness of assessments in terms of test takers and the Principle of Justice refers to just institutions that are responsible for administering assessments and making decisions based on test takers' scores. Specifically, ethical principles lead to general claims and these lead to sub-claims. Figure 6.1 shows the flow of the principles, claims, warrants, etc. In the example below, these claims and sub-claims are written with a fictitious *Assessment A* in mind.

Principle 1—The Principle of Fairness: Assessment (named A) ought to be fair to all test takers, that is, there is a presumption of providing every test taker with equal opportunities to demonstrate their abilities.

General Claim: *Assessment A* is fair to all test takers.

Sub-claim 1: Prior to taking *Assessment A*, adequate opportunity to learn and prepare is provided

Sub-claim 1.1: Prior to taking Assessment A, adequate opportunity to learn is provided.
Sub-claim 1.2: Prior to taking Assessment A, adequate time preparation is provided.
Sub-claim 1.3: Prior to taking Assessment A, adequate practice with new technology is provided.
Sub-claim 1.4: Prior to taking Assessment A, adequate semiotic embodied experience in the domain of the assessment is provided.

Sub-claim 2: *Assessment A* is both meaningful and consistent.

Sub-claim 2.1: Assessment A is meaningful in terms of the blueprint and specifications, or curriculum objectives.
Sub-claim 2.2: Assessment A is meaningful in terms of the constructs of the language ability in the assessment.
Sub-claim 2.3: Assessment A is meaningful in terms of the language variety, content, and topics of the assessment.
Sub-claim 2.4: Assessment A is meaningful in that it is able to predict performance in terms of external criteria.
Sub-claim 2.5: Assessment A is consistent within sets of items/tasks in terms of different constructs.
Sub-claim 2.6: Assessment A is consistent across multiple assessment tasks, forms and/or occasions of assessments (in different regions, offices, and rooms).
Sub-claim 2.7: Assessment A is consistent across multiple examiners/immigration officers involved in the assessment.

Sub-claim 3: *Assessment A is free of bias.*

Sub-claim 3.1: Assessment A is free of bias in terms of content or topic or language variety across test taker groups.
Sub-claim 3.2: Assessment A is free of differential performance by different test taker groups of similar ability (in terms of gender, age, race/ethnicity, and native language).
Sub-claim 3.3: Assessment A score-interpretation is based on defensible standard-setting procedures.

Sub-claim 4: *Assessment A uses appropriate access and administration.*

Sub-claim 4.1: Assessment A is affordable to test takers.
Sub-claim 4.2: Assessment A is administered at locations that are accessible to test takers.
Sub-claim 4.3: Assessment A is accessible to test takers with disabilities and has appropriate accommodations.
Sub-claim 4.4: Assessment A is accessible to test takers whose first language is not English for subject matter tests (e.g., science, mathematics, computer science).
Sub-claim 4.5: Assessment A is administered uniformly to test takers.
Sub-claim 4.6: Assessment A is administered without any fraud or breach of security.
Sub-claim 4.7: Assessment A decision-making is based on defensible grounds, including legal and ethical.

Principle 2—The Principle of Justice: The assessment institution that administers Assessment A ought to be a just institution as the assessment ought to be beneficial to society.

General claim: *Assessment A is administered by a just institution.*

Sub-claim 1: Assessment A is beneficial to the immediate community and larger society.

> Sub-claim 1.1: Assessment A-based decision-making is beneficial to immediate stakeholders (e.g., test takers, instructors in citizenship courses in community colleges, and college administrators).
> Sub-claim 1.2: Assessment A-based decision-making is beneficial to test takers (in terms of gender, age, race/ethnicity, size of community).
> Sub-claim 1.3: Assessment A-based decision-making is beneficial to the instructional program (e.g., teaching-learning and the learning environment, also known as "washback").
> Sub-claim 1.4: Assessment A-based decision-making is beneficial to the wider stakeholders (e.g., school district, community, province/state, country).

Sub-claim 2: *Assessment A*-based decision-making promotes positive values and advances justice.

> Sub-claim 2.1: Assessment A has provision for administrative remedies to challenge decisions such as rescoring or re-evaluation.
> Sub-claim 2.2: Assessment A has provision for legal challenges related to decision-making.
> Sub-claim 2.3: Assessment A-based decision-making is not detrimental to test taking groups and corrects existing injustice (if any) to test taking groups.
> Sub-claim 2.4: Assessment A institution promotes positive values and advances justice by providing public justification and reasoning for the assessment.

The claims and sub-claims that are the direct result of an ethics-based approach include the following: Opportunity-to-learn and free of bias under the Principle of Fairness, and beneficial assessment and positive values and advancement of justice under the Principle of Justice. These claims are typically not pursued under the Standards-based and Argument-based approaches except for Bachman and Palmer's focus on equitable decisions and beneficial consequences. At first glance, these claims and sub-claims may also seem to be obvious to researchers who use Standards-based and Argument-based approaches. But these unique principles are operationalized into claims and sub-claims that can be evaluated in terms of collected evidence. Further, they are articulated in a framework with supporting philosophical positions. These sub-claims, if they are part of assessments, can be examined through traditional quantitative and qualitative research methods.

Applications of an Ethics-Based Approach. Early applications of an ethics-based approach include a few general ideas that were proposed by educational and language assessment researchers. Davies' (1997) "Test virtues" approach made an early argument for "test virtues," reflecting Aristotelian virtue ethics. In essence, Davies argued that test developers or agencies ought to act as moral individuals or agents who have ethical principles by which they operate and therefore do the right thing for the right reasons.

Kunnan (1997) proposed a fairness agenda after reviewing 100 validation studies conducted by well-known language assessment researchers. He argued that "a social postmodernist view, in contrast, would value validation research that is attentive to social and cultural difference, not just by learning about differences among test takers or indulging in an easy relativism which in practice might result in not taking difference seriously, but by engaging in a research program that would incorporate social and cultural difference within the validation process" (p. 93).

Willingham and Cole (1997), in their study of gender and fair assessment, argued that "test fairness is an important aspect of validity…anything that reduces fairness also reduces validity…test fairness is best conceived of as comparability in assessment; more specifically, comparable validity for all individuals and groups" (pp. 6–7). Using the notion of comparable validity as the central principle, Willingham and Cole (1997) suggested three criteria for evaluating the fairness of a test: "comparability of opportunity for examinees to demonstrate relevant proficiency, comparable assessment exercises (tasks) and scores, and comparable treatment of examinees in test interpretation and use" (p. 11).

FairTest, a non-profit organization in the US, has devoted its entire work to the cause of fair assessments. Its mission is to advance "quality education and equal opportunity by promoting fair, open, valid and educationally beneficial evaluations of students, teachers and schools" (https://www.fairtest.org/about). FairTest also works to end the misuses and flaws of testing practices that impede those goals.

More recent research studies on a number of these claims and sub-claims have been completed. For example, studies focused on opportunity-to-learn by examining adequate opportunity, time, practice with technology, and experiences in the domain of the assessment (Kunnan, 2018); providing adequate feedback from automated systems (Hoang & Kunnan, 2016; Liu & Kunnan, 2016); and beneficial consequences of the US naturalization language assessments (Kunnan, 2009a, 2009b, 2012, in press). Research studies that need to be conducted in the future should generally take the two principles into consideration: (1) whether an assessment is fair to all test takers; and (2) whether an assessment is beneficial to the community where it is deployed and whether the institution using the assessment is promoting positive values and advancing justice.

Conclusions, Implications and Future Directions

The central thesis of this chapter is that an ethics-based approach to evaluation of language assessments has the scope to promote fairness of assessments and just institutions that are not clearly brought to the forefront in the Standards-based and Argument-based approaches. While the Standards-based approach provided the best educational assessment practice approach and the Argument-based approach offered a useful and clear framework for evaluating claims, they did not harness an ethical foundation to motivate assessment developers and researchers. An ethics-based approach as the one proposed here can be seen as a useful extension to the ongoing debate of the *what and why* principles that should be employed for language assessment development and evaluation.

In addition, the key point is that fairness and justice are necessary everywhere language assessments are conducted—in schools, colleges, and universities; in the workplace; in immigration, citizenship, and asylum; in all countries, big, medium, and small; and in well-developed, developing, and slow-developing communities. Every test taker in the world—young or old, man or woman, white, black, yellow, or brown, with disabilities or otherwise—needs to have fundamental rights to be treated equitably, so that they can experience fair language assessments and just assessment institutions throughout their lives. Thus, fair assessments and just institutions need to be ubiquitous everywhere in the world.

Such a global non-parochial approach should remind us of King's (1963) famous words written as a letter from a jail in Birmingham, Alabama, USA: "Injustice anywhere is a threat to justice everywhere. We are caught in the inescapable network of mutuality, tied in a single garment of destiny. Whatever affects one directly, affects all indirectly. Never again can we afford to live with the narrow, provincial 'outside agitator' idea."

Bachman's contributions in the Standards-based approach through the *Qualities of Test Usefulness* and in the Argument-based approach through the *Assessment Use Argument* stand out as stellar examples of clear and practical approaches in language assessment. These two contributions have been immensely useful to assessment developers and researchers in designing their assessments and planning and executing their research agendas. If we language assessment professionals pursue an ethics-based approach that incorporates fairness and justice for all, we would be making a substantial contribution to our communities and expanding on the legacy of Lyle Bachman's contributions to language assessment.

References

Alderson, J. C., Krahnke, K., & Stansfield, C. (Eds.). (1987). *Reviews of English language proficiency tests.* Washington, DC: TESOL.

American Educational Research Association, American Psychological Association & National Council on Measurement on Education. (1954). *Technical recommendations for psychological tests and diagnostic techniques.* Washington, DC: Author.

American Educational Research Association, American Psychological Association & National Council on Measurement in Education. (1955). *Technical recommendations for achievement tests.* Washington, DC: AERA.

American Educational Research Association, American Psychological Association & National Council on Measurement in Education. (1966). *Standards for educational and psychological tests and manuals.* Washington, DC: Author.

American Educational Research Association, American Psychological Association, & National Council on Measurement in Education. (1974). *Standards for educational and psychological tests.* Washington, DC: APA.

American Educational Research Association American Psychological Association, & National Council on Measurement in Education. (1985). *Standards for educational and psychological testing.* Washington, DC: APA.

American Educational Research Association, American Psychological Association, & National Council on Measurement in Education. (1999). *Standards for educational and psychological testing.* Washington, DC: AERA.

American Educational Research Association, American Psychological Association, & National Council on Measurement in Education. (2014). *Standards for educational and psychological testing.* Washington, DC: AERA.

Bachman, L. F. (2005). Building and supporting a case for test use. *Language Assessment Quarterly, 2,* 1–34.

Bachman, L. F., & Palmer, A. S. (1996). *Language testing in practice.* Oxford, UK: Oxford University Press.

Bachman, L. F., & Palmer, A. S. (2010). *Language assessment in practice.* Oxford, UK: Oxford University Press.

Chapelle, C. A., Enright, M. E., & Jamieson, J. (Eds.). (2008). *Building a validity argument for the test of English as a Foreign Language.* London, UK: Routledge.

Cronbach, L. J. (1988). Five perspectives on validity argument. In W. Howard & H. I. Braun (Eds.), *Test validity* (pp. 1–14). Hillsdale, NJ: Lawrence Erlbaum.

Davies, A. (1968). *Language testing symposium: A psycholinguistic approach.* Oxford, UK: Oxford University Press.

Davies, A. (Guest Ed.). (1997). Introduction: The limits of ethics in language testing. *Language Testing, 14,* 235–241.

FairTest. Retrieved February 26, 2020, from https://www.fairtest.org/about.

Hoang, G., & Kunnan, A. J. (2016). Automated essay evaluation for English language learners: A case study of *My Access. Language Assessment Quarterly, 13,* 359–376.

Kane, M. (1992). An argument-based approach to validity. *Psychological Bulletin, 112,* 527–535.

Kane, M. (2012). *Validating score interpretations and uses.* USA, Rosedale Road, Princeton, NJ: Educational Testing Service.

King, M. L. (1963, April 16). *Letter from a jail in Birmingham City Jail* (p. 2).

Kunnan, A. J. (1997). Connecting fairness and validation. In A. Huhta, V. Kohonen, L. Kurti-Suomo, & S. Luoma (Eds.), *Current developments and alternatives in language assessment* (pp. 85–109). Jyvaskyla, Finland: University of Jyvaskyla.

Kunnan, A. J. (2009a). Politics and legislation in citizenship testing in the U.S. *Annual Review of Applied Linguistics, 29,* 37–48.

Kunnan, A. J. (2009b). The U.S. naturalization test. *Language Assessment Quarterly, 6,* 89–97.

Kunnan, A. J. (2012). Language assessment for immigration and citizenship. In G. Fulcher & F. Davidson (Eds.), *The handbook of language testing* (pp. 152–166). NY, NY: Routledge.

Kunnan, A. J. (2018). *Evaluating language assessments.* New York, NY: Routledge.

Kunnan, A. J. (in press). The U.S. Naturalization test: Is it a barrier or beneficial? In G. Fulcher & L. Harding (Eds.), *The handbook of language testing* (2nd ed.). New York, NY: Routledge.

Lado, R. (1961). *Language testing.* London, UK: Longman.

Liu, S., & Kunnan, A. J. (2016). Investigating the application of automated writing evaluation to Chinese undergraduate English majors: A study of *WriteToLearn. CALICO Journal, 33,* 71–91.

Llosa, L. (2008). Building and supporting a validity argument for a standards-based classroom assessment of English proficiency based on teacher judgments. *Educational Measurement, 27,* 32–40.

Messick, S. (1989). Validity. In R. Linn (Ed.), *Educational measurement* (3rd ed., pp. 13–103). London, U.K.: Macmillan.

Plake, B. S., & Wise, L. L. (2014). What is the role and importance of the revised AERA, APA, NCME standards for educational and psychological testing? *Educational Measurement, 33,* 4–12.

Rawls, J. (1971). *A theory of justice.* Cambridge, MA: Harvard University Press.

Sen, A. (2009). *The idea of justice.* Boston, MA: Harvard University Press.

Stoynoff, S., & Chapelle, C. A. (Eds.). (2005). *ESOL tests and testing: A resource for teachers and administrators*. Alexandria, VA: TESOL.

Toulmin, S. (1958). *The uses of argument*. Cambridge, UK: Cambridge University Press.

Wang, H., Choi, I., Schmidgall, J., & Bachman, L. (2012). Review of the Pearson test of English academic: Building an assessment-use argument. *Language Testing, 29,* 603–619.

Willingham, W. W., & Cole, N. (1997). *Gender and fair assessment*. Mahwah, NJ: Lawrence Erlbaum Associates.

Chapter 7
Alignment as a Fundamental Validity Issue in Standards-Based K-12 English Language Proficiency Assessments

Mikyung Kim Wolf

Abstract In U.S. K-12 education, large-scale, standards-based English language proficiency (ELP) assessments have a far-reaching impact at many levels—from individual students to education systems. Validation for K-12 ELP assessments is undeniably crucial. One essential aspect of validation is a determination of how well the content of an assessment aligns with the target domain. Although this alignment has often been considered as a type of validity evidence based on test content, this paper highlights its extensive role pertaining to the consequences of K-12 ELP assessment uses. The paper discusses how Bachman and Palmer's Assessment Use Argument framework helps us integrate an expanded view of alignment by reinforcing consideration of the consequences of assessment uses in validity. A range of pressing areas of research on alignment evaluation for K-12 ELP assessments is also discussed.

Introduction

Over the past four decades, the fields of educational measurement and language testing have witnessed an evolving concept of and approaches to validity. While validity is generally seen as a judgement on the degree of appropriateness of interpretations and uses based upon test scores (American Educational Research Association, American Psychological Association, & National Council on Measurement in Education [AERA, APA, & NCME], 2014; Bachman & Palmer, 1996, 2010; Kane, 2001; Messick, 1989), the consequences resulting from test uses have been treated differently across validity frameworks. Some early frameworks, such as Messick's construct validity model as a unitary validity framework and Kane's interpretation/use argument, do mention consequences, but they do not assign consequences a central role, nor do they provide clear guidance on incorporating consequences into validation.

M. K. Wolf (✉)
Educational Testing Service, Rosedale Road, Princeton, NJ 08541, USA
e-mail: mkwolf@ets.org

© Springer Nature Singapore Pte Ltd. 2020   95
G. J. Ockey and B. A. Green (eds.), *Another Generation of Fundamental Considerations in Language Assessment*, https://doi.org/10.1007/978-981-15-8952-2_7

Building on previous validity concepts and frameworks, Bachman and Palmer (2010) proposed an Assessment Use Argument (AUA) framework where they brought consequences to the fore of validity and laid out a validation process linking assessment performance to consequences. In the AUA framework, any claim about intended consequences must be specified and supported by evidence. This means that consequences can be traced to a series of other interrelated assessment claims on decisions, interpretations, and assessment performance. Maintaining that assessment uses must be accountable to all stakeholders, Bachman and Palmer offered the AUA framework as an accountability mechanism.

The AUA framework is particularly instrumental to the validation of K-12 English language proficiency (ELP) assessments in U.S. K-12 educational settings. In U.S. K-12 education, large-scale, standards-based ELP assessments have drawn substantial attention from educators, researchers, policy makers, and advocacy groups due to the significant roles they play in students' academic lives. By federal law, schools must identify "English learner (EL)" students whose home language is not English and who experience difficulty accessing content learning in English-medium school settings due to their limited English language proficiency (U.S. Department of Education, 2016). Federal guidelines explicitly specify that a "valid and reliable ELP test" should be used to identify EL students and that schools must provide appropriate support and services to those EL students (U.S. Department of Justice and U.S. Department of Education, 2015; U.S. Department of Education, 2015).

Consequences of the use of K-12 ELP assessments are far-reaching—from individual students to education systems. While it is important to measure EL students' progress in English language development, unfortunately ELP assessments often function as gatekeepers for EL students attempting to exit the EL designation to take a mainstream educational pathway. Once officially identified as an EL based on ELP assessment results, students follow a track where English language development (ELD) instruction often takes place separately from mainstream classes at the expense of rigorous academic content learning, particularly at the secondary school level (Estrada, 2014; Umansky, 2016). EL students also must take an ELP assessment annually until they meet the proficiency level required to exit the EL designation (i.e., EL reclassification). At the local district and state levels, ELP assessments are also used to determine, for accountability and program evaluation purposes, the number of EL students and the extent of their progress in ELP attainment, which in turn leads to decisions about funding/resource allocation and program changes. Given these stakes and the wide range of stakeholders involved in the use of ELP assessments, a consideration of consequences must be integral to making a validity argument for ELP assessment uses.

This paper discusses how AUA provides a coherent validity framework for U.S. K-12 ELP assessments while taking consequences into explicit consideration. In particular, this paper focuses on alignment issues in U.S. K-12 ELP assessments. In the context of U.S. K-12 education, alignment between assessments and educational academic standards is of crucial importance. Although alignment has often been considered specific to test content only as a type of validity evidence, this paper highlights the implications of alignment for the consequences of K-12 ELP assessment uses. I will describe the construct of K-12 ELP assessments as a key element to understand the important role of alignment. Then, I will provide an overview of previous alignment research and discuss how alignment is tied to consequences from the use of K-12 ELP assessments. The AUA framework facilitates this connection. I will conclude this paper by delineating areas of research, particularly those related to alignment and consequences, that are critical to sustaining the validity of K-12 ELP assessments uses.

Constructs

There has been a long-standing use of K-12 ELP assessments primarily for EL designation purposes (i.e., EL identification and reclassification). However, the construct of these K-12 ELP assessments has varied over time. One major shift in the ELP construct is attributed to the 2001 reauthorization of the Elementary and Secondary Education Act, known as No Child Left Behind (NCLB, 2002). This federal legislation required all states to develop or adopt ELP standards that are aligned with academic standards and to annually measure EL students' attainment of English language proficiency for accountability purposes. This policy requirement led to the era of post-NCLB assessments of ELP, spawning the ELP or ELD standards and *standards-based* ELP assessments. Prior to NCLB, K-12 ELP assessments did not always measure the four language skills (i.e., listening, reading, speaking, and writing) consistently. They also tended to measure general, basic language skills, failing to measure the academic language skills needed in school settings (Stevens, Butler, & Castellon-Wellington, 2000). To comply with federal mandates, many states rushed to develop or adopt ELP standards and assessments, with little guidance on defining the ELP construct (Wolf et al., 2008; Boals et al., 2015). Some review studies have pointed out that states have differed in their approaches to developing ELP standards and operationalizing those standards into ELP assessment constructs and test items (Bailey & Huang, 2011; Forte, Kuti, & O'Day, 2011; Wolf, Farnsworth, & Herman 2008; Wolf & Farnsworth, 2014). For example, there were varied approaches to representing academic versus social language skills in post-NCLB ELP assessments (Abedi, 2007; Wolf & Faulkner-Bond, 2016).

The Common Core State Standards (CCSS), introduced in 2012 as new academic content standards, spurred another wave of substantial changes in instructing and assessing EL students' ELP. With the intent of preparing all students for college and careers, the CCSS feature higher academic rigor and greater language demands than previous standards. For instance, Bunch, Kibler, and Pimental (2012) discuss the major language and literacy demands in the CCSS for English language arts including (1) engaging complex texts (reading standards), (2) using evidence in writing and research (writing standards), (3) working collaboratively and presenting ideas (speaking and listening standards), and (4) developing linguistic resources to do the above-mentioned tasks effectively (language standards). The authors also highlight the strong interdisciplinary focus of the language and literacy requirements in the CCSS.

In efforts to equip EL students with the language skills to meet rigorous academic content standards, the two major ELP consortia in the United States (i.e., WIDA consortium and the English Language Proficiency Assessment for the 21st century [ELPA21] consortium) have developed new ELP standards including language skills and knowledge tied to the Common Core. Notably, the two consortia have taken different approaches to revising or developing their respective ELP standards (Wolf, Guzman-Orth, & Hauck, 2016). In revising its 2004 standards, WIDA maintained its original structure of four language domains (listening, reading, speaking, and writing) and added a description of how each standard is connected to CCSS content standards. In contrast, ELPA21's newly created ELP standards take the CCSS as their basis and reflect the prevailing view of integrated language skills in academic contexts. ELPA21's ELP standards are not divided into the traditional four language domains of listening, reading, speaking, and writing. Rather, the standards include descriptions of integrated language skills (i.e., oral proficiency that integrates listening and speaking, literacy skills that incorporate reading and writing, receptive skills that focus on listening and reading comprehension, and productive skills that focus on oral and written expression). This approach is also reflected in California's 2012 English Language Development Standards, which are divided into three communication modes (i.e., interpretive, productive, and collaborative modes) rather than four language skills.

A common approach to the current ELP assessment construct among these consortia and states reflects an emphasis on academic language proficiency in the context of disciplinary areas (e.g., mathematics, language arts, science, social studies). The ELP construct has been conceptualized with a focus on authentic interactions and more complex uses of language in order to correspond to the more rigorous language demands embodied in academic content standards such as the CCSS. On one hand, this approach is driven by the explicit policy requirement in the current Elementary and Secondary Education Act, the Every Student Succeeds Act (ESSA, 2015). ESSA stipulates that states should have ELP standards and ELP assessments that are aligned with academic content standards (ESSA, Sec. 1111(b)(2)(F)). On the other hand, this approach is intended to bring a close interconnection between ELP and disciplinary areas so that EL students can acquire necessary language skills within enriched contexts, moving away from traditional instruction of discrete language skills (e.g., phonics, morphology, vocabulary, grammar) in isolation. Taken together, the current approach to the K-12 ELP construct signifies the importance of alignment among standards, assessments, curriculum, and instruction. In the next section, I discuss how alignment is situated in previous validation research and how Bachman and Palmer's (2010) AUA framework can be utilized for linking alignment to consequences in validating K-12 ELP assessment uses.

Historical Perspectives

As described above, the ELP construct of U.S. K-12 ELP assessments has been heavily influenced by government policies and standards adopted in specific periods. The reliance of the ELP construct on standards for the past two decades is a manifestation of standards-based reforms enacted in U.S. K-12 education. As Porter (2002) explains, in standards-based education, standards drive an instructional system, determining what is taught and what is assessed. A coherent instructional system in close alignment with standards is expected to promote equity and student learning outcomes. A large body of educational assessment literature has emphasized the importance of such an alignment between standards and assessments. Indeed, this arrangement is crucial in ensuring that assessment results can accurately reflect student learning as well as inform instructional planning (e.g., Hamilton, Stecher, & Yuan, 2012; Herman, 2004; Webb, 1999). Assessments can provide a concrete way to view how standards are understood and implemented in practice. Therefore, the degree of alignment is an essential piece of validity evidence pertaining to test content as well as consequences for K-12 assessments.

In educational measurement research, alignment evaluation has primarily focused on comparing test content with the content expectations in academic standards of language arts, mathematics, and science. The cognitive demands of test items have also been an important element of comparison to ensure that assessments are aligned with standards in terms of their rigor. The breadth and depth of alignment between assessment and standards are thus commonly examined using well-known alignment methods such as Webb's alignment tool, the Surveys of Enacted Curriculum, and the Achieve alignment protocol (Porter, 2002; Rothman, Slattery, Vranek, & Resnick, 2002; Webb, 1999). While researchers delve into methodological issues in alignment (e.g., alignment criteria, rater reliability), test developers typically conduct alignment evaluations in order to provide evidence of the quality of their assessments. The focus on test content for alignment has become the norm for states' accountability assessments as the federal "Peer Review" process for state assessment systems specifies that states must provide validity evidence based on test content, particularly alignment (U.S. Department of Education, 2018).

Although previous literature acknowledges both content and consequences as issues around alignment (Hamilton et al., 2012; Herman, Webb, & Zuniga, 2007; Martone & Sireci, 2009), the federal Peer Review guidance has emphasized alignment only for test content, adopting the validity framework from the *Standards for Educational and Psychological Testing* (AERA, APA, & NCME, 2014). This practice mainly views alignment as evidence to support valid interpretations of test scores.

However, considering the intended, positive consequences from standards-based reform efforts, it is critical that alignment evaluation be expanded and connected systematically across standards, assessment, curriculum, and instruction. Bachman and Palmer's (2010) AUA framework helps us integrate an expanded view of alignment by reinforcing consideration of the consequences of assessment uses. As mentioned earlier, the underlying principle for the AUA framework is that assessment uses should be justified and that test developers and decision-makers should be held accountable for the decisions about and uses and consequences of assessments (Bachman, 2005; Bachman & Palmer, 2010). Bachman and Palmer contend that a validity argument must begin with an explicit articulation of consequences from the use of assessments.

In the AUA framework, a series of inferences are made within and across claims regarding assessment records (e.g., scores), interpretations of assessment records, decisions made based on interpretations, and consequences resulting from such decisions (Bachman & Palmer, 2010; Bachman, 2013). In this way, AUA offers a coherent and systematic model to collect a range of evidence to justify assessment uses. In the case of K-12 ELP assessments, the assessments have been created with the ultimate goal that EL students receive equitable education based on current standards and acquire appropriate language skills to successfully perform academic tasks in school settings. Additionally, the use of sound ELP assessments was intended to increase teachers' understanding of standards and of EL students' linguistic needs, thereby raising the quality of instruction. To realize the intended consequences, a host of alignment evidence needs to be gathered from standards, assessments, curriculum, and instruction.

To illustrate the use of AUA framework for validating K-12 ELP assessment uses, some example claims and the links among those claims are presented in Fig. 7.1. For each claim presented in Fig. 7.1, its pertinent warrants and evidence can be concerned with alignment. For instance, important evidence can be obtained to support claims about consequences, interpretations, and assessment records by examining the extent to which (1) teachers understand ELP assessment results in relation to ELP standards, (2) ELP assessments reflect language skills manifested in ELP standards, and (3) ELP standards represent target language use skills.

Notably, alignment research with U.S. K-12 ELP assessments is in its infancy. The next section will examine the critical issues that surround the alignment of ELP assessments to standards and instruction in order to increase validity.

Inferential Links   **Example Claims**

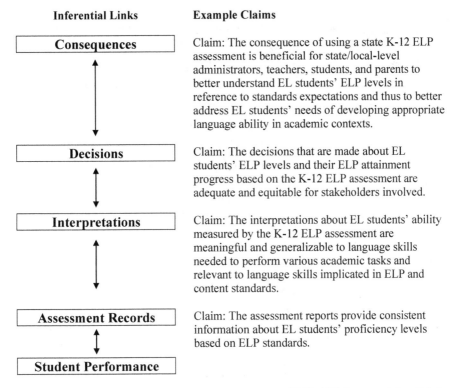

Claim: The consequence of using a state K-12 ELP assessment is beneficial for state/local-level administrators, teachers, students, and parents to better understand EL students' ELP levels in reference to standards expectations and thus to better address EL students' needs of developing appropriate language ability in academic contexts.

Claim: The decisions that are made about EL students' ELP levels and their ELP attainment progress based on the K-12 ELP assessment are adequate and equitable for stakeholders involved.

Claim: The interpretations about EL students' ability measured by the K-12 ELP assessment are meaningful and generalizable to language skills needed to perform various academic tasks and relevant to language skills implicated in ELP and content standards.

Claim: The assessment reports provide consistent information about EL students' proficiency levels based on ELP standards.

Fig. 7.1 An example of applying the Bachman and Palmer (2010) AUA framework in validating K-12 ELP assessment uses

Critical Issues

Expanding an Alignment Framework for ELP Assessments

As described earlier, the construct of U.S. K-12 ELP assessments should be formulated on the basis of ELP standards that states have adopted (i.e., alignment between ELP assessments and ELP standards). These ELP standards should also be aligned with academic content standards in accordance with the ESSA. The intent here is that ELP standards encompass the appropriate language knowledge and skills that EL students need to achieve proficiency in academic content standards. The alignment between ELP and content standards is a critical issue to be examined in order to support the use of ELP assessments for making EL reclassification decisions. An EL reclassification decision implies that a student is ready to exit language services (e.g., ELD instruction) to perform the academic tasks specified in the standards.

Furthermore, in order to evaluate how well ELP assessments measure appropriate language skills for EL students, the types of language demands involved in the curriculum and instruction also need to be examined. Curricular materials provide

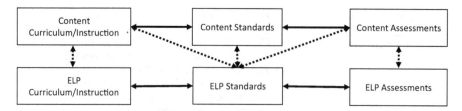

Fig. 7.2 An expanded framework of alignment for ELP standards and assessments

an essential way of understanding the extent to which standards are implemented in the classroom. Previous literature points out that the alignment of curricula with standards and assessments is critical to ensure that teachers have a clear understanding of the expectations placed on them and their students, and that students have ample opportunity to learn expected content and to be assessed fairly (Mohamud & Fleck, 2010; Martone & Sireci, 2009; Porter, 2002).

Thus, for a comprehensive alignment evaluation, standards, assessments, curriculum, and instruction in both ELP and content areas should be considered. This expanded approach not only provides important validity evidence but also yields empirical evidence to further improve the policy and practice of ELP standards and assessments (e.g., a better understanding of academic language proficiency in K-12 education settings). Figure 7.2 illustrates this expanded alignment framework in which standards, assessments, and curricula in ELP and content areas relate to one another in terms of alignment and correspondence of language demands. In Fig. 7.2, solid arrows represent alignment, while dotted lines represent correspondence. Note that the term *correspondence* is meant to indicate a conceptual difference with alignment as it has typically been used in the literature. Alignment refers to the comparison of artifacts from the same domain (e.g., mathematics standards to mathematics assessments), whereas correspondence refers to the comparison of artifacts from different domains (e.g., ELP standards to content standards) on particular aspects the artifacts might have in common (e.g., language demands) (Council of Chief State School Officers [CCSSO], 2012).

As shown in Fig. 7.2, in the current era of college- and career-ready (CCR) standards such as the Common Core State Standards and the Next Generation Science Standards in the United States, content-area standards are the drivers of other components in the educational system. They determine what ELP skills and knowledge are necessary for access to the curriculum, and thus are the drivers of the ELP components insofar as content standards also drive content instruction and assessment. In this framework, it is critical to identify explicit and implicit language skills and tasks embedded in new CCR-era content and ELP standards and then to examine how those language skills and tasks are measured in the CCR-era ELP assessments. Under the premise that content assessments and curriculum/instruction reflect the types of language demands embodied in content standards, an examination of the language demands in these elements (i.e., assessments and curriculum/instruction) between the content areas and ELP is also included in the framework.

Although much effort has been made to examine the alignment between content standards and assessments, or between ELP standards and assessments, there is little research available to comprehensively investigate the types of language skills implicated in standards, assessments, and curricular materials in both content and ELP areas from the perspectives of EL teaching and learning. Previous studies of alignment have been conducted in isolation from other important considerations (e.g., content and ELP standards without their associated assessments, textbooks, and standards without assessments). The framework presented here offers a useful model for alignment evaluation for the assessment of EL students, stressing that ELP alignment evaluation should encompass the examination of both alignment and correspondence between content and ELP. It can also aid in articulating any intended positive consequences from the use of standards-based ELP assessments.

Identifying Language Demands for Alignment Evaluation

Alignment research in the educational measurement field has strived to develop robust tools to evaluate the content and cognitive demands of content standards, assessments, and instruction (Porter, 2002; Rothman et al., 2002; Webb, 1999). Yet, it is notable that no alignment tools have been developed specifically to examine the language demands in standards, assessments, and curricular materials from the perspective of EL education despite the increased language demands that are apparent in CCR content and new ELP standards. A number of researchers point out the significance of examining alignment in terms of language demands. Cook (2005) argues that existing alignment tools need modifications in their applications to ELP standards and assessments. He suggests that the linguistic complexity of the standards and assessments is an important dimension, differing from dimensions examined in the alignment of content standards and assessments. Bailey, Butler, and Sato (2007) propose adding the dimension of language demands when examining the correspondence between content-area and ELP standards to develop ELP assessments. They define language demands in terms of specific linguistic skills (e.g., lexical, syntactic structures) and academic language functions (e.g., argument, comparison, evaluation, and explanation), and argue that prior standards-to-standards linkage studies have neglected this important dimension of learning.

To facilitate alignment evaluation for ELP assessments, the first crucial step is to identify the types of language demands entailed in various artifacts (standards, assessments, and curricular materials). It is a challenging undertaking because standards descriptions, particularly content standards, are not necessarily explicit about the language demands implicated in the standards. In addition, one single standard may include multiple language skills explicitly as well as implicitly (Llosa, 2011; Bailey & Wolf, 2012; Rothman et al., 2002; Wolf, Wang, Huang, & Blood, 2014). Take, for example, one reading standard from the Common Core State Standards for English language arts: "*Determine the meaning of words and phrases as they are used in a text, including analyzing how an author uses and refines the meaning of a key term over the course of a text.*" (Common Core State Standards for English Language Arts: Reading Standards for Literacy in History/Social Studies, 6–12, p. 61.) This standard explicitly describes the types of tasks students should accomplish with language as they read and comprehend disciplinary texts. While two language skills (i.e., vocabulary knowledge and analysis of an author's intentions) are overtly delineated, the standard presupposes a host of other language skills and knowledge, such as the conventions of formulating definitions and making inferences based on text comprehension, which are not explicitly mentioned (Bailey & Wolf, 2012).

There has been increasing research effort to provide a framework for analyzing the language demands in standards and curriculum/instruction (Bailey & Wolf, in press; CCSSO, 2012; Lee, 2017; Llosa, 2016; Uccelli et al., 2014). One approach is to identify a set of key practices of language use drawing from systemic functional linguistics and sociocultural theory. That is, the language demands can be characterized by identifying common language functions and language use contexts across disciplinary areas. For example, constructing an argument may be a common, key practice of language use manifested in standards, curriculum, instruction, and assessments. Such a core set of language demands can be instrumental in conducting a systematic alignment evaluation.

Examining the Relationship Between ELP and Content-Area Assessments

As noted in Fig. 7.2, an examination of the relationship between ELP and content assessments is another critical area for better understanding the alignment for ELP assessments. Investigating EL students' actual performance on content and ELP assessments can provide valuable insights into the impact of ELP on EL students' demonstration of content knowledge and skills. For example, using the NCLB-era ELP assessment of the WIDA consortium, Parker, Louie, and O'Dwyer (2009) employed hierarchical linear modeling to explore relationships between language domain scores in reading, writing, listening, and speaking, and academic content scores in reading, writing, and mathematics, for samples of fifth- and eighth-grade EL students from three states. They found that, after controlling for student- and school-level covariates, written language scores (reading and writing) were significant predictors of all three types of content assessment performance for both samples in all three states. Oral language scores (listening and speaking) predicted content outcomes for some grade levels and content areas, but in all cases, these relationships were significantly less strong than those observed for written language. The findings of the study have implications for ways to assess students' literacy and oral language skills in ELP assessments. That is, a content analysis is critical in this line of research to reveal how those language skills are represented in content and ELP assessments.

Wolf and Faulkner-Bond (2016) incorporated a content analysis in examining the relationship between ELP and content performance in three states using different ELP assessments. They found that the three states' ELP assessments measured different degrees of academic and social language proficiency. For example, one state's ELP assessment contained more social language items than did the other two states' ELP assessments. With respect to those other two states' ELP assessment , one ELP assessments was found to include more technical–academic language items (i.e., items including highly discipline-specific contexts with technical vocabulary and complex syntactic structures) than the other. These differences seemingly led to different relationships between ELP and content performance in the three states.

It is important to investigate precisely what language demands are included in content assessments and how EL students perform on assessment items with complex language demands. By the same token, it is crucial to examine whether new ELP assessments appropriately reflect the language demands of new CCR and ELP standards and whether they provide sufficient information to make fair and valid decisions about EL students. In order to better understand the relationship between ELP and content proficiency for EL students, it is essential to analyze the language demands and complexity of the various assessments (i.e., ELP and content) being used. This type of analysis can account for key patterns about EL students' performance on assessments measuring specific language skills.

Facilitating Professional Support to Enhance Alignment

In traditional alignment methods, experienced teachers typically take part in alignment evaluation for assessments. In this process, a common interpretation of standards is vital for the accuracy of alignment evidence. Taking the AUA framework for K-12 ELP assessments, for example, one claim about consequences of the use of ELP assessments is that they help teachers increase their understanding of standards. They are theorized to do so by communicating the standards' models and instantiating the standards' expectations concretely through assessment items. Assessment results are also intended to give teachers insights into their students' needs.

However, empirical research has demonstrated that much professional support is needed to build a common understanding of standards and implement the right expectations in practice (Llosa, 2011; McKay, 2006; Wolf et al., 2014). In discussing key challenges in using standards-based ELP assessments, Llosa (2011) revealed that teachers in her studies interpreted certain standards differently and even ignored some parts of the standards when they found standards descriptions ambiguous. Wolf et al. (2014) also found a wide variation of interpretations about standards among a sample of teachers, particularly for the primary objectives of a single standard as well as for terminology in the standards documents. The issue of ambiguous or general language in the standards' documents is problematic, adding complexity to alignment evaluation. Therefore, it is critical to provide professional development and resources to help teachers interpret standards in a consistent manner. Without teachers' appropriate understanding of standards, the fidelity of standards implementation in instruction and adequate use of assessment results is unlikely to be accomplished. It will also work against generating the intended consequences from assessment uses.

Conclusions, Implications, and Future Directions

In this paper, I have described the context of using large-scale, standards-based ELP assessments in U.S. K-12 education where policies on educational standards and assessments have a substantial impact on the development and use of ELP assessments. The consequences of the use of ELP assessments are significant at the individual, school, state, and system levels. ELP assessments disproportionately increase the testing burden on EL students compared to their native English-speaking peers who are assessed only for content knowledge and skills. While the stakes of content assessments are minimal at the individual level, those of ELP assessments are high for individual EL students' academic paths. Widespread criticism of the emphasis on accountability testing at the expense of instructional time has also been perpetuated. In this context, justifying ELP assessment uses and being accountable for those uses are paramount. That is, how well do ELP assessments serve the intended purposes of addressing EL students' needs and eventually raising the quality of EL education? Bachman (1990, 2005, 2013) and Bachman and Palmer (1996, 2010) have argued for this assessment justification and have drawn our attention to the consequences of assessment uses in making a validity argument. The emphasis on assessment justification is further echoed in Kunnan (2018) as a key starting point for evaluating language assessments, along with fairness. Adopting Bachman and Palmer's AUA framework, a comprehensive validity argument can be made for K-12 ELP assessments, linking the intended consequences (e.g., equity and improved student learning) to the uses of K-12 ELP assessments (e.g., EL identification and reclassification) as well as to the interpretations of the assessments (e.g., EL students' language ability to perform academic tasks).

In order to appropriately use K-12 ELP assessments and create the intended consequences, alignment provides indispensable evidence to be examined. I have discussed some major issues around alignment for the current standards-based K-12 ELP assessments: (1) the expansion of alignment evidence, (2) the need for identifying the language demands in standards, assessments, curriculum, and instruction in both content areas and ELP, (3) the inclusion of content analyses in examining the relationship between ELP and content assessments, and (4) the demand for professional development for alignment. The challenges in addressing these alignment issues point to areas in need of further research. I conclude this paper with a few pressing research areas to facilitate test developers and users in adequately gathering alignment evidence and to further improve the development and uses of K-12 ELP assessments.

The first main area deals with the construct for K-12 ELP assessments as the focal element of alignment evaluation. As discussed earlier, the construct of K-12 ELP assessments should reflect states' ELP standards that are supposedly based on the language demands implicated in academic content standards. The rigorous college-and career-ready content standards such as the Common Core embody sophisticated academic language uses. However, relatively little research is available to unpack the types of language demands that are entailed across various content and ELP standards. In the past two decades, researchers have strived to better understand the academic language in K-12 school contexts and have provided some theoretical frameworks to conceptualize academic language proficiency (e.g., Bailey, 2007; DiCerbo, Anstrom, Baker, & Rivera, 2014; Gottlieb, Katz, & Ernst-Slavit, 2009; Schleppegrell, 2004, 2012; Snow & Uccelli, 2009). At this juncture, an analysis of the current standards based on a robust framework is crucial in order to identify the types of language demands (e.g., types of language skills and tasks) in which students are expected to be involved. This line of investigation will provide pivotal information to define or evaluate the construct of U.S. K-12 ELP assessments. Notably, this information is necessary but not sufficient for providing a solid basis to formulate the ELP construct. This condition is largely due to the nature of the standards which are not developed for the purpose of assessment development and are not always developed by drawing from empirical evidence.

Thus, much more research is needed to systematically analyze a wide range of target language use (TLU) domains so as to characterize school language and inform the construct of K-12 ELP assessments. Addressing this need is a fundamental consideration in language testing, originating from Bachman and Palmer's (2010) seminal work. In addition to standards, the analysis of TLU domains should consider classroom discourse, curriculum materials, and various assessment materials to better understand the types of academic tasks and specific language demands involved in those TLU domains. This is a principal step to define the construct of interest and support an assessment claim about students' language ability (Bachman, 1990, 2007; Bachman & Palmer, 1996, 2010). There is growing research on analyzing the academic language from standards, curriculum materials (textbooks), and classroom talks in U.S. K-12 education contexts. The continued research in this area and the systematic organization of collective empirical findings will not only improve the practice of alignment evaluation but also yield empirical grounding to theorize academic language proficiency for K-12 ELP testing.

The second area of research concerns the alignment methods for K-12 ELP assessments. Beyond the challenge of identifying specific language knowledge and skills from standards, there is a lack of robust methods or tools to evaluate the alignment between ELP assessments and standards. As discussed earlier, existing alignment methods and tools are predominantly concerned with content assessments and standards, without attending to alignment in terms of language demands. Cook (2005) pointed out the inappropriate application of existing tools to ELP assessments. He proposed developing a rating scale of "Linguistic Difficulty Level" for ELP assessments in lieu of the depth of knowledge as in the Webb alignment method. The rationale of this proposal stems from the unique feature of ELP standards, that they postulate the language proficiency level in addition to the expected language proficiency to be achieved at each grade level. Cook argues that this dimension needs to be included for alignment evaluation for K-12 ELP assessments and that such a tool should be developed in consideration of second language acquisition theories. This is one critical area which merits further research for developing a sound alignment method for K-12 ELP assessments. In addition to rating dimensions, an array of issues including alignment panels, procedural steps, methods for summarizing the results, and criteria to evaluate the degree of alignment are yet to be investigated. It is also important to note that such methods and tools should consider the applications to curriculum and instruction for a comprehensive alignment evaluation of standards, assessments, curriculum, and instruction.

The third pressing area is the need to examine student performance data on ELP and content assessments. Alignment methods are limited to relying largely on expert judges to examine the language demands of assessments. To complement expert evaluation, EL students' performance on assessments supplies an important source to evaluate language demands. Owing to the establishment of a testing-based account-ability system, rich data are available for researchers. A deeper investigation of EL students' performance on those assessments accompanied by the content analysis of assessments has great potential to unveil the types of language demands and the progression of academic language development that EL students may experience. Information from this investigation will also offer valuable insights into the align-ment of language demands between ELP and content assessments. This type of information is critical for test developers as well as educators for the appropriate development and uses of ELP assessments.

These areas of further research would be beneficial for alignment evaluation as well as for the continuous improvement of the K-12 EL education system that spans standards, assessments, curriculum, and instruction. Bachman and Palmer's (2010) AUA framework provides guidance in conducting such research and helps connect collective information to improve the development and uses of K-12 ELP assessments (e.g., from defining the construct to ensuring intended positive consequences). Efforts in these areas also need to be made in a concerted way among language testing and educational measurement researchers given the connection of K-12 ELP assessments to content standards and associated assessments.

Acknowledgments The work presented here was supported in part by the William T. Grant Foun-dation grant ID187863 (An Investigation of the Language Demands in Standards, Assessments, and Curricular Materials for English Learners) to Educational Testing Service. The opinions expressed are those of the author and do not represent views of the Foundation.

References

Abedi, J. (2007). *English language proficiency assessment in the nation: Current status and future practice*. Davis, CA: University of California.
American Educational Research Association, American Psychological Association, & National Council on Measurement in Education. (2014). *Standards for educational and psychological testing*. Washington, DC: Author.

Bachman, L. F. (1990). *Fundamental considerations in language testing.* Oxford: Oxford University Press.

Bachman, L. F. (2005). Building and supporting a case for test use. *Language Assessment Quarterly,* 2(1), 1–34.

Bachman, L. F. (2007). What is the construct? The dialectic of abilities and contexts in defining constructs in language assessments. In J. Fox, M. Wesche, D. Bayliss, L. Cheng, C. E. Turner, & C. Doe (Eds.), *Language testing reconsidered* (pp. 41–71). Ottawa, Canada: Ottawa University Press.

Bachman, L. (2013). How is educational measurement supposed to deal with test use? *Measurement: Interdisciplinary Research and Perspectives, 11*(1–2), 19–23.

Bachman, L. F., & Palmer, A. S. (1996). *Language testing in practice.* Oxford: Oxford University Press.

Bachman, L. F., & Palmer, A. S. (2010). *Language assessment in practice: Developing language assessments and justifying their use in the real world.* Oxford: Oxford University Press.

Bailey, A. L. (2007). *The language demands of school: Putting academic English to the test.* New Haven, CT: Yale University Press.

Bailey, A. L., Butler, F. A., & Sato, E. (2007). Standards-to-standards linkage under Title III: Exploring common language demands in ELD and science standards. *Applied Measurement in Education, 20*(1), 53–78.

Bailey, A. L., & Huang, B. H. (2011). Do current English language development/proficiency standards reflect the English needed for success in school? *Language Testing, 28*(3), 343–365.

Bailey, A., & Wolf, M. K. (2012). *The challenge of assessing language proficiency aligned to the Common Core State Standards and some possible solutions.* Commissioned paper by the Understanding Language Initiative. Stanford, CA: Stanford University. Retrieved from http://ell.stanford.edu/papers/policy.

Bailey, A. L., & Wolf, M. K. (in press). The construct of English language proficiency in consideration of college and career ready standards. In M. K. Wolf (Ed.), *Assessing English language proficiency in K-12 U.S. Schools.* New York: Routledge.

Boals, T., Kenyon, D. M., Blair, A., Cranley, M. E., Wilmes, C., & Wright, L. J. (2015). Transformation in K 12 English language proficiency assessment changing contexts, changing constructs. *Review of Research in Education, 39*(1), 122–164.

Bunch, G. C., Kibler, A., & Pimental, S. (2012). *Realizing opportunities for English learners in the Common Core English language arts and disciplinary literacy standards.* Commissioned paper by the Understanding Language Initiative. Stanford, CA: Stanford University. Retrieved from http://ell.stanford.edu/papers/practice.

Cook, H. G. (2005). *Aligning English language proficiency tests to English language learning standards.* Washington, DC: Council of Chief State School Officers.

Council of Chief State School Officers. (2012). *Framework for English Language Proficiency Development Standards corresponding to the Common Core State Standards and the Next Generation Science Standards.* Washington, DC: Author.

DiCerbo, P., Anstrom, K., Baker, L., & Rivera, C. (2014). A review of the literature on teaching academic English to English language learners. *Review of Educational Research, 84*(3), 446–482.

Estrada, P. (2014). English learner curricular streams in four middle schools: Triage in the trenches. *The Urban Review, 46*(4), 535–573.

Every Student Succeeds Act. (2015). Public Law No. 114-354.

Forte, E., Kuti, L., & O'Day, J. (2011). *A review of states' English language proficiency standards, volume I—National evaluation of Title III implementation.* Washington, DC: U.S. Department of Education.

Gottlieb, M., Katz, A., & Ernst-Slavit, G. (2009). *Paper to practice: Using the English language proficiency standards in PreK–12 classrooms.* Alexandria, VA: Teachers of English to Speakers of Other Languages (TESOL), Inc.

Hamilton, L. S., Stecher, B. M., & Yuan, K. (2012). Standards-based accountability in the United States: Lessons learned and future directions. *Education Inquiry, 3*(2), 149–170.

Herman, J. L. (2004). The effects of testing in instruction. In S. Fuhrman & R. Elmore (Eds.), *Redesigning accountability systems for education* (pp. 141–165). New York: Teachers College Press.

Herman, J. L., Webb, N., & Zuniga, S. (2007). Measurement issues in the alignment of standards and assessments: A case study. *Applied Measurement in Education, 20*(1), 101–126.

Kane, M. (2001). Current concerns in validity theory. *Journal of Educational Measurement, 38*(4), 319–342.

Kunnan, A. J. (2018). *Evaluating language assessments.* New York: Routledge.

Lee, O. (2017). Common Core State Standards for ELA/literacy and Next Generation Science Standards: Convergences and discrepancies using argument as an example. *Educational Researcher, 46*(2), 90–102.

Llosa, L. (2011). Standards-based classroom assessments of English proficiency: A review of issues, current developments, and future directions for research. *Language Testing, 28*(3), 367–382.

Llosa, L. (2016). Assessing students' content knowledge and language proficiency. In E. Shohamy & I. Or (Eds.), *Encyclopedia of language and education* (Vol. 7, pp. 3–14). New York, NY: Springer International Publishing.

Martone, A., & Sireci, S. G. (2009). Evaluating alignment between curriculum, assessment and instruction. *Review of Educational Research, 79,* 1–76.

McKay, P. (2006). Research into the assessment of school-age language learners. *Annual Review of Applied Linguistics, 25,* 243–263.

Messick, S. (1989). Validity. In R. L. Linn (Ed.), *Educational measurement* (3rd ed., pp. 13–103). New York: Macmillan.

Mohamud, A., & Fleck, D. (2010). Alignment of standards, assessment and instruction: Implications for English language learners in Ohio. *Theory Into Practice, 49,* 129–136.

No Child Left Behind Act of 2001, Pub. L. No. 107-110, 115 Stat. 1425 (2002).

Parker, C., Louie, J., & O'Dwyer, L. (2009). *New measures of English language proficiency and their relationship to performance on large-scale content assessments* (Issues & Answers Report No. REL 2009–No. 066). Washington, DC: U.S. Department of Education, Institute of Education Sciences, National Center for Education Evaluation and Regional Assistance, Regional Educational Laboratory Northeast and Islands. Retrieved from http://ies.ed.gov/ncee/edlabs.

Porter, A. C. (2002). Measuring the content of instruction: Uses in research and practice. *Educational Researcher, 31*(7), 3–14.

Rothman, R. Slattery, J. B., Vranek, J.L., & Resnick, R. (2002). Benchmarking and alignment of standards and testing. (*CSE Technical Report 566*). Los Angeles: University of California, National Center for Research on Evaluation, Standards, and Student Testing (CRESST).

Schleppegrell, M. J. (2004). *The language of schooling: A functional linguistics perspective.* Mahwah, NJ: Lawrence Erlbaum.

Schleppegrell, M. J. (2012). Academic language in teaching and learning: Introduction to special issue. *The Elementary School Journal, 112*(3), 409–418.

Snow, C. E., & Uccelli, P. (2009). The challenge of academic language. In D. R. Olson & N. Torrance (Eds.), *The Cambridge handbook of literacy* (pp. 112–133). Cambridge: Cambridge University Press.

Stevens, R. A., Butler, F. A., & Castellon-Wellington, M. (2000). *Academic language and content assessment: Measuring the progress of English language learners (ELLs)* (CSE Report 552). Los Angeles, CA: University of California, Los Angeles, National Center for Research on Evaluation, Standards, and Student Testing (CRESST).

Uccelli, P., Barr, C. D., Dobbs, C. L., Galloway, E. P., Meneses, A., & Sánchez, E. (2014). Core academic language skills (CALS): An expanded operational construct and a novel instrument to chart school—Relevant language proficiency in pre-adolescent and adolescent learners. *Applied Psycholinguistics, 36,* 1077–1109.

Umansky, I. M. (2016). Leveled and exclusionary tracking: English Learners' access to core content in middle school. *American Educational Research Journal, 53*(6), 1792–1833.

U. S. Department of Justice and U.S. Department of Education. (2015, January). Dear colleague letter: English learner students and limited English proficient parents. Retrieved from https://www2.ed.gov/about/offices/list/ocr/letters/colleague-el-201501.pdf.

U. S. Department of Education. (2015). Tools and resources for identifying all English learners. Retrieved from https://www2.ed.gov/about/offices/list/oela/english-learner-toolkit/chap1.pdf.

U. S. Department of Education. (2016). Non-regulatory guidance: English learners and title III of the Elementary and Secondary Education Act (ESEA), as amended by the Every Student Succeeds Act (ESSA). Washington, DC: Author. Retrieved from https://www2.ed.gov/policy/elsec/leg/essa/essatitleiiiguidenglishlearners92016.pdf.

U.S. Department of Education. (2018). A state's guide to the U.S. Department of Education's assessment peer review process. Retrieved from https://www2.ed.gov/admins/lead/account/saa/assessmentpeerreview.pdf.

Webb, N. (1999). Alignment of science and mathematics standards and assessments in four states (*Research Monograph No. 18*). Madison, WI: National Institute for Science Education University of Wisconsin-Madison.

Wolf, M. K., & Farnsworth, T. (2014). English language proficiency assessments as an exit criterion for English learners. In A. Kunnan (Ed.), *The companion to language assessment* (Vol. 1, pp. 303–317). New York, NY: Wiley-Blackwell.

Wolf, M. K., Farnsworth, T., & Herman, J. L. (2008). Validity issues in assessing English language learners' language proficiency. *Educational Assessment, 13*(2–3), 80–107.

Wolf, M. K., & Faulkner-Bond, M. (2016). Validating English language proficiency assessment uses for English learners: Academic language proficiency and content assessment performance. *Educational Measurement: Issues and Practice, 35*(2), 6–18.

Wolf, M. K., Guzman-Orth, D., & Hauck, M.C. (2016). *Next-generation summative English language proficiency assessments for English learners: Priorities for policy and research* (ETS Research Report No. RR-16-08). Princeton, NJ: Educational Testing Service.

Wolf, M. K., Kao, J., Herman, J. L., Bachman, L. F., Bailey, A., Bachman, P. L., et al. (2008). *Issues in assessing English language learners: English language proficiency measures and accommodation uses-Literature review* (CRESST Technical Report 731). Los Angeles, CA: University of California, National Center for Research on Evaluation, Standards, and Student Testing (CRESST).

Wolf, M. K., Wang, Y., Huang, B. H., & Blood, I. (2014). Investigating the language demands in the Common Core State Standards for English language learners: A comparison study of standards. *Middle Grades Research Journal, 9*(1), 35–51.

Chapter 8
Validating a Holistic Rubric for Scoring Short Answer Reading Questions

Sara T. Cushing and Rurik Tywoniw

Abstract This study presents an investigation of the validity of a practical scoring procedure for short answer (sentence length) reading comprehension questions, using a holistic rubric for sets of responses rather than scoring individual responses, on a university-based English proficiency test. Thirty-three previously scored response sets were rescored by the researchers at the item level, with ratings for completion, fidelity to the source text, and overlap with source text language. Results confirm that holistic section-based scores are predicted by fidelity ratings only, providing evidence to support the scoring inference of the validity argument.

Introduction

In his influential book, *Fundamental Considerations in Language Testing*, Bachman states: "As test developers and test users, … it is our responsibility to provide as complete evidence as possible that the tests that are used are valid indicators of the abilities of interest and that these abilities are appropriate to the intended use, and then to insist that this evidence be used in the determination of test use" (1990, p. 285). Bachman's insistence on this responsibility is fleshed out further in a (2005) article in *Language Assessment Quarterly*, in which he poses two fundamental questions: "How convincing is the argument for using the assessment in this way?" and "How credible is the evidence that supports this argument?" (p. 5).

Expanding on these ideas even further, Bachman and Palmer (2010) lay out a useful framework for outlining an Assessment Use Argument (AUA) to justify the use of any given assessment. Such an AUA consists of four general claims, involving (1) the consequences of using an assessment and of the decisions based on the

S. T. Cushing (✉)
Department of AL/ESL, Georgia State University, P.O. BOX 4099, Atlanta, GA 30302-4099, USA
e-mail: stcushing@gsu.edu

R. Tywoniw
Department of Linguistics, University of Illinois at Urbana-Champaign, 4080 Foreign Languages Building, 707 S Mathews Avenue, Urbana, IL 61801, USA
e-mail: rtywoniw@illinois.edu

© Springer Nature Singapore Pte Ltd. 2020
G. J. Ockey and B. A. Green (eds.), *Another Generation of Fundamental Considerations in Language Assessment*, https://doi.org/10.1007/978-981-15-8952-2_8

assessment; (2) the decisions themselves, which are based on (3) the interpretation about the ability assessed; and (4) the consistency of assessment records (verbal and numeric) across different tasks, raters, and groups of test takers.

In the spirit of formulating and investigating an AUA, this chapter presents an investigation of the credibility of evidence supporting the use of a practical scoring procedure for short answer reading comprehension questions as part of a university-based English language proficiency examination. We first describe the context, the test itself—focusing specifically on the short answer portion—and how the test is used. Following our literature review, we then lay out an argument structure for the specific scoring procedure, following Bachman and Palmer (2010). In framing our study in this way, we hope to contribute to the literature on argument-based approaches to test validation (e.g., Llosa, 2008; Jamieson, Eignor, Grabe, & Kunnan, 2008).

Context of the Study

The purpose of our study is to seek validity evidence for the use of section-based holistic scores to evaluate sets of responses to short answer questions in the reading/writing section of the Georgia State Test of English Proficiency (GSTEP), a locally developed English proficiency test for academic purposes (see Weigle, 2004, for a complete description of the test). The GSTEP, until 2015, was used for two main purposes: as evidence of English proficiency for admission to local colleges and universities at the undergraduate level, and as a placement test for international graduate students to determine whether they needed additional English language support. In 2015, the Georgia Board of Regents ruled that locally developed tests like the GSTEP could no longer be used for admission, so since then, only the latter use of the test is permitted.

In the short answer section of the GSTEP, test takers read two short passages presenting opposing perspectives on a topic and respond to eight comprehension questions: three main idea or detail questions on each passage and two synthesis questions, which require test takers to compare the views of the two authors. The instructions to test takers state that they should use complete sentences in their responses and to write at least ten words in response to each question. Test takers are also informed that their answers will be scored on content (how accurate and complete their response is) and language (the accurate use of academic English and the avoidance of copying directly from the text). The short answer section is followed by an essay prompt, in which students are asked to take a position on the issue presented in the readings, using information from at least one of the readings to support their position. The short answer section is thus intended to assess reading to learn and reading to integrate information, two essential purposes for academic reading (Enright et al., 2000).

When the test was developed, the original intent was to score each of the eight items individually, on how accurate and complete the response was, on one hand, and on the writer's facility with English, including the ability to paraphrase information from the source text appropriately, on the other. However, pilot testing revealed that this scoring method was highly impractical, given the amount of resources required to create detailed scoring guides for each item and to train raters (typically graduate students without a great deal of assessment experience) to score them reliably. Instead, the test developers decided on a simpler approach. Instead of scoring each item separately, raters provide a single score for content and another score for language, taking into consideration the entire response set, using a five-point scale (see Table 8.1 for the scoring rubric). The content score is intended to tap into reading comprehension and is combined with scores on a multiple-choice reading section to provide a reading score, while the language score is combined with scores on the essay for a writing score.

While the holistic section-level scoring method has been found to be both reliable and practical (see Weigle, 2004), questions have arisen about its validity, particularly in terms of the degree to which content scores represent the construct of interest. Anecdotally, raters have occasionally been misled into providing higher scores than are warranted for at least two reasons: when writers write lengthy answers that include some relevant information from the source text but do not answer the question posed, or when writers copy extensively from the source text in their responses, including extraneous information that does not respond to the question. We were also interested in exploring the degree to which scores were consistent across the

Table 8.1 Short answer rubric

	Content	Language
5	Responses demonstrate full and sophisticated understanding of both texts. All items addressed completely and accurately	Responses demonstrate excellent command of English. Few errors in grammar or vocabulary; responses consist primarily of student's own words
4	Responses demonstrate good understanding of both texts. Most items addressed completely and accurately, though some responses may be undeveloped	Responses demonstrate good command of English. Some errors present that do not interfere with comprehension; there may be some reliance on source text language
3	Responses demonstrate minimally adequate understanding of both texts. Some responses may be brief or off-target; at most one or two items are not attempted	Responses suggest minimally adequate command of English. There may be several distracting errors but responses are generally comprehensible; there may be heavy reliance on source text language
2	Responses demonstrate partial misunderstanding of at least one text. Several answers may be brief and/or off-target but some responses are accurate	Responses suggest lack of command of English. Many errors, some of which interfere with comprehension; extensive copying from source texts
1	Responses demonstrate inadequate understanding of both texts. Several items not answered or responses are off-target	Responses demonstrate lack of command of English. Responses that are present are mostly incomprehensible or are copied from source texts

two main populations of test takers (resident prospective undergraduate students and matriculated international graduate students) since a recent study of the essay portion of the test revealed some discrepancies in rater behavior across these two groups (Goodwin, 2016).

In terms of an AUA, these questions relate to Claims 3 (interpretation) and 4 (consistency). To be valid indicators of the reading construct, higher scores should represent response sets that answer the questions thoroughly and accurately, and do not rely heavily on copying from the source text. Furthermore, scores should reflect responses to all eight items and should not be heavily influenced by one or two items.

Literature Review

Constructs

As noted above, the intended construct for the short answer section (in terms of the content scores) is academic reading, which involves reading to learn, i.e., reading which focuses on understanding the content of a message and not reading which focuses on mastering language mechanics (Carver, 1997; Trites & McGroarty, 2005). Most reading scholars distinguish between low-level reading processes such as word recognition, syntactic parsing, and local activation of semantic knowledge, and higher-level processes such as inferencing, activating background knowledge, and evaluating the usefulness of textual information (Perfetti, 2007). Higher-level processing is seen to occur at two levels: creating a text model, or a model of the propositional content of a text, and a situation model, which connects the text to the reader's background knowledge, allowing the reader to construct the overall meaning of the text (Kintsch, 1998; Grabe, 2009). Reading comprehension is also affected by reader purpose, intersecting with rate (faster vs. more slowly) and strategy (careful vs. expeditious) (Carver, 1992; Weir, 1993).

Second language reading ability is widely thought to be affected both by L1 reading ability and L2 proficiency with L2 proficiency typically being a stronger predictor of L2 reading scores (Carson, Carrell, Silberstein, Kroll, & Kuehn 1990; Carrell, 1991; Jiang, 2011; Pae, 2017). Skills specific to L2 reading include strategies for approaching unfamiliar language- and register-specific text structures and using context to guess word meaning (Grabe, 2009).

In terms of assessing academic reading, a useful framework for defining the construct comes from the TOEFL 2000 Reading Framework (Enright et al., 2000), which uses reader purpose as an organizing principle. This framework identifies four main reading purposes: reading for information, reading for basic comprehension, reading to learn, and reading to integrate information across texts. Each reading purpose is associated with specific reading abilities, task types, and text types. As noted above, the short answer questions on the GSTEP are intended to tap all four of these purposes but particularly reading to learn and reading to integrate information across texts.

Reading Assessment Tasks

Reading can be assessed through numerous task types (see, e.g., Brown & Abey-wickrama, 2010; Green, 2014a, for taxonomies). Multiple-choice tests, in particular, have drawn criticism for being susceptible to guessing and more suitable for low-level reading skills (see, for example, Rupp, Ferne, & Choi, 2006). The task type that we call short answer questions (SAQ) are perhaps more appropriately categorized as extended response or reading-into-writing (Green, 2014a). According to Green (2014b), such tasks are suitable for assessing higher order skills such as inferencing and intertextual relationships as well as basic propositional content. However, a disadvantage of this task type is that it presupposes at least a baseline level of writing ability for students to provide complete answers; furthermore, if students are able to copy stretches of text from the source material, the degree to which the response demonstrates comprehension is not clear. Scoring sentence-length short answer responses can also be prohibitively time-consuming.

Methods

Using Bachman and Palmer's (2010) framework, the first AUA claim our study addresses is Claim 3, Warrant 4a: "The procedures for producing an assessment record focus on those aspects of the performance that are relevant to the construct we intend to assess" (Bachman & Palmer, 2010, p. 226). Our adapted warrant is that the scoring rubric and training procedures for the content score focus on key elements of the construct of reading comprehension. Using Toulmin's (2003) argument structure, the warrant, our first research question, can be summarized in Fig. 8.1. The claim we are making is that the holistic section-based content scores are an accurate reflection of the quality of the short answer responses in terms of reflecting comprehension of the reading passages. Our backing is the correlation between analytic scores of completion and accuracy (described below), and rebuttal data would come from evidence of a strong relationship between holistic scores and overlap with the source texts; i.e., inappropriate copying or evidence of a strong relationship between holistic scores and mere completeness of response length in terms of meeting the minimum word requirement.

We were further interested in whether these relationships would hold true for the two different populations of test takers—prospective undergraduate students, who were primarily Georgia residents taking the test in lieu of the TOEFL or other international test, and matriculated graduate students, who were primarily international students. These two groups of test takers took the GSTEP at different times and raters

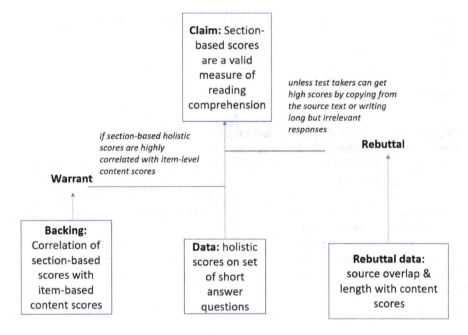

Fig. 8.1 Argument structure for the Claim 3, Warrant A4

were aware which group they were scoring at any given time. While rater training emphasized using the same standards across both groups, Goodwin's (2016) study suggests that differences in expectations of performance across the two groups may have led to differences in scoring on a different test task (the essay). This research question thus addresses Claim 4, Warrant 4: "Raters are trained to avoid bias for or against different groups of test takers" (Bachman & Palmer, 2010, p. 243).

The research questions are as follows:

1. What are the relationships between holistic content scores of response sets with response completion, fidelity, and source overlap scores on individual items?
2. To what extent are these relationships mediated by test taker population?

Participants

A stratified random sample of 33 scripts was selected from tests on a single topic taken between 2015 and 2016. Scripts were selected so that they represented all possible score bands, with two scripts at the ends of the score range (1 and 5) and three to five scripts at each half-point interval between the endpoints. Twenty of the test takers were matriculated graduate students taking the test for language class placement purposes and 13 were prospective undergraduate applicants. The topic of the two texts on the short answer section was about natural resources: one text discussing environmental policy and the dangers of overusing natural resources, and another text discussing the improvements of humanity in the face of resource usage. The eight short answer questions asked test takers to identify main ideas and details, as well as compare and contrast the two passages' authors' viewpoints and make predictions. Test takers were told that answers should be complete sentences and include at least ten words. The passages and instructions were the same for both the graduate and undergraduate test takers.

Ratings

Holistic Ratings. As noted above the holistic rubric descriptors refer to an accurate representation of text content, relevance to the question, and completeness of the answer (see Table 8.1). Descriptors for Levels 3 and below refer to the possibility of some questions not being answered. Low-proficiency students frequently leave one or more questions blank, either because they are not sure of the answer or because they run out of time. The use of source text language in response is covered in the language score, not the content score, as the content score is intended to measure the construct of reading. The holistic scores used in the study were the scores given by the original raters, as it was our intention to investigate rating under operational rather than experimental conditions.

As part of the normal GSTEP scoring procedure, short answer sections were each rated by two raters, with the average of the two scores used as the final score. If raters disagreed by more than one point, a third rater rated the writing and the reported score was the average between the third rating and the rating closest to it. Thus, holistic scores for this study ranged from 1 to 5 by half-points.

Individual Item Ratings. The individual items for each set of eight short answer responses selected for this study were rerated by the researchers in three ways. The 33 answer sets were rated for completion and fidelity: three raters each rated a randomly selected (without replacement) group of 11 sets of answers, and then a second rated another rater's set. First, to investigate whether raters were unduly influenced by lengthy responses that might not have fully answered the question, each item was given a completion score of one or zero based on whether it consisted of at least ten words or not, as the instructions specify. Raters manually counted the words of each response for this score. Second, each item was rated using a fidelity scale that was intended to reflect the intended construct, i.e., complete and accurate responses to the question. Table 8.2 provides a comparison between the section-level scale and individual item fidelity scale; the content scale addresses the response set as a whole while the individual item scale focuses on the qualities of individual item responses. Unlike the holistic scale, the fidelity scale does not include descriptors for levels 2 and 4; those levels were assigned to responses that fell in between the levels with descriptors.

Table 8.2 Comparison between section-level content scale and individual item fidelity rating scale

	Section-level content scale	Individual item fidelity rating scale
5	Responses demonstrate full and sophisticated understanding of both texts. All items addressed completely and accurately	Well-developed answer which addresses multiple points expected in the response and is consistent with the source material
4	Responses demonstrate good understanding of both texts. Most items addressed completely and accurately, though some responses may be undeveloped	
3	Responses demonstrate minimally adequate understanding of both texts. Some responses may be brief or off-target; at most one or two items are not attempted	Response is consistent with information in the source, but does not address the question with specific enough information
2	Responses demonstrate partial misunderstanding of at least one text. Several answers may be brief and/or off-target but some responses are accurate	
1	Responses demonstrate inadequate understanding of both texts. Several items not answered or responses are off-target	Response neither addresses the question nor is consistent with the information in the source

Finally, to investigate the overlap between test takers' short answers and the integrated writing source texts, the degree of overlap was measured and scored using an automated text analysis program designed specifically for this study using the free statistical software system R. Motivated in part by Keck's (2006) taxonomy of source overlap, this program calculated two types of overlap: total lexical overlap in a pairing of source and test taker writings, and clusters of words in test taker writing which corresponded exactly to a single occurrence in the source (what Keck refers to as "direct links"). Examining the overlapping language of a text which has only one occurrence in a source text sifts out much of the incidental overlap that occurs in source-based writing; that is, a phrase that occurs frequently in a source text might easily be repeated without paraphrasing in a written summary of that text. See Table 8.3 for examples of each type of overlap. Total overlap scores were recorded for each test taker's writing as a percentage of that text's total length which occurred in the source text, and direct link overlap scores were recorded as a percentage of a text which is created from direct links to the source.

In summary, for each examinee, the data include a single holistic score (which is the average of two rater scores), eight completion scores (one for each response), eight fidelity scores, eight total source overlap scores, and eight direct link source overlap scores. The first three scores were assigned by human raters and the source overlap scores were calculated automatically. The analytic scores were then averaged across the eight items for comparison with the holistic score.

Table 8.3 Examples of total overlap (bolded) and direct links (underlined)

Source text	Examinee writing	Percentage overlap (total) (%)	Percentage overlap (direct links) (%)
… "**our world is** at present faced with two unprecedented **and** supreme dangers:" One of these dangers **is** "the devastating effect of **modern industrialization and overpopulation** on the **world**…" … global environment **to** which Kennan refers **has** a scale … the earth's climate **and** biogeochemical cycles, …, loss of **forests, and** the decline of ecological communities	**Our world is** having a bad **pollution** related **to modern industrialization and overpopulation**	77	46
Since **World** War II, **growth** in human **population and** economic activity **has been unprecedented.** The **world's population** now exceeds six billion, **and** the gross **world** product **has increased** fourfold since 1950. With these **increases in population and** economic activity have come large **increases** in both **pollution and** pressure on natural resources	**World population growth has been unprecedented.** It <u>has been</u> a huge increase	75	50
Air pollution today poses problems … As use of fossil fuels **has increased, so have emissions of** sulfur and nitrogen oxides **and other** harmful gases. Acid rain, ozone, **and other** ills born of this **pollution** are now damaging public health **and** harming **forests**, fish, **and** crops over large areas of the globe These **and other** atmospheric issues constitute the most serious **pollution** threat in history. Simultaneous **and** gradual. … These **air pollution** issues are also … In the future, **energy** policy **and** environmental policy should be made together	**As use of energy has increased, so have emissions of other** fields like **air, public health, and forests**	89	44

Note: Source text has been abridged.

Data Analysis

Descriptive statistics were calculated for the holistic scores for short answer content and averaged analytic scores for completion, fidelity scores, and the amount of source overlap per author and per response. These measurements were tested for normality. Pairwise correlations were calculated between the holistic scores for test taker short answers and each of the completion, fidelity, and overlap scores. Spearman's Rho was chosen as the correlation statistic as some measurements were not normally distributed. Finally, to investigate whether any correlated analytic measures predict holistic content scores in short answer writing, a linear model was constructed.

Results

Descriptive Statistics

Holistic Scores. Each test taker's short answer section was given a holistic content rating in the original administration of the test. Average holistic scores are shown in Table 8.4. The average holistic score for all test takers was 3.05 (out of 5), with a standard deviation of 1.16.

Item Scores. Mean analytic scores and standard deviations for completion, fidelity, and source overlap are displayed in Table 8.5. The average completion score for all test takers was 7.3 (out of 8), with a standard deviation of 1.11, and the average per item score was 0.91. The average fidelity score for all test takers was 22.86 with a standard deviation of 9.17 (2.86 out of 5 per item). The average percent of total overlap between test taker answers and source text was 72.92%, and the average percent of source overlap in test taker answers with a direct link to the source text was 30.31%.

Table 8.4 Holistic content scores: descriptive statistics by student group	N	Mean holistic content score	SD
Graduate students	20	3.53	0.92
Undergraduate applicants	13	2.31	1.13
Total	33	3.05	1.16

Table 8.5 Item scores: descriptive statistics by student group

	Completion (Max = 8)		Fidelity (Max = 40)		Total overlap (percentage)		Direct link overlap (percentage)	
	M	SD	M	SD	M	SD	M	SD
Graduate students	7.8	0.52	27.38	7.46	0.75	0.06	0.32	0.08
Undergraduate students	6.6	1.39	15.92	8.49	0.69	0.17	0.28	0.10
Total	7.3	1.11	22.87	9.17	0.73	0.12	0.30	0.09

Correlations: Holistic and Analytic Scores

Before calculating correlations, Shapiro–Wilk tests for normality were performed on each variable, and these results are shown in Table 8.6. Due to non-normal distributions for some of the measurements, Spearman's Rho correlations were calculated for each mean measurement in the analytic rubric along with the holistic content scores. The correlation matrices are presented in Tables 8.7, 8.8, and 8.9. Among all test takers, holistic content scores were very strongly positively correlated with the fidelity ratings, $r = 0.90$ ($r = 0.82$ for graduates, $r = 0.91$ for undergraduates). Holistic content score was also significantly positively correlated with item completeness, $r = 0.76$ This significance held for the undergraduate testing group, $r = 0.78$, but not the graduates. Neither overlap measure had a significant correlation with content scores, although direct link overlap had a medium, but non-significant, negative correlation with holistic content scores for graduate test takers only ($r = -0.43$).

Table 8.6 Shapiro-Wilk tests of normality for short answer test measurements

	Completion	Fidelity	Total overlap	Direct link overlap	Holistic Content score
Graduate	0.45*	0.96	0.97	0.73*	0.96
Undergraduate	0.87	0.92	0.92	0.79	0.91
Total	0.66*	0.96	0.90	0.80*	0.96

*Significant at $p < 0.001$. Indicates non-normality

Table 8.7 Spearman's Rho correlations between item scores and the holistic content score for all test takers ($N = 33$)

	Completion	Fidelity	Total overlap	Direct links
Fidelity	0.77*			
Total overlap	0.02	0.14		
Direct inks	−0.01	−0.13	0.32	
Content	0.76*	0.90*	0.09	−0.12

*Significant at $p < 0.0017$. The alpha of 0.0017 was chosen via Bonferroni Correction to adjust for multiple comparisons

Table 8.8 Spearman's Rho correlations between mean item scores and the holistic content score for graduate test takers ($N = 20$)

	Completion	Fidelity	Total overlap	Direct links
Fidelity	0.62			
Total overlap	−0.09	0.00		
Direct links	−0.52	−0.58	−0.10	
Content	0.61	0.82*	−0.01	−0.43

*Significant at $p < 0.0017$. The alpha of 0.0017 was chosen via Bonferroni Correction to adjust for multiple comparisons

Table 8.9 Spearman's Rho correlations between mean analytic scores and holistic content score for undergraduate testtakers ($N = 13$)

	Completion	Fidelity	Total overlap	Direct links
Fidelity	0.75			
Total overlap	0.23	0.37		
Direct links	0.05	−0.12	0.56	
Content	0.78*	0.91*	0.15	−0.23

*Significant at $p < 0.0017$. The alpha of 0.0017 was chosen via Bonferroni Correction to adjust for multiple comparisons

Regression Analysis: Predicting Holistic Scores

The stepwise regression model constructed to confirm that variance in holistic scores could be predicted using relevant analytic scores was found to be significant and is shown in Table 8.10. The table shows the one predictive measure and both standardized (B) and unstandardized (β) coefficients. Only one predictor variable was used to construct the final model, fidelity scores. Completion and direct links were removed due to non-significant predictive power, and total overlap was further removed due to non-significant predictive power in the model. Fidelity scores were a significant predictor of holistic scores, with $r^2 = 0.85$, indicating strong predictive power.

Table 8.10 Linear regression model using analytic ratings to predict holistic score

	B	SE B	β	t	p	r^2
Intercept	0.38	0.22		1.73	0.09	
Fidelity	0.12	0.01	0.92	13.19*	<0.01	0.85

Discussion

We set out to examine the claim that section-based holistic scores (i.e., assigning a single score to a set of item responses) were an appropriate representation of student performance (Claim 3, Warrant 4a in an Assessment Use Argument; Bachman & Palmer, 2010). We collected data to examine both the warrant: item-level fidelity scores, and data that could rebut the claim: length and source overlap scores. Our findings provide evidence in support of the claim: we found that the holistic content score is most closely related to the individual fidelity scores, with a Spearman correlation of 0.90. No other item-level measure was significantly predictive of the overall content score. This suggests that raters are applying the rubric as intended; that is, they appear to be weighing the accuracy of all items equally in their scores and do not appear to be unduly influenced by copied material from the source texts or by unduly long responses that do not answer the question directly.

Neither total source overlap nor direct links to the source were found to correlate significantly with content scores, indicating that for short answer content scores, considered part of the reading comprehension construct in this test, source overlap is appropriately treated as a language or writing matter, and discounted in ratings of content accuracy.

Our second research question addressed Claim 4, Warrant 4: "Raters are trained to avoid bias for or against different groups of test takers" in an AUA (Bachman & Palmer, 2010, p. 243). For both graduate and undergraduate students, the fidelity score had the strongest relationship with the content scores, providing some support for this warrant. We note that the completion scores were more strongly related to the holistic content scores for undergraduate students than for graduate students, which might be interpreted as rebuttal evidence for this warrant. However, there was twice as much variance in the completion scores for undergraduate students as for graduate students, suggesting that more test takers wrote shorter responses or skipped items altogether in this test taker group, thus leading to lower content scores and a larger correlation coefficient. Actual word counts of responses (rather than a binary distinction between those responses that met the ten-word requirement and those that did not) might have provided stronger evidence to support this warrant, as would more qualitative evidence from rater verbal protocols. There was also a stronger relationship between total source overlap and holistic content scores for undergraduate students only, and a negative relationship between direct link borrowing and content scores for graduate students. These results complement the findings of Weigle and Parker (2012), who studied textual borrowing on GSTEP essays and found that, for one topic in particular, undergraduate students tended to borrow more from the source text, and lower proficiency students in general tended to borrow longer strings of text than did higher proficiency students. Furthermore, Weigle and Parker (2012) concluded that students' use of borrowed language from the source text was not so extensive that it prevented raters from accurately evaluating their facility with the language in GSTEP essays; our study suggests that the same is true for the content scores on the short answer section of the test, which are intended to be a measure of reading comprehension, not writing ability.

Conclusions, Implications, and Future Directions

Our study suggests that, for the purposes, we are using this test, the holistic section scores are adequate reflections of the intended construct. Given the relatively low stakes of the section in terms of the overall decision to be made, the amount of resources available for scoring, and the safeguards in place to review borderline or inconsistent scores, we feel confident that there is little to be gained from scoring items individually.

Our results may serve to inform the development of automated programs for assessing short answer responses. Carr and Xi (2010) discuss a number of operational difficulties with automating scoring for such items. For example, misspellings of key lexical items can lead to inaccurate scores, as can elegant but unusual paraphrases of the source text. In their study, they found that human raters did not always agree on whether a response containing extraneous information from the source material should be given full credit. It may be that algorithms that cannot reliably score individual items may in fact score them adequately in the aggregate so that decisions can be made with reasonable confidence.

Of course, our study has limitations. First, the study utilizes a small sample size, examining response data of just 33 test takers. It is thus likely that the statistical analyses performed to understand the relationship between the ratings have low power. Considering the strength of the findings and the systematic inclusion criteria of writing samples, inclusion of further response data would likely not create drastically different results. Second, the analysis relies on test taker responses for a single topic (natural resource use). It is possible that with different topics and with text prompts of different levels of complexity, the relative contribution of individual items to overall scores may change, as well as the relative importance of response length and copying. Finally, our study includes examination of only three analytic constructs. There are any number of identifiable constructs which may influence rater judgments in holistic scoring, and we only utilized three that relate to explicit instructions in the test. Further research utilizing more rating constructs in the analytic ratings can be conducted to understand the complete picture of holistic rating of short answer reading questions.

As Xi (2010) notes, the aspects of a validity argument that should be fully supported with data depend on the use to which the assessment is put; essentially, the higher the stakes, the more robust the evidence required to support a validity argument. Our test, particularly now that it is no longer being used for admissions, has relatively low stakes and thus provides little impetus for use of a detailed, yet potentially cumbersome, analytic rubric. Although other avenues, such as automated scoring, exist for increasing the practicality of rating writing in such a circumstance, numerous problems with automated scoring that may cause it to apply poorly to short answer source-based written responses exist (Carr & Xi, 2010). In particular, insofar as the content of source-based writing is the basis for evaluation, this study shows that accuracy vis-à-vis the source text, outside of any linguistic linkages to the source text, is the most important aspect of scoring, so perhaps a holistic set-based score is a better avenue to take than trying to crack the nut of automated scoring, at least for the time being.

In sum, this study examines variability in rubric-based judgments of raters on a language assessment, an important aspect of test validity (Bachman, Lynch, & Mason, 1995). In this approach, we hoped to understand if variability in rater judgements of reading-to-write short answer questions were due to construct-relevant features (Messick, 1989) of the content test taker responses (i.e., content accuracy and relevance) or construct-irrelevant features (language mechanical features, e.g., response length, source overlap). We use this information to make informed decisions about test structure considering not only construct validity, by investigating the validity of different types of rubrics but also consequential validity (Bachman, 2000) of using a more practical but seemingly less-thorough rating method. Our findings contribute to the understanding of rubric design, and also contribute to the understanding that validation and validity issues are pervasive throughout all aspects of a language test, from the measurement of the intended construct, down to the decision to use certain formats of rubrics.

References

Bachman, L. F. (1990). *Fundamental considerations in language testing.* Oxford University Press.

Bachman, L. F. (2000). Language testing at the turn of the century: Making sure that what we count counts. *Language Testing, 17*(1), 1–42.

Bachman, L. F. (2005). Building and supporting a case for test use. *Language Assessment Quarterly: An International Journal, 2*(1), 1–34.

Bachman, L. F., & Palmer, A. S. (2010). *Language assessment in practice.* Oxford: Oxford, UK.

Bachman, L. F., Lynch, B. K., & Mason, M. (1995). Investigating variability in tasks and rater judgements in a performance test of foreign language speaking. *Language Testing, 12,* 238–257.

Brown, H. D., & Abeywickrama, P. (2010). *Language assessment: Principles and classroom practices.* NY: Pearson Longman.

Carr, N. T., & Xi, X. (2010). Automated scoring of short-answer reading items: Implications for constructs. *Language Assessment Quarterly, 7*(3), 205–218.

Carrell, P. L. (1991). Second language reading: Reading ability or language proficiency? *Applied Linguistics, 12*(2), 159–179.

Carson, J. E., Carrell, P. L., Silberstein, S., Kroll, B., & Kuehn, P. A. (1990). Reading-writing relationships in first and second language. *TESOL Quarterly, 24*(2), 245–266. https://doi.org/10.2307/3586901.

Carver, R. (1992). Reading Rate: Theory, research, and practical implications. *Journal of Reading, 36*(1), 84–95.

Carver, R. P. (1997). Reading for one second, one minute, or one year from the perspective of Rauding theory. *Scientific Studies of Reading, 1*(1), 3.

Enright, M., Grabe, W., Koda, K., Mosenthal, P., Mulcahy-Ernt, P., & Schedl, M. (2000). *TOEFL 2000 reading framework*. Princeton, NJ: Educational Testing Service.

Goodwin, S. (2016). A Many-Facet Rasch analysis comparing essay rater behavior on an academic English reading/writing test used for two purposes. *Assessing Writing, 30*, 21–31.

Grabe, W. (2009). *Reading in a second language: Moving from theory to practice*. Cambridge University Press.

Green, A. (2014a). Online resources for *Exploring language assessment and testing: Language in action*. Routledge. Retrieved August 1, 2019, from https://routledgetextbooks.com/textbooks/_author/rial/language.php.

Green, A. (2014b). *Exploring language assessment and testing: Language in action*. Routledge.

Jamieson, J. M., Eignor, D., Grabe, W., & Kunnan, A. J. (2008). Frameworks for a new TOEFL. In Chapelle, Enright & Jamieson (Eds.), *Building a validity argument for the test of English as a Foreign language*™ (pp. 69–110). Routledge.

Jiang, X. (2011). The role of first language literacy and second language proficiency in second language reading comprehension. *Reading Matrix: An International Online Journal, 11*(2), 177–190.

Keck, C. (2006). The use of paraphrase in summary writing: A comparison of L1 and L2 writers. *Journal of second language writing, 15*(4), 261–278.

Kintsch, W. (1998). *Cognition: A paradigm for cognition*. Cambridge: Cambridge University Press.

Llosa, L. (2008). Building and supporting a validity argument for a standards-based classroom assessment of English proficiency based on teacher judgments. *Educational Measurement: Issues and Practice, 27*(3), 32–42.

Messick, S. (1989). Meaning and values in test validation: The science and ethics of assessment. *Educational Researcher, 18*(2), 5–11.

Pae, T.-I. (2017). Effects of task type and L2 proficiency on the relationship between L1 and L2 in reading and writing: An SEM Approach. *Studies in Second Language Acquisition, 40*(1), 1–28.

Perfetti, C. (2007). Reading ability: Lexical quality to comprehension. *Scientific Studies of Reading, 11*(1), 357–383.

Rupp, A. A., Ferne, T., & Choi, H. (2006). How assessing reading comprehension with multiple-choice questions shapes the construct: A cognitive processing perspective. *Language testing, 23*(4), 441–474.

Toulmin, S. E. (2003). *The uses of argument*. Cambridge University Press.

Trites, L., & McGroarty, M. (2005). Reading to learn and reading to integrate: New tasks for reading comprehension tests? *Language Testing, 22*(2), 174–210).

Weigle, S. C. (2004). Integrating reading and writing in a competency test for non-native speakers of English. *Assessing writing, 9*(1), 27–55.

Weigle, S. C., & Parker, K. (2012). Source text borrowing in an integrated reading/writing assessment. *Journal of Second Language Writing, 21*(2), 118–133.

Weir, C. J. (1993). *Understanding and developing language tests*. New York: Prentice Hall.

Xi, X. (2010). Automated scoring and feedback systems: Where are we and where are we heading? *Language Testing, 27*(3), 291.

Chapter 9
The Curse of Explanation: Model Selection in Language Testing Research

Ikkyu Choi

Abstract Language testing researchers often use statistical models to approximate and study a true model (i.e., the underlying system that is responsible for generating data). Building a model that successfully approximates the true model is not an easy task and typically involves data-driven model selection. However, available tools for model selection cannot guarantee successful reproduction of the true model. Moreover, there are consequences of model selection that affect the quality of inferences. Introducing and illustrating some of these issues related to model selection is the goal of this chapter. In particular, I focus on three issues: (1) uncertainty due to model selection in statistical inference, (2) successful approximations of data with an incorrect model, and (3) existence of substantively different models whose statistical counterparts are highly comparable. I conclude with a call for explicitly acknowledging and justifying model selection processes, as laid out in Bachman's research use argument framework (2006, 2009).

Introduction

Language testing researchers use statistical models to learn about the underlying system that is responsible for generating data. This underlying system can be conveniently called the true model (be it real or imagined), and statistical models can be understood as approximations of the corresponding true models. Sometimes the approximation is intentionally bad (e.g., a straw-man null hypothesis to reject), whereas at other times approximations are based on rigorous reviews of relevant literature to ensure that they are as close to the true model as possible (e.g., a structural model with variables representing constructs). In this chapter, I focus on the latter type of modeling.

Building a model that successfully approximates a true model is not an easy task. Even a thorough review of relevant theories and empirical findings may fail to provide sufficient information to specify a well-fitting model a priori. It is thus

I. Choi (✉)
Educational Testing Service, Princeton, New Jersey, USA
e-mail: ichoi001@ets.org

© Springer Nature Singapore Pte Ltd. 2020
G. J. Ockey and B. A. Green (eds.), *Another Generation of Fundamental Considerations in Language Assessment*, https://doi.org/10.1007/978-981-15-8952-2_9

common for researchers to employ iterative procedures to build towards a satisfactory model using available data. A typical practice consists of the following steps (Berk, Brown, & Zhao, 2010). First, on the basis of prior knowledge, a few competing models are proposed and fit to the data at hand. In the second step, the models are compared in terms of their fit and substantive interpretability. The third step involves the selection of the temporary best model and additional examinations of whether further improvements are possible. Changes made to the temporary model are evaluated by moving iteratively between the second and third steps. In the fourth (and final) step, the final model is obtained and deemed to be an approximation of the true model. In this chapter, the second and third steps are referred to as model selection.

Model selection is integral when the primary goal of research is to learn about the true model. Understanding the true model is made possible by understanding the final statistical model. Thus, obtaining a final model that is as close as possible to the true model is crucial. The distance between the final model and the true model is evaluated by comparing what would have happened if a proposed model were the true model (i.e., fitted values) to what actually happened (i.e., data available). Many tools and workflows are available to formalize and guide the model selection process, but they cannot guarantee successful reproduction of the true model. Moreover, there are consequences of model selection that affect the quality of inferences based on the final model.

Introducing and illustrating some of these issues related to model selection is the goal of this chapter. In particular, I focus on three issues: (1) uncertainty due to model selection in statistical inference, (2) successful approximations of data with a wrong model, and (3) existence of substantively different models whose statistical counterparts are highly comparable. These three issues by no means form an exhaustive list. Rather, they are chosen because they present interesting conundrums for different aspects of common practices in language testing research. In the remainder of this chapter, each issue is discussed with an example designed to illustrate the issue in a simple setting (data and code used for the examples are available upon request). I then discuss another modeling framework, in which model selection can be avoided. Finally, I conclude with some implications of issues arising from model selection and future directions.

Literature Review

Challenges in Model Selection

Difficulties of model selection in social sciences is well-documented in the statistical and methodological literature. The fundamental problem is that the system responsible for generating the data (i.e., the true model) is not only unknown to researchers but may not be accessible at all. As the famous quote goes, "all models are wrong" (Box, 1976). This ontological problem renders model selection complicated: in reality, the search for the true model is effectively the search for an approximation to the true model. It is up to researchers to determine how to find the best approximation.

In addition to this fundamental problem, several major difficulties have been identified and emphasized. Some are technical in nature, such as the curse of dimensionality (Bellman, 1961): in a given data set, one can continue improving model fit by positing more and more complex models (e.g., MacKay, 1992). Other problems have to do with the variables included in data. Examples of this sort include failure to include important variables (e.g., Cox & Snell, 1974) and measurement errors (e.g., Cudeck & Henly, 1991). Lastly, there are issues that have to do with the discrepancy between ideal data collection mechanisms that are imposed to allow statistical inference, which are often quite restrictive (e.g., random sampling from a well-defined population of interest), and actual data collection mechanisms, which are almost always based on convenience and availability. The following statement by Berk and Freedman (2003) in their discussion of models in criminal justice research may apply to language testing research as well: "the data in hand are simply the data most available" (p. 236). Each of the three specific issues discussed in this chapter arises from one or more of these major difficulties.

It is a common practice that statistical inferences are made after model selection based on the p-values and/or confidence intervals from the selected model. Warnings against such post-selection inferences are not new (Brown, 1967; Buehler & Feddersen, 1963; Cox & Snell, 1974; Sen, 1979). The warnings are due to the model-specific nature of statistical inference and the lack of well-developed statistical tools to address "uncertainty about the structure of the model" (Chatfield, 1995, p. 421). An exacerbating factor is that many variables used for modeling are correlated, and therefore, whether a variable is selected can change the sampling distributions for other variables in the model. Consequently, the "correct" sampling distribution of a parameter estimate amounts to a mixture of different sampling distributions under different models. Formal studies of these mixture distributions have been undertaken (e.g., Berk et al., 2010; Kabalia, 1998; Leeb & Pötscher, 2005, 2006, 2008), and it is understood that this issue arises regardless of "how" models are selected (Leeb & Pötscher, 2005) and that it is in general difficult to obtain correct mixture distributions of interest in practice (Leeb & Pötscher, 2006, 2008). The first illustrative example in this chapter is adopted with some minor changes from an example given by Berk et al. (2010).

The goal of model selection is to find a well-performing model and, through that model, to learn about the corresponding true model (Breiman, 2001a). However, this lofty goal is elusive regardless of how well a model fits the data, which is the second issue discussed in this chapter. Substantive aspects of this issue are well-documented: available theories are weak and underspecified whereas the corresponding true models are in all likelihood very complex (e.g., Cudeck & Henly, 1991; Meehl & Waller, 2002). There is also a statistical side, which was sharply presented by Gelman and Nolan (2002): "A fundamental problem in statistics is that it can be easy to fit the wrong model to data but difficult to notice the problem"

(p. 145). This difficulty can be due to well-known culprits such as small sample size and noisy measurements. However, even when the sample size is large and measurements are highly precise, deducing the data generating system based on data analysis is not straightforward. Gelman and Nolan illustrate this with a linear regression example (Chap. 9, pp. 145–146). This example is used with little change as the second illustrating example in this chapter.

It is not an easy task to operationalize substantive theories and hypotheses into testable statistical models (Berk & Freedman, 2003). Models that differ in a substantively meaningful manner may, from a statistical perspective, prove to be equivalent or highly comparable. Statistically equivalent models with different substantive meanings have received attention in the factor analysis literature, among others (e.g., Lee & Hershberger, 1990; MacCallum, Wegener, Uchino, & Fabrigar, 1993). Moreover, substantively different models that are not statistically equivalent can still yield highly comparable performances in a given data set (McCullagh & Nelder, 1989). This is the third issue of this chapter. Even when a unique model is identified as the "best-performing" under a given criterion, there can be many other models that perform almost equally well. In the context of parameter estimation, multiple sets of estimates that yield performances that are almost identical to that of the best-performing set are called "fungible" parameters. They can be obtained and examined as a type of sensitivity analysis (Lee, MacCallum, & Browne, 2018; Waller, 2008; Waller & Jones, 2009). As model selection can be viewed as an estimation problem (Kadane & Lazar, 2004), we expect to find models that are only very slightly worse than the best-performing one. These slight differences may have little practical impact. This issue is illustrated in the third example of this chapter.

Statistical models have served multiple purposes, the most prominent of which include providing explanations for the data generating process of interest (modeling for explanation) and making predictions for new observations (modeling for prediction). It has long been acknowledged that the practice of modeling should depend on the purpose. For example, Cox and Snell (1974) distinguished modeling for explanation and prediction and provided separate sets of advice. Consequences of optimizing for one purpose over the other have become better understood over the years, culminating in focused review papers such as Breiman (2001a) and Shmueli (2010). Despite being almost a decade apart, Breiman and Shmueli share core messages. First, explanation and prediction represent different goals. Modeling for explanation is the dominant, if not exclusive, paradigm in most social science disciplines. Lastly, model selection is inherent in modeling for explanation such that researchers can interpret the final model and generalize the interpretation to the domain of interest. Each of these messages will be discussed in more detail after the illustrating examples.

Bachman's Work on Statistical Models

The use of statistical models has been an integral part of Bachman's empirical research program. Bachman and Palmer's (1981) study was one of the earliest applications of structural equation modeling (SEM) published in the applied linguistics literature and was followed by a series of influential SEM studies (Bachman, 1982; Bachman & Palmer, 1982; Fouly, Bachman, & Cziko, 1990) that effectively demonstrated the methodology's potential and formed the empirical basis for Bachman's (1990) influential framework of communicative competence. The explicit connection between substantive hypotheses and their testable statistical counterparts appears to have played a central role in this methodological choice. For example, Bachman viewed "the explicitness with which research hypotheses and assumptions must be stated" (Bachman & Palmer, 1982, p. 463) in constructing a model as facilitating the construction and evaluation of hypotheses. The why and how of modeling are also clear from the first SEM paper: "for statistically evaluating the extent to which different causal models explain the relationships observed in a body of data" (Bachman & Palmer, 1981, p. 77). This focus on modeling for explanation and empirical model selection is a constant throughout Bachman's career (see, e.g., Bae & Bachman, 2010, for a recent example of his use and descriptions of modeling). Another constant is his preference towards parsimonious and interpretable models: when different models were similar in terms of data fit, he made clear arguments for models that provided more structured explanations (Bachman & Palmer, 1981; Fouly et al., 1990; Bae & Bachman, 1998, 2010).

Although Bachman made critical contributions to the widespread application of statistical models in language testing and applied linguistics research, he has repeatedly emphasized the importance of understanding their limitations (Bachman, 2000, 2013). His research use argument (RUA) framework makes it explicit that researchers are responsible for justifying their analytical choices and acknowledging the associated limitations (Bachman, 2006, 2009). The RUA framework also provides a conceptual context in which the importance of model selection can be highlighted: Processes of model selection involve substantive judgments that need to be justified and have direct impacts on the final model whose outputs will be interpreted and potentially used in the real world.

Issue 1: Post-selection Inference

Making statistical inferences after model selection is a common practice. For example, a regression model can be constructed through stepwise procedures (i.e., model selection), and the importance of each predictor can be interpreted in terms of statistical significance based on the corresponding t-test (i.e., statistical inference). Unfortunately, this practice leads to a distorted view of the actual uncertainty associated with parameter estimates. The sampling distributions of parameter estimates obtained from any given model are based on the assumption that that model was the only one considered. This assumption clearly does not hold when a model was selected through data-driven search, in which there exists uncertainty associated with model selection. Unless predictors are independent of one another, introducing a new predictor to a model or removing an existing predictor leads to changes to the sampling distributions of the remaining predictors. As a result, the estimated sampling distributions from the selected model can be quite different from sampling distributions resulting from proper consideration of the uncertainty due to model selection. In the remainder of this section, I illustrate this difference in the context of a regression model. As noted earlier, this example is based on simulations done by Berk et al. (2010).

Suppose a simple true model in which an outcome variable y is generated linearly and additively as the weighted sum of three predictors, x_1, x_2, and x_3. For convenience, I use *predictor* and *outcome* as generic terms to denote input and output variables, respectively, in this chapter. This use does not imply that models are used only for prediction. Assuming that y is measured with normally distributed noise with constant positive variance, but x_1, x_2, and x_3 are perfectly measured, the outcome variable y_i of the observation unit i has the form

$$y_i = \beta_0 + \beta_1 x_{1i} + \beta_2 x_{2i} + \beta_3 x_{3i} + \epsilon_i,$$

where x_{1i}, x_{2i}, and x_{3i} stand for the x_1, x_2, and x_3 values for the unit i, respectively, and ϵ_i denotes the normal measurement error for y_i with positive variance. In other words, the true model above is the normal theory multiple regression model. If a researcher knows this model a priori and fits it to data randomly sampled from the population, all is fine. Because the true model is known, the only uncertainty comes from the random sampling of data. Consequently, the estimated sampling distributions for the usual ordinary least squares estimates $\hat{\beta}_1$, $\hat{\beta}_2$, and $\hat{\beta}_3$ correctly represent the actual uncertainty.

Language testing researchers rarely encounter such an ideal case. On the contrary, a common scenario would involve many predictors that are substantively plausible. Identifying a set of plausible predictors that leads to generation of the outcome y is often a primary goal. To reflect this reality without complicating the illustration too much, suppose the researcher has the three predictors available but does not know whether all three are needed to explain the outcome. Now model selection comes into the picture because the true model is not fully known. The goal of analysis is to reverse-engineer the true model using data. The probability of success in this endeavor depends on multiple factors, including the representativeness and size of available data, the magnitude of the parameters, relationships among the three predictors, and tools and logic used for model selection.

For this illustration, I assumed a simple random sample of 200 data points and used 0.1, 0.5, and 0.3 as the values for β_1, β_2, and β_3, respectively. The error ϵ_i was a normal variable with mean zero and standard deviation equal to 0.5. These conditions were designed to roughly reflect somewhat noisy predictors that have differential impact on the outcome, but the choice of these specific values was largely arbitrary.

The values for the three predictors were randomly drawn from a multivariate normal distribution with zero mean vector and the following covariance matrix:

$$\begin{pmatrix} 1 & 0.5 & 0.7 \\ 0.5 & 1 & 0.6 \\ 0.7 & 0.6 & 1 \end{pmatrix}$$

I used the above setup to generate 10,000 simulated data sets. For each data set, I conducted forward stepwise search using AIC (Akaike, 1974) as the criterion. The search was limited to additive models such that the total number of possible models was eight: the null model without any predictor, three models with one of the three predictors, three models with two of the three predictors, and the full (and correct) model with all three predictors. The data generation and the stepwise search were conducted using R (R Core Team, 2019).

Consider first what would have resulted if the true model were known a priori. Because statistical inference for each coefficient is often made based on the corresponding t-statistic, I focused on that statistic instead of looking at both the point estimate and the standard error. The t-statistic for each of the estimates, $\hat{\beta}_1$, $\hat{\beta}_2$, and $\hat{\beta}_3$, still varies across the data sets due to sampling variability. The distributions of these statistics are shown as solid lines in Fig. 9.1. The solid lines differ across the three panels in terms of the range. The 97.5-th percentile for a t variate with one degree of freedom is approximately two. Therefore, most of the t-statistics for the first predictor would be deemed not significantly different from zero, whereas most of the t-statistics for the second and third predictors would be declared as being significantly different from zero. This reflects the power of the t-tests for the predictors; because the sample size was fixed at 200, the power of each test is solely determined by the respective effect sizes (i.e., the difference between the true β values and zero). In other words, the solid lines characterize the uncertainty surrounding the estimates due to sampling and the true effect sizes, if there were no model selection. If the distributions of "post-model-selection" statistics are comparable to the solid lines, we can conclude that model selection would have little impact on statistical inference.

Unfortunately, that is not the case. Consideration of model selection complicates the sampling distributions of $\hat{\beta}_1$, $\hat{\beta}_2$, and $\hat{\beta}_3$. The distribution of $\hat{\beta}_j$, $1 \leq j \leq 3$, is defined only in models in which x_j is included. Among the 10,000 data sets, the true model was found 2,825 times. The second predictor x_2 was always included. The first predictor x_1 was included in the model 3,606 times, and the third predictor x_3 was included 9,198 times. Moreover, the t-statistics for $\hat{\beta}_j$ were also affected by whether the other two predictors were included. Consequently, the distribution of the t-statistics becomes a mixture of multiple distributions. Figure 9.1 also gives these distributions as dotted lines. The solid lines and the dotted lines are different from each other, even for the second predictor x_2 that was included every time. The difference was substantial for the first predictor x_1.

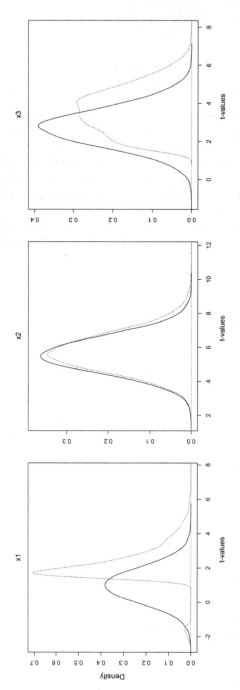

Fig. 9.1 The distributions of the t-statistics for the three predictors. The solid lines represent the distributions resulting from fitting the true model to all 10,000 data sets, and the dotted lines represent post-selection t-statistics calculated from data sets in which the given predictor was selected (3,606, 10,000, and 9,198 data sets for x_1, x_2, and x_3, respectively)

This example shows that statistical inference would in general be incorrect if uncertainty due to model selection is ignored. It has been proposed to broaden confidence intervals to acknowledge the model selection uncertainty (e.g., Berk, Brown, Buja, Zhang, & Zhao, 2013), but these proposals have yet to be implemented in applied research. Making post hoc adjustments to address this issue is inherently difficult because the true model is not known in practice, and thus actual sampling distributions of estimates may not be attainable (Leeb & Pötscher, 2005). Consequently, researchers are left with an inconvenient truth that, after model selection, sampling distributions from the final model are incorrect, without an accessible means to obtain correct sampling distributions.

There are several remedies. From a theoretical perspective, this issue can be avoided by constructing a model that is (almost) certainly selected. Figure 9.1 shows that the two lines are quite similar for the second predictor x_2 that has a large impact on the outcome variable and was thus always selected. This is, however, seldom feasible in language testing research, in which a typical study involves many potentially important and inter-related variables that are measured with a relatively large amount of noise (e.g., scores on a language assessment, the amount and type of exposure to target language input, the level of motivation). A practical solution is to use separate data sets for model selection and statistical inference: one data set only for model selection and another data set for making statistical inference for the estimated parameters. For example, in a regression context, researchers can determine which predictors and their interactions should be included in the model using one data set and then make statistical inferences based on the output obtained by fitting the selected model to another data set. Ideally, these data sets are distinct realizations from the same population under investigation. Obtaining such data sets may be difficult, and an even more practical alternative may be splitting a single data set into two random sets. However, data splitting introduces another source of uncertainty (due to the random subsetting), and its effectiveness depends on the sample size and the level of pre-specification for model building (Berk et al., 2010; Faraway, 2016). In sum, there is no convenient remedy for this problem outside of the conventional wisdom: We need specific theories, precise measurements, and strong data.

Issue 2: True Model and Well-Fitting Model

Models are evaluated on the basis of how well they approximate data at hand, not on how close they are to the true model. The indirect nature of model evaluation is a practical necessity, for the true model is unknown and can only be approximated using available theories, analytical tools, and data. However, it also puts an inherent limitation to our access to the true model through statistical models. Although very close approximations to data may be achieved, such results indicate only that the model under consideration yielded fitted values highly comparable to observed outcome values; it does not guarantee that the hypothesized relationships among variables in the model are close to the true relationships. In fact, even models that yield fitted

Table 9.1 Data Excerpts for the Second Example

	Data set 1			Data set 2		
Unit #	y	x_1	x_2	y	x_1	x_2
1	20.20	11.09	16.89	20.09	10.73	16.99
2	18.55	9.86	15.71	20.40	11.49	16.85
3	16.83	9.71	13.75	21.48	12.33	17.58
4	18.81	10.87	15.36	20.50	11.12	17.22
...	...	...	...	...	...	...
200	19.26	11.46	15.49	20.65	12.67	16.30

values that are almost identical to observed outcome values may be far from the true model. In the remainder of this section, I illustrate this point using another linear regression example. As noted earlier, this example is based on an example given by Gelman and Nolan (2002, Chap. 9).

Suppose data consisting of an outcome variable, y, and two predictors, x_1 and x_2. There are 200 observation units, each of which is denoted by a subscript i, $1 \leq i \leq 200$, such that y_i stands for the outcome variable for unit i and x_{1i} and x_{2i} are similarly defined. An excerpt of this data set is given in Table 9.1. Further suppose that it is known a priori that the two predictors x_1 and x_2 were the only inputs used to generate the outcome variable y in the true model. The primary goal of the analysis is thus to approximate the mechanism that generated the outcome variable using the predictors.

As a first step towards this goal, bivariate plots between these variables can be examined, as can be seen in Fig. 9.2. The plots do not suggest any major deviations from linear relationships between y and either of the x variables, and the correlation between the two predictors x_1 and x_2 seems miniscule (at 0.02). Consequently, it is reasonable to fit a multiple regression model of the following form:

$$y_i = \beta_0 + \beta_1 x_{1i} + \beta_2 x_{2i} + \epsilon_i,$$

where ε_i is assumed to follow the normal distribution with zero mean and constant positive variance.

Fitting this regression model yielded the estimates of the β coefficients in Table 9.2. The estimates $\hat{\beta}_1$ and $\hat{\beta}_2$ are both positive and significantly different from zero at the 1% level. The resulting fitted values, obtained by $0.04 + 0.56 \times x_1 + 0.83 \times x_2$, are plotted against the observed y values in the left panel of Fig. 9.3. The fitted values are almost perfectly aligned to the observed values. The R^2 value (0.99) is almost perfect as well. All these indicate an extremely close approximation.

Perhaps this great performance could be due to chance. Examining whether this were the case requires a separate data set generated from the same true model. Suppose there is such a data set, an excerpt of which is also given in Table 9.1. The fitted values from the new x_1 and x_2 values, again obtained by $0.04 + 0.56 \times x_1 +$

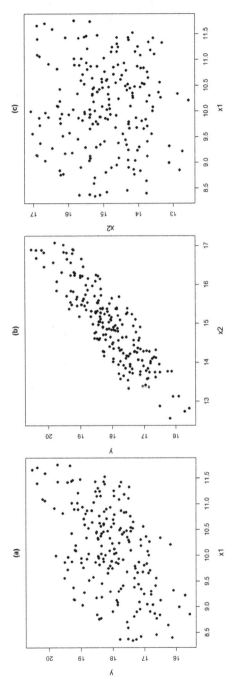

Fig. 9.2 Bivariate relationships among the outcome variable y and the predictors x_1 and x_2

Table 9.2 Point estimates, standard errors, and t-statistics from the regression model

	Estimate	Standard error	t-statistic (p-value)
β_0	0.04	0.03	1.02 (0.31)
β_1	0.56	0.002	260.12 (<0.01)
β_2	0.83	0.002	455.58 (<0.01)

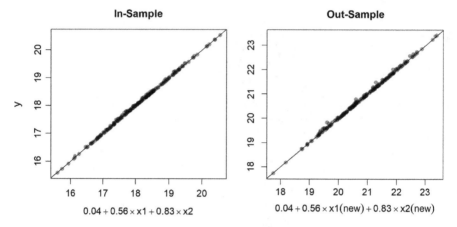

Fig. 9.3 Relationships between the fitted values (x-axis) and the outcome values (y-axis) in the first (left panel) and second (right panel) data sets. The solid lines represent the least squares lines estimated from the first data set

$0.83 \times x_2$, are still almost perfectly aligned to the new y values, as can be seen in the right panel of Fig. 9.3. The R^2 value (0.99) is still almost perfect despite the use of the estimates obtained from a different data set. This model looks even better now. In light of these findings, it may be tempting to claim that this model is close to the true model.

That claim would have been false. The true model used to generate y from x_1 and x_2 was the Pythagorean equation:

$$y_i^2 = x_{1i}^2 + x_{2i}^2.$$

where $x_{1i} \sim N(10, 1)$ and $x_{2i} \sim N(15, 1)$. Although the linear model yielded fitted values that were highly comparable to y, it was not close in form to the true model. The true model was neither linear in the x variables nor affected by normally distributed noise.

From a technical perspective, this example highlights the power of linear approximation: despite the major differences in form between the true model and the linear model, the latter was able to produce highly comparable approximations. On the other hand, the might of linear approximation can make it difficult to explain substantive aspects of the true model, because good approximations in terms of fitted values, which all model selection tools evaluate, do not guarantee a close agreement between the fitted model and the true model. Any model can be wrong, even the ones that fit very well.

Issue 3: Substantive Model and Statistical Model

The third issue has to do with discordance between substantive and statistical models when the fit of the latter is used as evidence to justify the former. In particular, models that are distinct from a theoretical perspective may be quite similar in a statistical sense in that they yield highly comparable fitted values. Statistical comparisons between those models may be of little value. This discordance, however, may not be properly manifested during model selection. In the remainder of this section, I illustrate this issue with an example in an SEM context.

Language assessments often consist of multiple sections, each of which is designed to measure a dedicated mode (e.g., reading) or domain (e.g., academic) of language use. For convenience, these constructs will be called section constructs. Scores from these sections are often highly correlated, and it is of substantive interest whether the high correlation can be attributed to a single common construct across sections. SEM allows researchers to explicitly model relationships among section constructs and thus provides a statistical framework for tackling this question.

Consider the following incarnation of this general research question. The TOEFL iBT test is designed to measure one's "ability to use and understand English at the university level" (Educational Testing Service, 2019). The test consists of four sections: Reading, Listening, Speaking, and Writing. Test takers receive section scores (each on the scale of 0–30) as well as a total score (the sum of all section scores). A subset of scored responses from 1,000 test takers to one operational form of the test is available as part of the TOEFL iBT public use data set. As expected, the section scores in this data set are highly correlated (ranging from 0.54 to 0.77). Is it reasonable to attribute the high correlations to a single governing construct, say academic English proficiency?

To address this question, two models that share the same measurement model (i.e., a model for the relationship between observed variables and latent variables) but differ in their structural components can be formed. The common measurement model conforms to the test structure and involves four latent variables representing the four section constructs. As the measurement model is shared across the two models of interest and thus does not affect the primary outcome of this illustration, I made two simplifying steps. First, I summed up item scores within each passage and used the resulting sum scores (sometimes called parcel scores) as indicator variables for the Reading and Listening sections. Second, I assumed that each item loaded only on the factor that represents the section it belongs to. The resulting measurement model specification is summarized in Table 9.3.

The primary interest lies in the structural models (i.e., a model for the relationship among latent variables). In the first model, factor correlations are unstructured.

Table 9.3 Common
measurement model
specification for the two
models

Observed variables	Section constructs
Reading passage 1	Reading
Reading passage 2	
Reading passage 3	
Listening passage 1	Listening
Listening passage 2	
Listening passage 3	
Listening passage 4	
Listening passage 5	
Listening passage 6	
Speaking item 1	Speaking
Speaking item 2	
Speaking item 3	
Speaking item 4	
Speaking item 5	
Speaking item 6	
Writing item 1	Writing
Writing item 2	

Because the four section constructs form six unique pairs, there are six correlation coefficients freely estimated from data. The second model, on the other hand, represents an additional assumption of a higher-order construct, called academic English proficiency for convenience, that is responsible for the correlations among the section constructs. The section constructs all load on this higher-order construct, and therefore the structural component has four loadings freely estimated from data. Thus, the second model has two fewer parameters than the first model. The first and second models are called the correlated-factors model and the higher-order model, respectively, in the remainder of this section. The two models are visually summarized in Fig. 9.4.

I fit the two models to the data and estimated model parameters via normal-theory maximum likelihood. The correlated-factors model yielded the likelihood ratio test (LRT) statistic of 288.79 with 113 degrees of freedom, and the corresponding statistic for the higher-order factor model was 371.75 with 115 degrees of freedom. The fit of neither model is satisfactory in terms of the LRT statistic, but few models would satisfy this criterion at this sample size. In this context, the LRT statistics are more useful for comparing the two models. The difference in the LRT statistics between the correlated-factors model and the higher-order model is 82.96 with two degrees of freedom. The 99-th percentile for a chi-square variable with two degrees of freedom is approximately nine, and thus this difference is significant at the 1% level. This may be regarded as statistical evidence against attributing the section construct correlations to the common construct of academic English proficiency.

Correlated-Factors Model

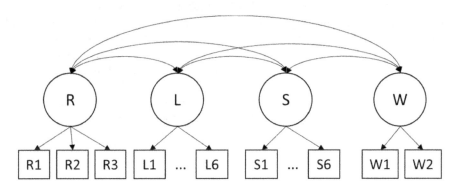

Higher-Order Model

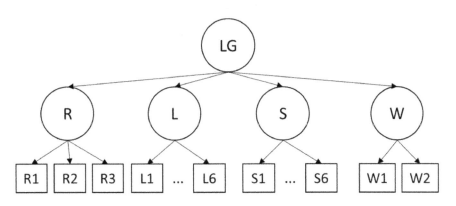

Fig. 9.4 Conceptual diagrams for the correlated-factors model and the higher-order model. The letters R, L, S, and W represent reading, listening, speaking, and writing, respectively. The letters LG in the higher-order model represents academic English proficiency

This evidence, however, becomes less convincing when we look under the hood. In the normal-theory maximum likelihood context, the LRT statistic is obtained by $(N - 1) \times d_m$, where N stands for the sample size and d_m is the minimized normal-theory maximum likelihood discrepancy function between the observed covariance matrix (denoted by S) and the fitted covariance matrix from a given model m (denoted by Σ_m):

$$d_m = log(|\Sigma_m|) - log(|S|) + tr\left(S\Sigma_m^{-1}\right) - p,$$

where $|A|$ denotes the determinant of matrix A, $tr(A)$ denotes the trace function for matrix A, and p denotes the number of variables in the covariance matrix. That is, the LRT statistic is determined by the sample size and the distance between the observed covariance matrix and the fitted covariance matrix. The minimized discrepancy function value is used in virtually all fit indices (see, e.g., Cudeck & Henly, 1991), but I focus on the LRT statistic in this chapter because of its popularity and space limitations. As mentioned earlier, the sample size of the TOEFL iBT public use data set is 1,000 and thus $N - 1 = 999$. Let the minimized discrepancy functions for the correlated-factor model and the higher-order factor model be denoted by d_c and d_h, respectively. Then $999 \times d_h - 999 \times d_c = 82.96$. It follows that $d_h - d_c$, the difference between the two minimized discrepancy functions, was $82.96/999 \approx 0.08$. In fact, the distance between the two fitted covariance matrices directly measured by the discrepancy function was 0.086.

This value is on a rather abstract scale and is thus difficult to interpret. However, it does not appear large, especially considering that it synthesizes the differences between two 17×17 covariance matrices. To gauge its magnitude, I compared this distance to sampling variability of the observed covariance matrix, which was obtained via nonparametric bootstrapping with 1,000 bootstrapped samples. Let the covariance matrix of a bootstrapped sample b, $1 \leq b \leq 1,000$, be denoted by S_b. The distance between the observed covariance matrix and each of the 1,000 resulting bootstrapped covariance matrices, denoted by d_b, was calculated by plugging in S_b in place of Σ_m in the above equation for d_m. The distribution of d_b is presented in Fig. 9.5, which also shows the distance between the fitted covariance matrices

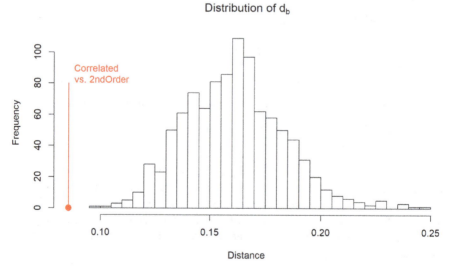

Fig. 9.5 The distribution of distances between the observed covariance matrix and its bootstrapped samples. The red dot represents the distance between the fitted covariance matrices from the correlated-factors model and the higher-order model

from the two models. Figure 9.5 puts the distance between the two fitted covariance matrices in a more interpretable context: the two fitted covariance matrices were closer to each other than was the observed covariance matrix and its closest bootstrapped sample out of 1,000. In other words, the distance between the correlated-factors model and the higher-order factor model appears smaller than the sampling variability of the observed covariance matrix itself. I interpret this as an indication that the two models are too close to each other to be empirically distinguished based on the available data. This interpretation is specific to the models and the data set for this example and is not a general rebuke to the SEM methodology, which provides a framework for meaningful model comparisons. For example, the distance between the fitted covariance matrix from the correlated-factors model and the fitted covariance matrix from a unidimensional model (in which all observed variables load on one factor) was 0.95, which was almost eleven times larger than the distance between the correlated-factors model and the higher-order model and almost four times larger than the distance between the observed covariance matrix and its farthest bootstrapped sample out of 1,000. The comparison between the correlated-factors model and the unidimensional model thus appears quite meaningful.

This example demonstrates at least two noteworthy aspects. The first is, as mentioned earlier, discordance between the substantive models and those of the statistical models that were compared. Although the substantive models were different in a meaningful way, the fitted values from the statistical models were highly comparable. The second lies in model selection tools, which enable only statistical meaning. When competing models yield highly comparable fitted values, model selection tools provide little value in making substantive claims. Even worse, as was the case with the LRT statistics in this example, they may portray a false sense of convincing evidence during the model selection process. The difference in the LRT statistics between the two compared models appeared large enough to portray solid statistical evidence for the less interpretable correlated-factors model, until we looked under the hood.

Modeling for Explanation and Modeling for Prediction

In language testing research, statistical models are used to understand and explain the true model. This goal leads researchers to model selection procedures, through which the final model is selected and interpreted as an approximation to the true model. The pursuit of explanation thus necessitates model selection, which can be fraught with difficulties such as those shown in the illustrative examples. For this reason, I playfully call model selection the curse of explanation.

Modeling for explanation is a dominant paradigm in most social science disciplines (Breiman, 2001a; Shmueli, 2010). However, it is not the only paradigm. Modeling for prediction is a separate paradigm that focuses on prediction of new or future observations without attempting to explain how those observations were generated and is predominantly used in multiple disciplines such as bioinformatics and natural language processing (Shmueli, 2010). In the language testing literature, automated scoring of constructed responses (e.g., essays, speech samples) is a topic for which modeling for prediction is primarily used. This is not coincidental, for natural language processing is integral to automated scoring of language output. A proper introduction to modeling for prediction goes beyond the scope of this chapter, but the key difference between the two paradigms can be summarized as follows. Both paradigms share commonalities at the beginning (model building) and the end (model evaluation) of analysis: explanatory and predictive models are both built based on a functional relationship between predictors and outcomes and are evaluated in terms of the distance between observed outcomes and fitted values. They diverge in the middle. In modeling for explanation, the primary goal is to obtain a good approximation to the "true" functional relationship. The goodness of fit is used as evidence for the quality of this approximation. A successful study provides a better understanding of (some aspects of) the true relationship. On the other hand, the relationship between predictors and outcomes in modeling for prediction is merely a means to the end, which are fitted values that closely match target outcomes. Here, a successful study produces effective and/or efficient predictions. The true relationship remains a black box even at the end.

The difference between the two paradigms has led to different conventions. It is possible to keep improving prediction in a given data set by using more complex models. To address this issue, in modeling for prediction, it is standard to evaluate the quality of predictions on a separate data set. In modeling for explanation, on the other hand, this issue is addressed in a less explicit manner by preferring parsimonious models. Parsimony is also important for explanation because complex models are difficult to interpret. On the other hand, interpretability is less of a concern in modeling for prediction, and therefore, highly complex models are routinely used.

The distinction most relevant to this chapter is that model selection is integral in modeling for explanation but not in modeling for prediction. If there is no need to interpret predictive models, then there is no need to select only one model either. Instead, predictions from multiple models can be synthesized to obtain better predictions than those that can be obtained from any one model. Several well-established approaches to modeling for prediction, such as random forests (Breiman, 2001b) and boosting (Schapire, 1999), exploit this freedom from model selection: They build a committee of models and rely on the consensus from the committee.

Moreover, the three issues discussed in this chapter would not amount to difficult challenges for researchers focusing on modeling for prediction. The post-selection inference issue vanishes when models are evaluated on a separate data set, which is a standard practice in modeling for prediction. The second and third issues have to do with mistaken confidence in the explanatory capabilities of the final model. If models are used only for prediction, researchers do not need to worry about explanatory capabilities or selecting one final model among many similarly performing ones.

Conclusions, Implications, and Future Directions

People say prediction is hard. In this chapter, I argued that explanation is harder, at least in the context of statistical modeling. The pursuit of explanation requires model selection, which brings about difficult challenges. Examples of such challenges include, but are not limited to, the issues illustrated in this chapter. Sampling distributions of parameter estimates from the selected model are not reflective of uncertainty due to model selection. In addition, tools used for model selection may provide unwarranted confidence in the closeness between the selected model and the true model and/or in the superiority of the selected model over other alternatives. These challenges can be avoided if model selection can be avoided, which some approaches in the modeling for prediction paradigm have successfully exploited.

To be clear, I am not arguing for abandoning modeling for explanation and using models only for prediction. As evidenced by Bachman's influential research on the multi-componential nature of language proficiency (Bachman, 1982, 1990; Bachman & Palmer, 1981, 1982; Bae & Bachman, 1998, 2010; Fouly et al., 1990), explanation plays a central role in language testing research. Many important research questions in language testing require understanding of an underlying system that connects learners' language proficiency to a host of relevant factors known about them. Simply providing well-performing predictions would not address those research questions. We should not abandon statistical modeling for such important research questions because of technical challenges.

Instead, I believe that there are concrete lessons from successful applications of predictive models in other fields to facilitate statistical modeling practices in language testing research. Use of separate data sets for model building and evaluation does not require a separate paradigm. It is simply a good practice. There are also ways to more actively utilize modeling for prediction in language testing research. Predictive models can serve as a powerful tool for exploratory data analysis to help formulate substantive hypotheses (Berk, 2016). Moreover, even when the primary goal of research is to explain data generating mechanisms, there may be parts of analysis that only require good predictive performance (e.g., estimation of propensity scores). For those parts, researchers can benefit from borrowing successful algorithms optimized for producing good predictions. Lastly, and perhaps most importantly, researchers should recognize and acknowledge that explanation does not come from data or mathematics (with the notable exception of randomized experiments); it comes from models, which are based on a set of assumptions that are, implicitly or explicitly, made by researchers. As Bachman makes clear in the RUA framework (Bachman, 2006, 2009), these assumptions need to be stated and justified.

Advancements in computing power and algorithms have brought about substantial changes to model selection practices. Today, fitting and comparing complex models involving structural relationships among multiple latent variables presents little difficulty. This increased accessibility towards complex models, combined with complex substantive theories, can lead researchers to a complicated path that involves difficult model selection tasks. To a certain degree, this simply reflects the nature of research questions language testing and applied linguistics researchers encounter, as noted by Bachman (2006): "I'm inclined to advise my students to go into some simpler endeavor, something less complex and relatively straight-forward, like rocket science. After all, launching an electronic explorer on a trajectory to rendezvous with a distant planet in 25 years' time is a piece of cake compared to identifying the specific learning challenges for a given language learner, determining what kinds of language use activities will provide the most effective interactions for him or her, how a teacher can best implement these, and then assessing how much language that learner has learned after a program of instruction" (p. 166). It is because of the difficulty and importance of these research questions that language testing researchers must recognize and acknowledge the limitations of statistical modeling practices and peruse outputs from statistical models with such limitations in mind.

References

Akaike, H. (1974). A new look at the statistical model identification. *IEEE Transactions on Automatic Control, 19,* 716–723.

Bachman, L. F. (1982). The trait structure of cloze test scores. *TESOL Quarterly, 16,* 61–70.

Bachman, L. F. (1990). *Fundamental considerations in language testing.* Oxford: Oxford University Press.

Bachman, L. F. (2000). Modern language testing at the turn of the century: Assuring that what we count counts. *Language Testing, 17,* 1–42.

Bachman, L. F. (2006). Generalizability: A journey into the nature of empirical research in applied linguistics. In M. Chalhoub-Deville, C. A. Chapelle, & P. Duff (Eds.), *Inference and generalizability in applied linguistics: Multiple perspectives* (pp. 165–207). Dordrecht, The Netherlands: John Benjamins.

Bachman, L. F. (2009). Generalizability and research use arguments. In K. Ercikan & W-M. Roth (Eds.), *Generalizing from educational research* (pp. 127–148). New York, NY: Tayler & Francis.

Bachman, L. F. (2013). Ongoing challenges in language assessment. In A. J. Kunnan (Ed.), *The companion to language assessment.* Wiley-Blackwell: Hoboken, NJ.

Bachman, L. F., & Palmer, A. S. (1981). The construct validation of the FSI oral interview. *Language Learning, 31,* 67–86.

Bachman, L. F., & Palmer, A. S. (1982). The construct validation of some components of communicative proficiency. *TESOL Quarterly, 16,* 444–465.

Bae, J., & Bachman, L. F. (1998). A latent variable approach to listening and reading: Testing factorial invariance across two groups of children in the Korean/English two-way immersion program. *Language Testing, 15,* 380–414.

Bae, J., & Bachman, L. F. (2010). An investigation of four writing traits and two tasks across two languages. *Language Testing, 27,* 213–234.

Bellman, R. E. (1961). *Adaptive control processes.* Princeton, NJ: Princeton University Press.

Berk, R. A. (2016). *Statistical learning from a regression perspective* (2nd ed.). New York, NY: Springer.

Berk, R. A., Brown, L., Buja, A., Zhang, K., & Zhao, L. (2013). Valid post-selection inference. *The Annals of Statistics, 41,* 802–837.

Berk, R. A., Brown, L., & Zhao, L. (2010). Statistical inference after model selection. *Journal of Quantitative Criminology, 26,* 217–236.

Berk, R. A., & Freedman, D. A. (2003). Statistical assumptions as empirical commitments. In T. G. Blomberg & S. Cohen (Eds.), *Law, punishment, and social control: Essays in honor of Sheldon Messinger* (pp. 235–254). New York, NY: Aldine de Gruyter.

Box, G. E. P. (1976). Science and statistics. *Journal of the American Statistical Association, 71,* 791–799.

Breiman, L. (2001a). Statistical modeling: The two cultures. *Statistical Science, 16,* 199–231.

Breiman, L. (2001b). Random forests. *Machine Learning, 45,* 5–32.

Brown, L. D. (1967). The conditional level of Student's t test. *The Annals of Mathematical Statistics, 38,* 1068–1071.

Buehler, R. J., & Feddersen, A. P. (1963). Note on a conditional property of Student's t. *The Annals of Mathematical Statistics, 34,* 1098–1100.

Chatfield, C. (1995). Model uncertainty, data mining and statistical inference. *Journal of the Royal Statistical Society, Series A, 158,* 419–466.

Cox, D. R., & Snell, E. J. (1974). The choice of variables in observational studies. *Journal of the Royal Statistical Society, Series C, 23,* 51–59.

Cudeck, R., & Henly, S. J. (1991). Model selection in covariance structures analysis and the "problem" of sample size: A clarification. *Psychological Bulletin, 109,* 512–519.

Educational Testing Service. (2019). About the TOEFL iBT® test. https://www.ets.org/toefl/ibt/about.

Faraway, J. J. (2016). Does data splitting improve prediction? *Statistics and Computing, 26,* 40–60.

Fouly, K., Bachman, L. F., & Cziko, G. (1990). The divisibility of language competence: A confirmatory approach. *Language Learning, 40,* 1–21.

Gelman, A., & Nolan, D. (2002). *Teaching statistics: A bag of tricks.* Oxford: Oxford University Press.

Kabalia, P. (1998). Valid confidence intervals in regression after variable selection. *Econometric Theory, 14,* 463–482.

Kadane, J. B., & Lazar, N. A. (2004). Methods and criteria for model selection. *Journal of the American Statistical Association, 99,* 279–290.

Lee, S., & Hershberger, S. (1990). A simple rule for generating equivalent models in covariance structure modeling. *Multivariate Behavioral Research, 25,* 313–334.

Lee, T., MacCallum, R. C., & Browne, M. W. (2018). Fungible parameter estimates in structural equation modeling. *Psychological Methods, 23,* 58–75.

Leeb, H., & Pötscher, B. M. (2005). Model selection and inference: Facts and fiction. *Econometric Theory, 21,* 21–59.

Leeb, H., & Pötscher, B. M. (2006). Can one estimate the conditional distribution of post-model-selection estimators? *The Annals of Statistics, 34,* 2554–2591.

Leeb, H., & Pötscher, B. M. (2008). Model selection. In T. G. Anderson, R. A. Davis, J. P. Kreib, & T. Mikosch (Eds.), *The handbook of financial time series* (pp. 785–821). New York, NY: Springer.

MacCallum, R. C., Wegener, D. T., Uchino, B. N., & Fabrigar, L. R. (1993). The problem of equivalent models in applications of covariance structure analysis. *Psychological Bulletin, 114,* 185–199.

MacKay, D. J. C. (1992). Bayesian interpolation. *Neural Computation, 4,* 415–447.

McCullagh, P., & Nelder, J. A. (1989). *Generalized linear models* (2nd ed.). London: Chapman & Hall.

Meehl, P. E., & Waller, N. G. (2002). The path analysis controversy: A new statistical approach to strong appraisal of verisimilitude. *Psychological Methods, 7,* 283–300.

R Core Team. (2019). *R: A language and environment for statistical computing [Computer software].* Vienna, Austria: R Foundation for Statistical Computing.

Schapire, R. E. (1999). A brief introduction to boosting. In *Proceedings of the Sixth International Joint Conference on Artificial Intelligence* (pp. 1401–1406). Stockholm, Sweden.

Sen, P. K. (1979). Asymptotic properties of maximum likelihood estimators based on conditional specification. *Annals of Statistics, 7,* 1019–1033.

Shmueli, G. (2010). To explain or to predict? *Statistical Science, 25,* 289–310.

Waller, N. G. (2008). Fungible weights in multiple regression. *Psychometrika, 73,* 691–703.
Waller, N. G., & Jones, J. A. (2009). Locating the extrema of fungible regression weights. *Psychometrika, 74,* 589–602.

Part III
Understanding Internal Structures
of Language Assessments

Chapter 10
Developing Summary Content Scoring Criteria for University L2 Writing Instruction in Japan

Yasuyo Sawaki

Abstract This study examined the functioning of two types of summary content scoring methods (content point scores and a holistic summary content rating scale called Integration) for low- to medium-stakes uses in university L2 academic writing instruction in Japan from the perspective of Bachman and Palmer's (*Language assessment in practice*, Oxford University Press, Oxford, 2010) assessment use argument (AUA) framework. Results of a multivariate generalizability theory analysis of summaries written by 130 Japanese university students suggested a satisfactory level of score dependability of the Integration rating scale for the intended uses, supporting the rating consistency warrant for the assessment record claim in the AUA, while the evidence concerning the score dependability of the content point scores was mixed. Meanwhile, summary content scores based on both scoring methods were distinct from a language quality score. This suggests that employing either one with the language quality rating would enhance the representation of the summary writing construct, supporting the meaningfulness warrant for the test score interpretation claim in the AUA.

Introduction

The last decade witnessed a rapid increase of studies that examined the process and product of L2 learners' performance on academic writing tasks that require the incorporation of information from a source text(s) into written responses. Among them is summary writing, a frequent and important language use task type in the academic domain (e.g., Rosenfeld, Leung, & Oltman, 2001). Summarization is involved in many academic writing tasks such as annotated bibliography and source-based research paper writing. In performing such tasks, succinct and yet accurate representation of the source text content is critical because summarization serves as a vehicle for building, demonstrating, and sharing disciplinary knowledge in the target language use domain (TLU domain; Bachman & Palmer, 1996). Indeed, some

Y. Sawaki (✉)
Waseda University, Tokyo, Japan
e-mail: ysawaki@waseda.jp

© Springer Nature Singapore Pte Ltd. 2020
G. J. Ockey and B. A. Green (eds.), *Another Generation of Fundamental Considerations in Language Assessment*, https://doi.org/10.1007/978-981-15-8952-2_10

153

recent L2 assessment studies have indicated the critical role source-text comprehension plays in integrated writing performance (Plakans & Gebril, 2012; Sawaki, Quinlan, & Lee, 2013). Thus, scoring learner summary task responses specifically for source-text content representation would illuminate the importance of this critical L2 academic literacy skill that deserves more attention of learners and their teachers. Despite this, previous L2 integrated writing assessment studies focusing on summary content or its relationship to various measures of writing ability are relatively limited in number (Plakans, 2015). A potential reason might be the oft-adopted conceptualization of summarization in L2 assessment as a measure of writing ability that contributes to a writing score, not to a comprehension score.

In order to address the research gap above, the present study explored the functioning of criterion-referenced summary content scoring criteria. This study is part of a larger research project that aimed to design, develop, and validate summarization rating scales for academic writing instruction at a university in Japan. The results reported herein were obtained in the initial stage of the project that focused on low- to medium-stakes uses of the proposed scoring criteria. Previously there was no standard assessment criteria in use for the source-based writing component of the curriculum. Thus, the aims of designing rating scales including those discussed in this paper were to promote instructors' and students' understanding of the instructional goals and to streamline the criteria for learner feedback, course grading, and evaluating instructional effectiveness. The entire project employed Bachman and Palmer's (2010) Assessment Use Argument (AUA) as the theoretical framework for building a validity argument for using the rating scales. While argument-based approaches to test validation including the AUA have often been applied to high-stakes assessment settings (e.g., Chapelle, Enright, & Jamieson, 2008), Bachman and Damböck (2018) suggest their relevance to classroom-based assessment settings as well. In this phase of the project, two types of scoring criteria were compared against each other concerning two fundamental measurement issues. One is the degree to which the two types of scoring criteria compare to each other in score dependability, relevant to the assessment record claim (Claim 4). The other is the relationships among the summary content scoring criteria to a scale of language quality, which corresponds to the test score interpretation claim (Claim 3). The ultimate goal of this initial investigation was to explore an optimum approach to assessing summarization performance that promotes learning.

Literature Review

Constructs

Explicitly defining the target assessment construct is a central tenet that determines the interpretability of test scores in Bachman and Palmer's (2010) AUA cited above. Various empirical studies addressing the convergent and discriminant validity of language measures that Bachman and his associates conducted over the years employing multitrait-multimethod analyses and factor analyses (e.g., Bachman, Davidson, Ryan & Choi, 1995; Bachman & Palmer, 1981, 1982) furthered our understanding that L2 language ability comprises a range of highly correlated yet distinct subconstructs. This position has been supported by a number of subsequent factor analytic studies of L2 ability measures across different modalities (e.g., Kunnan, 1995; Llosa, 2007; Sasaki, 1996; Sawaki, Stricker, & Oranje, 2009; Shin, 2005).

The multicomponential nature of language ability is particularly relevant to the present investigation because whether a psychometrically distinct subconstruct of summary writing can be identified is essential in designing performance feedback that sheds light on multiple, critical aspects of summarization performance. A study that supported this direction is Sawaki et al.'s (2013) confirmatory factor analysis of the TOEFL iBT integrated writing task performance data. By modeling analytic content and language scores and automated measures of writing for the integrated writing task along with the TOEFL iBT reading and listening section data, Sawaki et al. identified correlated yet distinct factors for comprehension/content, productive vocabulary, and sentence conventions. This result suggests that combining content assessment criteria with conventional writing measures may yield meaningful performance feedback on source-based writing performance. However, given the limited number of investigations in this area, further research is required to explore how source-text comprehension should be operationalized, how content scoring criteria should be designed, and how consistently such criteria can be applied to scoring learner responses.

The Process of Text Comprehension and Summary Production

In operationalizing the construct of L2 summary writing, a thorough understanding of the process involved in the comprehension of a source text and the generation of its gist is required. To date, many studies relevant to this issue have been conducted in the fields of text processing and L1/L2 reading. By far the most influential theoretical framework applied to previous summarization studies is Kintsch and van Dijk's text comprehension and production process model (Kintsh & van Dijk, 1978; van Dijk & Kintsch, 1983; Kintsch, 1998). Kintsch (1998) describes how the reader/listener develops a text gist (macrostructure), an abstract semantic map of main ideas in a text resulting from cyclical processing of semantic links across propositions. Kintsch and van Dijk also explicated the operations a comprehender might employ to generate the macrostructure as a set of macrorules. They are (1) *deletion,* or omitting unnecessary details; (2) *generalization*, or substituting a group of ideas with a superordinate expression; and (3) *construction,* or creating a superordinate expression that combines different pieces of information across sentences and paragraphs. Once the gist is constructed, the comprehender can then generate a recall or summary of it through reproducing and reconstructing the source text information as well as making metastatements about it, along with potential transformations of the original information in the source text (e.g., paraphrasing).

Following Kintsch and van Dijk's (1978) model above, previous L1/L2 summarization studies examined the content of learner-produced summaries generally by taking two approaches. One of them focused on the coverage and accuracy of important pieces of information. For this purpose, a source text is segmented first into smaller meaning units such as propositions and idea units (Carrell, 1985; Kroll, 1977). Then, learner summary responses are scored for the coverage and accuracy of relatively important meaning units (e.g., Cordero-Ponce, 2000; Hare & Borchardt, 1984; Johns & Mayes, 1990; Kim, 2001; Winograd, 1984). The other approach focused on the use of Kintsch and van Dijk's (1978) macrorules described above. In this approach, a scoring key that identifies specific points in the source text to which the macrorules could be applied is prepared. Each summary protocol can then be scored for appropriate macrorule application frequencies (e.g., Brown & Day, 1983; Cordero-Ponce, 2000; Hare & Borchardt, 1984; Johns & Mayes, 1990; Kim, 2001; Winograd, 1984).

Previous research adopting these two approaches explicated the nature of summarization performance, such as distinguishing characteristics between expert/experienced summarizers and novices in the selection of information from the source text and application of the macrorules (e.g., Brown & Day, 1983; Winograd, 1984) as well as the trainability of learners for macrorule use as summarization strategies (Brown & Day, 1983; Cordero-Ponce, 2000; Hare & Borchardt, 1984). Despite these contributions, however, these scoring methods have not been applied directly to L2 writing assessment. For one reason, many of these studies were conducted either in L1 reading/writing or L2 reading comprehension research, involving summaries written in L1s of the summary writers. Another reason is the resource-intensive nature of the content analyses of summary protocols required (e.g., text segmentation to meaning units, analyzing each summary for instances of macrorule use), which limits the practicality of the two methods above for day-to-day assessment use.

Developing Content Assessment Criteria for L2 Summary Writing

Compared to the summary content scoring methods developed in the text processing and L1/L2 reading literature reviewed above, those proposed in the recent L2 assessment literature are more practical in nature. Notably, such methods do not rely heavily on the resource-intensive process of segmenting summary protocols into smaller meaning units or conducting their content analyses. Instead, the basis of many approaches of this type is an empirical analysis of summaries written by a group of experts (but see Yu, 2007) to identify specific points in the source text covered in high proportions of the expert summaries. The empirically derived list of important

Table 10.1 Summary scoring criteria employed in previous studies

Author (year)	L1/L2	Main ideas	Gist representation	Paraphrasing
Cohen (1993)	L1	Content points		N/A
Sawaki (2003)	L1	Main idea coverage	Integration	N/A
		Main idea accuracy		
Yu (2007)	L1 & L2	Right statement credit	Summary-source text relationship	
Li (2014)	L2	Main idea coverage	Integration	Source use
Sawaki et al. (2013)	L2	Specific points	Framing point	N/A
Yamanishi et al. (2019)	L2	Content (selection of main ideas)		Paraphrase quantity
				Paraphrase quality

content points can then be transformed into scoring schemes that assess summary content from different perspectives. Table 10.1 shows how summary content was operationalized in previous L2 assessment studies. While there are variations in the breadth of the construct definition, in general, scoring criteria employed in these studies tapped into three major subconstructs. One of them is main idea coverage and accuracy, which were assessed in the form of separate scores assigned to individual content points or a holistic score for the overall effectiveness of main idea representation. A second component concerns the appropriateness of text gist representation. The Integration rating scale adopted by Sawaki (2003) and Li (2014) concerned effective macrorule applications (Kintsch & van Dijk, 1978), while other studies also examined different aspects of text gist representation. Another aspect assessed in three of these studies is paraphrasing, an optional transformation that may take place in summary writing (Kintsch & van Dijk, 1978). While not treated as a focal quality in reading comprehension studies (e.g., Cohen, 1993; Sawaki, 2003), paraphrasing is a key component of the construct from the writing perspective because representing source-text gist in one's own words, without plagiarism, is a critical academic literacy skill. Previous L2 integrated writing studies on source use also have suggested the frequent use of effective paraphrasing as a feature distinguishing high-scoring learners from low-scoring learners (e.g., Cumming et al., 2005; Gebril & Plakans, 2013; Plakans & Gebril, 2013).

As can be seen above, various efforts to design criteria for assessing content of learner-produced summaries have been made during the last two decades. It is fair to say, however, that the empirical evidence supporting the construct validity and scoring consistency for those assessment criteria is limited. First, while the construct of summary writing may comprise multiple, conceptually distinct dimensions from one another, more studies investigating their psychometric distinctness are in order. For instance, the observed spearman's ρ correlations among the Content,

Paraphrase Quantity, Paraphrase Quality, and Language ratings reported by Yamanishi et al. (2019) suggested their relative distinctness from one another, but the analysis was based on a small sample (n = 16). Meanwhile, correlation coefficients among multiple measures of summary content reported in other studies were extremely high (e.g., observed correlations ranging from 0.88 to 0.90 in Yu, 2007; virtually unity universe-score correlations based on generalizability theory in Sawaki, 2003). These results suggest the need to identify an optimal grain size at which feedback regarding summary content should be provided to learners.

Second, only some of the studies reported score reliability of the proposed scoring criteria, while the available reliability estimates are mixed. Specifically, Cohen (1993) articulated inherent difficulties in scoring summary responses based on his results showing varying degrees of inter-rater consistency across different content points included in his scoring key developed for Hebrew-speaking EFL learners. While some other studies reported higher inter-rater consistency reliability estimates (Sawaki, 2003; Sawaki et al., 2013; Yu, 2007), more investigations into rating consistency for summary content scoring are in order.

With this background, the present study addressed two research questions relevant to the test score interpretation claim and the assessment record claim in Bachman and Palmer's (2010) AUA. The first research question concerns score dependability, which hinges on inter-rater consistency in terms of rating severity and rank-ordering consistency of examinees in criterion-referenced assessment. Thus, empirical evidence supporting an acceptable level of score dependability for the intended score uses provides backing for the inter-rater consistency warrant that elaborates on the assessment record claim (Warrant 6, Claim 4). The second research question focuses on the relationships among analytic scores on summarization content and language quality. Demonstrating that these scoring criteria tap into empirically distinct dimensions of summarization performance provides backing for a meaningfulness warrant that specifies the need to assess aspects of summarization performance that are relevant to the target construct (Warrant A4, Claim 3).

1. How dependable are summary content ratings assigned by Japanese EFL writing instructors?
2. To what extent and in what ways do different types of summary content and language quality scoring criteria relate to one another?

Methods

Participants

Participants of this study were 130 undergraduate English majors at a private university in Tokyo. At the time of their study participation, all students were enrolled in an academic writing course as a second-year requirement or an elective TOEFL preparation course, which were part of the EAP curriculum offered to prepare English majors for English-medium instruction (EMI) courses. Prior to this study, the courses had covered summarization. Therefore, the participants were reasonably familiar with the notion of summary writing. The mean independent essay score obtained from the Criterion® Writing Program (ETS) for placement into the 2nd-year writing course was 4.11 on the 6-point scale ($SD = 1.01$). The mean TOEFL ITP score for the second-year students was 500.3 ($SD = 49.4$).

All raters who scored the learners' responses were native speakers of Japanese. Six of them were university faculty members of EFL and one was a doctoral student specializing in L2 writing. All of them had extensive experience teaching L2 writing at the high school or undergraduate level, and five of them were instructors of the academic writing and TOEFL preparation courses described above.

Materials

Two summary writing tasks, each based on a single source text, were employed in this study. The source texts (Texts A and B) were adopted from the reading section of previously administered Eiken Grade 2 test forms. Eiken, developed and administered by Eiken Foundation of Japan, is a suite of English language proficiency certification tests used primarily in Japan. According to the Eiken website (http://ste peiken.org/), the Grade 2 test corresponds to the B1 level of the Common European Framework of Reference for Languages (Council of Europe, 2001). These texts were selected from a larger pool of publicly available Eiken Grade 2 reading test materials on the Eiken website and in an Eiken test preparation book (Seibido, 2016) due to their comparability in terms of the topic (both were on new environmental technologies) as well as some key linguistic features (rhetorical structure, length, numbers of paragraphs/sentences, vocabulary level, and readability), as shown in Table 10.2. The directions for the task were provided in Japanese, instructing the participant to write a summary of the source text of around 60 words in length in English. Also included in the directions were to use the participant's own words and to avoid including his/her own opinions. Note-taking and dictionary use were allowed.

Table 10.2 Linguistic features of the source texts for the summary tasks

Task	A	B
Rhetorical structure	Problem/solution	
Length (in words)	345	371
Paragraphs/sentences	4/21	4/20
Vocabulary level	4,000	4,000
Readability (Flesch-Kinkaid Grade Level)	9.0	9.5

Procedures

The summary tasks were required writing assignments in the courses. Each student completed a summary task based either on Text A or Text B randomly assigned to them in class or as a take-home assignment. All students read the source texts provided on paper, word-processed their summaries, and submitted them via a web-based learning management system (LMS) within 40 min. The project staff visited each class to request permissions for analyzing the students' task responses for this study. Only data from 130 students (80.2% of all students enrolled) who agreed to make their data available to this study were analyzed. While the students received grades for these tasks from their respective course instructors, the scoring for this study was conducted independently from course activities by compiling summary responses across classes for blind scoring. Thus, the obtained scores did not affect students' course grades in any way.

Scoring Criteria Development

As mentioned above, two types of summary content assessment criteria were developed in two steps. In Step 1, following previous studies that empirically derived scoring criteria based on expert summaries (Brown & Day, 1983; Cohen, 1993; Winograd, 1984; Yu, 2007), the author analyzed summaries of the two source texts written by the seven raters and three additional doctoral students in applied linguistics to identify content points shared among them and develop a draft master outline of each source text. Then, the outlines were finalized based on the discussion of their correspondence to the expert summaries among the raters. The resulting master outlines comprised three main points for Text A and four for Text B. For each text, the outline also included a framing point representing the problem/solution structure depicted in each source text, following Sawaki et al. (2013).

In Step 2, two types of summary content scoring criteria were developed employing the agreed-upon master outlines of the source texts. The first type, similar to the criteria employed by Cohen (1993), Sawaki et al. (2013), and Yu (2007), were scoring keys for assessing the coverage and accuracy of individual content points included in the master source-text outlines on the scale of 0–3 (Appendices A and B). A strength of this approach is that it enables the generation of specific feedback that identifies the exact locations of summary content problems. Some drawbacks are, however, the time required for scoring summaries for individual content points and its prompt-specific nature that makes it difficult to compare scoring results across different source texts.

The other type of scoring criteria, adapted from Li (2014) and Sawaki (2003), was a holistic four-point (1–4) scale for assessing overall content appropriateness (Appendix C). This rating scale, Integration, combined different aspects of summary content considered in the previous studies into one. The primary aspect assessed was the succinctness of the representation of the main ideas and their relationships reflective of appropriate macrorule use (Kintsch & van Dijk, 1978). Detailed rules for scoring the main ideas were developed for each text based on the master source-text outlines described above. Also taken into account in this holistic rating scale was the appropriateness of paraphrasing, where excessive verbatim copying was penalized. While a demerit of this approach is the loss of fine-grained information about different aspects of summary content, a notable advantage is that, unlike the content point scoring keys above, this holistic rating scale enables the comparison of scoring results across source texts.

In addition to the two types of summary content scoring criteria described above, a language quality rating scale was also devised. The rating scales focusing on the appropriateness and variety of vocabulary and syntactic structures employed by Li (2014) and Yamanishi et al. (2019) were adapted for developing a four-point (1–4) Language scale (Appendix D).

All scoring criteria were conceptualized as criterion-referenced. Score 2 on the content point scoring and Score 3 on the Integration and Language rating scales were designated as the provisional target levels for achievement in the EAP program.

Rater Training and Scoring

All seven raters attended a 1.5-day rater training session. At the beginning of the session, the author explained the purpose of this project and the two types of content scoring methods. Following this, the raters discussed and finalized the master outlines of the two source texts and developed detailed scoring rules for both types of summary content scoring methods, as described above. After that, they rated 10 sample student responses and discussed their scoring results and rationales for each scoring method, which resulted in further revisions of the initial scoring rules. As for the Language rating scale, the author explained the rating scales to the raters, followed by practice scoring of 10 sample summaries. After that, the raters discussed their rating results to resolve discrepancies in their understanding of the different score levels.

After the rater training session, the raters independently rated learner-produced summaries. Summaries based on each source text were randomly assigned to two blocks. Different rater pairs were assigned to each block for each of content point scoring, Integration scoring, and Language scoring. Two ratings were obtained for each summary on all the scoring criteria studied.

Analyses

Summaries based on the two texts were analyzed separately because the content points identified for each source text were not directly comparable across the texts. Descriptive statistics were calculated for individual scoring criteria. Then, to address the two research questions, a multivariate generalizability theory analysis (G theory; Brennan, 2001) was conducted. The software mGENOVA (Brennan, 1999) was used for the analysis. The design adopted for the G-theory analysis was the "subdividing" method employed by Lin (2017) and Xi (2007), where variance and covariance component estimates are first obtained for each block of responses scored by a specific rater pair, and the obtained estimates are averaged across blocks. This approach is particularly useful for a rating design such as the present one, where each rater pair scored only part of the examinee responses. This enables the modeling of the rater effect as crossed with other facets, generating more information than when it is modeled as nested within persons. In this study, the individual scoring methods were specified as the levels of the fixed facet, while persons (p) and raters (r) were modeled as random facets crossed with each other as well as with the fixed facet (the $p^\bullet \times r^\bullet$ design). A G study was conducted for this design for each block across all the scoring criteria, and then the decision study (D study) for two raters was conducted across the blocks.

Results

Table 10.3 presents descriptive statistics for all scoring criteria for each source text. As for the content point scores, while the means for Text A were generally higher than those for Text B, they were all close to the designated target level (Score 2). In contrast, concerning the Integration and Language mean ratings, those for the Language rating scales were consistently higher and closer to the target level (Score 3) than those for the Integration rating scale. Moreover, score variability was greater for the Integration rating scale than that for the Language rating scale for both texts. These results suggest the students' generally low and varied achievement levels on the aspects of summary writing performance that the Integration rating scale tapped into (i.e., paraphrasing and appropriate macrorule use for succinct and balanced representation of the gist).

Tables 10.4, 10.5, 10.6 and 10.7 summarize results of the D study for the $p^\bullet \times r^\bullet$ design with two raters. Table 10.4 presents the estimates of the index of dependability (Φ) for each scoring criterion. These results are discussed along with Table 10.5, which presents the proportions of the total score variance explained by variance

Table 10.3 Descriptive statistics for the content and language scoring criteria

Text (n)	Statistic	Content point (0–3)					Integration (1–4)	Language (1–4)
		1	2	3	4	Frame		
A (74)	Mean	2.28	2.32	2.01		2.43	1.95	2.82
	SD	0.72	0.59	0.66		0.60	0.71	0.61
B (56)	Mean	1.88	1.97	1.95	2.01	2.27	1.90	2.69
	SD	0.75	0.82	0.78	0.83	0.43	0.76	0.59

Table 10.4 Index of dependability (Φ) for $p^\bullet \times r^\bullet$ decision studies (2 raters)

Text	Sample (n)	Content point (0–3)					Integration (1–4)	Language (1–4)
		1	2	3	4	Frame		
A	All (74)	0.75	0.65	0.62		0.64	0.76	0.54
B	All (56)	0.77	0.72	0.71	0.76	0.14	0.82	0.53

Table 10.5 D-study variance component estimates for the $p^\bullet \times r^\bullet$ design (2 raters)

	Text	Source of variation	Content point					Integ	Lang
			1	2	3	4	Frame		
% variance explained	A	Persons (p)	74.6	65.1	62.3		63.5	76.4	53.8
		Raters (r)	4.3	8.1	2.9		0.5	0.0	14.9
		pr, e	21.1	26.8	34.9		36.0	23.6	31.4
		Total	100.0	100.0	100.0		100.0	100.0	100.0
	B	Persons (p)	77.0	71.6	71.2	76.2	14.2	81.7	53.4
		Raters (r)	0.0	6.6	7.4	3.2	25.9	0.1	4.4
		pr, e	23.0	21.8	21.4	20.6	59.8	18.3	42.1
		Total	100.0	100.0	100.0	100.0	100.0	100.0	100.0

Notes p = persons, r = raters, e = error, Integ = Integration, Lang = Language

Table 10.6 Universe-score correlations across the scoring criteria (Text A)

	P1	P2	P3	Frame	Integ.
Point 2	−0.01				
Point 3	0.07	0.23			
Frame	0.75	0.40	0.64		
Integration	0.18	−0.01	0.22	0.25	
Language	0.17	0.28	0.75	0.55	0.35

Table 10.7 Universe-score correlations across the scoring criteria (Text B)

	P1	P2	P3	P4	Frame	Integ.
Point 2	0.09					
Point 3	0.45	0.47				
Point 4	0.25	0.02	0.14			
Frame	*1.38*	*0.85*	*1.21*	*0.90*		
Integration	0.01	−0.18	−0.09	0.15	*0.06*	
Language	0.49	0.23	0.15	0.46	*0.79*	0.28

Note The universe-score correlations involving the framing point score (highlighted in italic) will not be interpreted due to its extremely low dependability (Table 10.5)

components for persons (representing learner ability differences), raters (representing rater severity differences), and person-by-rater interaction (representing learner rank-ordering differences confounded with undifferentiated error). First, a great variation is observed in the size of the Φ coefficient across the content point scores. They were mostly in the low 0.60 s to the mid 0.70 s, while one estimate (for the framing point for Text B) was extremely small (0.14). As seen in Table 10.5, the relatively low estimates for Point 2 for Text A and Points 2 and 3 for Text B were partly due to non-negligible rater severity differences accounting for 6.6–8.1% of the total score variance, and those for Point 3 and the framing point for Text A to sizable person rank-ordering differences across raters confounded with error (34.9–36.0%). The extremely low coefficient for the framing point for Text B was due to both large rater severity differences (25.9%) and person rank-ordering differences confounded with undifferentiated error (59.8%). An inspection of the scoring results revealed a peculiar pattern observed for one rater, who awarded the lowest rating (1) to many summaries to which the other rater awarded higher scores (2 or 3). While written comments provided by the raters involved were few, this may reflect discrepancies in the understanding of the scoring rules among them. Second, the coefficients for the Integration rating scale were moderate to high (0.76–0.82), featured by negligible rater severity differences as well as relatively small person-by-rater rank-ordering differences confounded with error. As for the Language rating scale, the phi-coefficients (in Table 10.4) were quite low (0.53–0.54). As shown in Table 10.5, this was found to be due to the presence of quite sizable proportions of the observed total score variance explained by rater severity differences (particularly for Text A) and the person rank-ordering differences across raters confounded with undifferentiated error (particularly for Text B).

Tables 10.6 and 10.7 present the universe-score correlations across the scoring criteria for each text. Note that some of the universe-score correlations involving the framing point for Text B (Table 10.7) were out of range, exceeding 1.0. These are partly attributable to the extremely small person variance component estimate for this framing point (Table 10.5), which contributes to the calculation of the universe-score correlations. Given the resulting extremely low dependability for this framing point, the universe-score correlations involving it will not be considered further. Some notable patterns can be observed in the remaining universe-score correlations for both texts. First, the correlations among the individual content points varied, ranging from near zero to moderate. Second, most of the correlations between the individual content points with the corresponding framing point were small to moderate, while those between these two types of content points and the Integration rating scale were minimal (from −0.01 to 0.25 for Text A, and from −0.18 to 0.15 for Text B). Third, the universe-score correlations of the Language rating scale to the individual content points and the framing point (from 0.17 to 0.75 for Text A, and from 0.15 to 0.49 for Text B) and the Integration rating scale (0.35 for Text A and 0.28 for Text B) were low to moderate, suggesting that both types of content scoring criteria tapped into psychometrically distinguishable dimensions from the Language rating scale.

Discussion

The purpose of the present study was to examine the functioning of two types of criterion-referenced summary content scoring methods (a content point scoring key and a holistic rating scale of overall summary content called Integration) developed for university EAP writing instruction in Japan. A multivariate G-theory analysis was conducted on summaries written by 130 Japanese university students to address two specific research questions. In terms of the first research question concerning score consistency, the Integration rating scale consistently exhibited a higher level of score dependability across source texts than content point scores. Thus, from the perspective of Bachman and Palmer's (2010) AUA, the Integration scale provided the stronger backing for the rating consistency warrant for the assessment record claim (Claim 4). As for the second research question concerning the interrelationships among the two types of summary content scoring methods and a language quality rating scale, their universe-score correlations were generally low to moderate. Moreover, the overall patterns of the relationships suggested that (1) the Integration rating was quite distinct from the content point ratings despite some conceptual overlap between them and that (2) the content measures were weakly correlated to but psychometrically distinct from the Language rating. Interpreted from the perspective of the test score interpretation claim (Claim 3) in the AUA, the above results support the discriminant validity of both types of summary content scoring methods from a language quality score, providing backing for the meaningfulness warrant for this claim. This in turn suggests that devising summary content scoring criteria such as those examined in this study would enhance construct representation, providing support for the meaningfulness warrant for this claim.

At least three issues concerning the findings are worth further discussion. First, the divergent G-theory analysis results between the two source texts, particularly the aberrant pattern observed in the inter-factor correlations for Text B, is worth noting. As indicated above, this text involved more content points than Text A. It may be the case that the length limit for the task (around 60 words) was too stringent for Text B, which might have resulted in unwanted rater variations in applying the criteria for assessing the coverage and accuracy of individual content points. Second, the relative instability of the content point scores compared to the Integration rating scale in terms of score dependability requires further exploration. These findings for the content point scores were consistent with Cohen's (1993), while those for the Integration rating mirrored Yu's (2007) results on his holistic rating scale. One possible explanation for this contrasting finding between the two methods is the difference in their grain size. More specifically, the relative stability of the Integration rating scale might reflect the fact that multiple pieces of information regarding summary content contribute to this rating, while only one piece of information contributes to each content point score and is affected greatly by discrepancies in raters' application of specific scoring rules. However, given that other studies employing content point scoring have reported higher rater consistency estimates (e.g., Sawaki et al., 2013;

Yu, 2007), further investigations are required to explore factors affecting the rating consistency.

Third, the nature of the construct covered by the Integration rating scale requires further exploration. As noted above, this rating scale conceptually overlaps the content point scores. However, given its relative distinctness from the other content scores, the contribution of the other two components included in the construct definition (paraphrasing and macrorule use) appears to be quite large. One point of consideration is whether paraphrasing should be part of this construct (similar to Yu, 2007) or should be scored separately as done by Li (2014) and Yamanishi et al. (2019). In this study, paraphrasing was included in the Integration scale for three reasons. One was for practicality and administrative efficiency in scoring for summary content. Second, even if learners receive a separate rating(s) on paraphrasing, the feedback may not necessarily be specific enough for them to understand the nature of the problem. Thus, learners might benefit from receiving more specific feedback that identifies instances of insufficient paraphrasing, along with the holistic score. The third was to avoid crediting a summary protocol that selects important pieces of source-text information appropriately but does so by excessive copying. In a sense, the inclusion of paraphrasing in the Integration rating scale signifies that paraphrasing is an integral part of the construct of summary content. However, an additional analysis of learner summary responses reported elsewhere identified great variation across students in the degree of reliance on copying. While this variability seemed to have contributed to suppressing the universe-score correlations of the Integration rating scale to the others, the presence of this variability might also suggest that learners may benefit from receiving a paraphrasing score separately to explicate the nature of the problem.

Despite the fact that this study yielded some useful insights into the functioning of the two summary content scoring methods, the results should not be overinterpreted due to some limitations in the design of the study. One is the between-subject design, where each participant wrote a summary of only one source text to ensure practicality. Having the students complete both tasks as in a repeated-measures design would have allowed to take full advantage of the multivariate G-theory analysis. Moreover, this study employed only a single measure of writing ability (language quality). Further studies should examine the relationship of summary content measures to a wider range of writing measures to investigate the nature of the summary writing construct from a broader perspective.

Conclusions, Implications, and Future Directions

The present study yielded some initial empirical evidence supporting the use of criterion-referenced summary content scoring criteria for low- to medium-stakes purposes in university EAP writing instruction in Japan based on Bachman and Palmer's (2010) assessment use argument (AUA) framework. The results showed that, when content point scores and a holistic content rating were compared, the latter provided stronger backing for both the assessment record consistency claim and the meaningfulness warrant for the test score interpretation claim. In addition, the present results suggest that combining summary content and language quality rating scales would enable the provision of dependable and yet meaningful feedback from distinct perspectives for the intended uses in the target EAP instructional program. While the present study suggests the limited dependability of the content point scoring, it does not necessarily mean, however, that they do not have a place in summary writing instruction. One possibility is, for instance, to supplement Integration and Language rating results with descriptive feedback on the content point coverage (e.g., instructor's written comments).

As potential future directions, score dependability and construct validity of the Integration and Language rating scales should be explored further to enhance the AUA for their uses in this academic writing instruction context. For instance, further information regarding rater behaviors and the functioning of the scoring criteria should be obtained, for example, from a many-facet Rasch measurement analysis (Linacre, 1989), and a more thorough investigation into the convergent/discriminant validity of subconstructs for summary writing based on factor analyses. More-over, stakeholder perspectives are essential in examining how introducing summary content scoring criteria such as those considered in this study could facilitate the development of summary writing ability. In this respect, empirical investigations such as the above should be combined with learners' and teachers' perceptions of the usefulness of the summary content scoring criteria for learning and teaching as well as how they are implemented as part of L2 writing instruction in the classroom.

Acknowledgements This study was funded by the Japan Society for the Promotion of Science (JSPS) Grant-in-Aid for Scientific Research (C) awarded to the author (No. 16K02983). The author's special thanks go to Yutaka Ishii and Tatsuro Tahara at Waseda University for their help in various aspects of data collection and organizing scoring sessions. Part of the results reported in this chapter also appeared in Sawaki and Xi (2019).

Appendix A: Scoring Criteria for Each Specific Main Point

Score	Description
3	The response covers the given main point fully and accurately
2	The response covers the given main point only partially or inaccurately. However, the discrepancy is minor, not hindering the comprehension of the point
1	The response covers the given main point only partially or inaccurately. The discrepancy is major, hindering the comprehension of the point
0	The response does not cover the given point

Appendix B: Scoring Criteria for Each Framing Point

Score	Description
3	The response represents the relationships among main points of the text fully and accurately
	The representation of the different main points is well-balanced, allowing the understanding of the overall text meaning
2	The response represents the relationships among main points of the text only partially or inaccurately
	The representation of the different main points is not well-balanced
	For either or both of the above, the discrepancy from the text is minor, not hindering the understanding of the overall text meaning
1	The response represents the relationships among main points of the text only partially or inaccurately
	The representation of the different main points is not well-balanced
	For either or both of the above, the discrepancy from the text is major, hindering the understanding of the overall text meaning
0	The response does not cover the given point

Appendix C: The Integration Rating Scale

Score	Description
4	The response demonstrates effective and appropriate integration throughout
3	The response demonstrates effective and appropriate integration most of the time
2	The response contains some effective integration, possibly with some instances of inappropriate use that obscure meaning
1	The response may contain some integration, but EITHER they are mostly inappropriate or misleading OR there is little evidence of the use of integration

Appendix D: The Language Rating Scale

Score	Description
4	The response demonstrates consistent control of language with syntactic variety and appropriate word choice
3	The response demonstrates control of language with syntactic variety and word choice most of the time
	There are occasional noticeable errors in structure or word form that are minor, not interfering with meaning
2	The response demonstrates inconsistent control of sentence formation and word choice
	There may be frequent noticeable errors in structure or word form that result in lack of clarity and obscurity of meaning
1	The response lacks control of vocabulary and/or grammar
	Meaning is obscure due to a number of minor and major errors

References

Bachman, L. F., & Damböck, B. (2018). *Language assessment for classroom teachers*. Oxford: Oxford University Press.

Bachman, L. F., Davidson, F., Ryan, K., & Choi, I.-C. (1995). *An Investigation into the comparability of two tests of English as a foreign language: The Cambridge-TOEFL comparability study*. Cambridge: University of Cambridge Local Examinations Syndicate and Cambridge University Press.

Bachman, L. F., & Palmer, A. (1981). The construct validation of the FSI oral interview. *Language Learning, 31*, 67–86.

Bachman, L. F., & Palmer, A. (1982). The construct validation of some components of communicative proficiency. *TESOL Quarterly, 16*, 449–465.

Bachman, L. F., & Palmer, A. (1996). *Language testing in practice*. Oxford: Oxford University Press.

Bachman, L. F., & Palmer, A. (2010). *Language assessment in practice*. Oxford: Oxford University Press.

Brennan, R. L. (1999). *mGENOVA, Version 2.0*. [Computer software].

Brennan, R. L. (2001). *Generalizability theory*. New York, NY: Springer.

Brown, A. L., & Day, J. D. (1983). Macrorules for summarizing texts: The development of expertise. *Journal of Verbal Learning and Verbal Behavior, 22*, 1–14.

Carrell, P. L. (1985). Facilitating ESL reading by teaching text structure. *TESOL Quarterly, 19*(4), 727–753.

Chapelle, C. A., Enright, M. K., & Jamieson, J. M. (2008). *Building a validity argument for the Test of English as a Foreign Language™*. New York, NY: Routledge.

Cohen, A. (1993). The role of instructions in testing summarizing ability. In D. Douglas & C. Chapelle (Eds.), *A new decade of language testing research* (pp. 132–160). Alexandria, VA: TESOL.

Cordero-Ponce, W. L. (2000). Summarization instruction: Effects on foreign language comprehension and summarization of expository texts. *Reading Research and Instruction, 39*(4), 329–350. https://doi.org/10.1080/19388070009558329.

Council of Europe. (2001). *Common European framework of references for languages: Learning, teaching, assessment*. Cambridge, UK: Cambridge University Press.

Cumming, A. H., Kantor, R., Baba, K., Eouanzoui, K., Erdosy, U. M., & James, M. (2005). *Analysis of discourse features and verification of scoring levels for independent and integrated prototype written tasks for the New TOEFL*. (TOEFL Monograph Series, No. MS-30). Princeton, NJ: ETS.

van Dijk, T. A., & Kintsch, W. (1983). *Strategies of discourse comprehension*. New York: Academic Press.

Gebril, A., & Plakans, L. (2013). Toward a transparent construct of reading-to-write tasks: The interface between discourse features and proficiency. *Language Assessment Quarterly, 10*(1), 9–27. https://doi.org/10.1080/15434303.2011.642040.

Hare, V. C., & Borchardt, K. M. (1984). Direct instruction of summarization skills. *Reading Research Quarterly, 20,* 62–78.

Johns, A. M., & Mayes, P. (1990). An analysis of summary protocols of university ESL students. *Applied Linguistics, 11*(3), 253–271.

Kim, S.-A. (2001). Characteristics of EFL readers' summary writing: A study with Korean university students. *Foreign Language Annals, 34*(6), 569–581.

Kintsch, W. (1998). *Comprehension: A paradigm for cognition*. Cambridge, U. K.: Cambridge University Press.

Kintsch, W., & van Dijk, T. A. (1978). Toward a model of text comprehension and production. *Psychological Review, 85,* 363–394.

Kroll, B. (1977). Combining ideas in written and spoken English: A look at subordination and coordination. In E. O. Keenan, & T. L. Bennett (Eds.), *Discourse across time and space*. Los Angeles, Calif.: University of Southern California, S.C.O.P.I.L. No. 5.

Kunnan, A. J. (1995). *Test taker characteristics and test performance: A structural modeling approach*. Cambridge: Cambridge University Press.

Li, J. (2014). Examining genre effects on test takers' summary writing performance. *Assessing Writing, 22,* 75–90.

Lin, C.-K. (2017). Working with sparse data in rated language tests: Generalizability theory applications. *Language Testing, 34*(2), 271–289.

Linacre, J. M. (1989). *Many-facet Rasch measurement*. Chicago, IL: MESA Press.

Llosa, L. (2007). Validating a standards-based classroom assessment of English proficiency: A multitrait-multimethod approach. *Language Testing, 24*(4), 489–515.

Plakans, L. (2015). Integrated second language writing assessment: Why? What? How? *Language and Linguistics Compass, 9*(4), 159–167. https://doi.org/10.1111/lnc3.12124.

Plakans, L., & Gebril, A. (2012). A close investigation into source use in integrated second language writing tasks. *Assessing Writing, 17,* 18–34.

Plakans, L., & Gebril, A. (2013). Using multiple texts in an integrated writing assessment: Source text use as a predictor of score. *Journal of Second Language Writing, 22,* 217–230.

Rosenfeld, M., Leung, S., & Oltman, P. K. (2001). *The reading, writing, speaking, and listening tasks important for academic success at the undergraduate and graduate levels* (TOEFL Monograph Series No. 21). Princeton, NJ: ETS.

Sasaki, M. (1996). *Second language proficiency, foreign language aptitude, and intelligence: Quantitative and qualitative analyses*. New York: Peter Lang.

Sawaki, Y. (2003). *A comparison of summarization and free recall as reading comprehension tasks in web-based assessment of Japanese as a foreign language*. Unpublished doctoral dissertation. University of California, Los Angeles.

Sawaki, Y., Quinlan, T., & Lee, Y.-W. (2013). Understanding learner strengths and weaknesses: Assessing performance on an integrated writing task. *Language Assessment Quarterly, 10*(1), 73–95.

Sawaki, Y., Stricker, L., & Oranje, A. (2009). Factor structure of the TOEFL Internet-based Test (TOEFL iBT). *Language Testing, 26,* 5–30.

Sawaki, Y., & Xi, X. (2019). Univariate generalizability theory in language assessment. In V. Aryadoust & M. Raquel (Eds.), *Quantitative data analysis for language assessment* (Vol. 1, pp. 30–53). New York: Routledge.

Seibido (Ed.). (2016). *Eiken nikyuu kako rokkai mondaishu'16 nendoban* [Retired six operational Eiken test forms, 2016 edition]. Tokyo: Author.

Shin, S.-K. (2005). Did they take the same test? Examinee language proficiency and the structure of language tests. *Language Testing, 22,* 31–57.

Winograd, P. N. (1984). Strategic difficulties in summarizing texts. *Reading Research Quarterly, 19*(4), 404–425.

Xi, X. (2007). Evaluating analytic scores for the TOEFL® Academic Speaking Test (TAST) for operational use. *Language Testing, 24*(2), 251–286.

Yamanishi, H., Ono, M., & Hijikata, Y. (2019). Developing a scoring rubric for L2 summary writing: a hybrid approach combining analytic and holistic assessment. *Language Testing in Asia, 9*(13), 1–22.

Yu, G. (2007). Students' voices in the evaluation of their written summaries: Empowerment and democracy for test takers? *Language Testing, 24*(4), 539–572.

Chapter 11
Consistency of Computer-Automated Scoring Keys Across Authors and Authoring Teams

Nathan T. Carr

Abstract This study relates to computer-automated scoring of limited-production tasks. It examines the extent to which scoring keys written by different authors are comparable, as well as the degree to which keys written by different teams of authors are comparable. Multivariate generalizability studies revealed that while a single-author scoring key may initially appear to provide a satisfactory level of scoring consistency, modeling a key author facet revealed that such keys can be insufficiently reliable or dependable for high-stakes decisions. This problem can be solved, however, by using authoring teams to draft the key. Qualitative descriptions of problems encountered with single-author scoring keys help to highlight some of the issues that should receive attention when training key authors.

Introduction

The present study involves the consistency of scores given to short-answer reading comprehension questions. Specifically, it considers the degree to which keys produced by different authors, and by different teams of authors, yield comparable scores. The study is rooted in several areas of Bachman's scholarly work. Specifically, it relates first to specifying criteria for correctness and procedures for scoring test responses, two of the components of his language task characteristic framework (Bachman, 1990; Bachman & Palmer, 1996, 2010). As a result, it also clearly relates to issues of validity and reliability, notions he has dealt with extensively in his research over the years, and which are included in the test usefulness framework (Bachman & Palmer, 1996) and subsumed within the assessment use argument framework (Bachman, 2005; Bachman & Palmer, 2010). Finally, the study involves automated scoring of a web-based constructed response test, a project that Bachman himself led (Bachman et al., 2000, 2002).

N. T. Carr (✉)
California State University, Fullerton, USA
e-mail: ncarr@fullerton.edu

© Springer Nature Singapore Pte Ltd. 2020
G. J. Ockey and B. A. Green (eds.), *Another Generation of Fundamental Considerations in Language Assessment*, https://doi.org/10.1007/978-981-15-8952-2_11

Literature Review

This section provides some background for the study, emphasizing how it has been informed by several areas of Bachman's writing. It then discusses the constructs assessed in the present study, provides some brief background on web-based testing (WBT), and gives an overview of computer-automated scoring (CAS) research as it relates to the present study. It concludes by posing the research questions addressed by this study.

Grounding of the Present Study in Bachman's Work

A noteworthy feature of Bachman's work has been his development of a systematic framework for describing test tasks, in both his theoretical work (Bachman, 1990; Bachman & Palmer, 1996, 2010; Bachman & Dambӧck, 2017) and in empirical studies grounded in that theory (e.g., Bachman, Davidson, Ryan, & Choi, 1995; Bachman, Davidson, & Milanovic, 1996; see also the example projects in Bachman & Palmer, 1996, 2010). Referred to initially as test method facets (Bachman, 1990; Bachman et al., 1995), a clear reference to generalizability theory (e.g., Brennan, 1983), the framework was briefly referred to as test method characteristics (Bachman, et al., 1996), before taking on the label of task characteristics (Bachman & Palmer, 1996, 2010), and is currently referred to as language task characteristics, test task characteristics, or simply task characteristics, depending on the context and audience.

The task characteristics framework includes five categories: characteristics of the setting, the rubric (instructions, structure, time allotment, and scoring or recording method), the input, the expected response, and the relationship between the input and the response (Bachman & Palmer, 1996, 2010). Elements of the scoring method or recording method of particular relevance to the present study include the criteria for correctness; the procedures for producing an assessment record (i.e., for scoring); and recorders (i.e., scorers/raters), which can include computer scoring algorithms. Clearly, concerns over differences among scoring keys produced to score a given test relate to these task characteristics.

Another important area of Bachman's thought has involved reliability and validity. In *Fundamental Considerations in Language Testing* (1990), he treated reliability and validation in separate chapters, but noted that reliability was necessary in order to achieve validity, and argued "that the investigation of reliability and validity can be viewed as complementary aspects of identifying, estimating, and interpreting different sources of variance in test scores" (pp. 238–239). Bachman here viewed validity as a unitary concept, following Messick (1989). In *Language Testing in Practice* (Bachman & Palmer, 1996), Bachman's thinking had evolved, treating reliability as a necessary but insufficient precondition for construct validity, and seeing both as necessary qualities for test usefulness.

The subsequently developed assessment use argument (AUA) framework (Bachman, 2005; Bachman & Palmer, 2010; Bachman & Damböck, 2017) is very much concerned with the same issues as previous conceptualizations. However, rather than conceptualizing reliability and validity as independent concepts, it focuses instead on types of evidence supporting the use of a test for a particular purpose, including evidence for the consistency of scores (Claim 4). It also includes evidence for the meaningfulness of score interpretations—i.e., that interpretations of scores (or assessment records) provide stakeholders with information about the ability to be assessed—and evidence for the relevance of interpretations—the degree to which score interpretations provide stakeholders with the information necessary to make decisions (elements of Claim 3). However the concerns are formulated, though, the underlying issues are clearly the focus of the present study.

Finally, the statistical methodology used in this study was primarily generalizability theory. Generalizability theory has been used rather frequently in language assessment in recent decades, including in several of Bachman's own studies (e.g., Bachman, et al., 1996; Bachman, Lynch, & Mason, 1995), and was included in his book on statistical analyses (Bachman, 2004).

Constructs Assessed in the Present Study

The test used in the present study was the reading portion of the Web-Based English as a Second Language Placement Examination (ESLPE), developed and eventually used at the University of California, Los Angeles. Bachman was the ESLPE Director at that time, and starting in the summer of 1999, launched a project to convert the existing written test to a web-based format. The WBT system, dubbed the Web-Based Language Assessment System (WebLAS), was used by Japanese and Korean placement testing projects at UCLA as well, and for Spanish placement testing at the University of California, Davis (Pardo-Ballester, 2010). WebLAS contained modules for creating tasks, combining them into tests, computer-automated scoring of limited production responses (Bachman & Palmer, 1996, 2010), and storage and reporting of scores (Bachman et al., 2000, 2002). While the system could handle multiple-choice items, there was a strong desire, particularly within the ESL portion of the project, to use as many limited production items as possible for assessing reading and listening.

The target language use domain (Bachman & Palmer, 1996) for the reading portion of the ESLPE WebLAS was the use of English in academic coursework, specifically reading introductory-level academic texts in English. The construct to be measured included the areas of language ability required to comprehend academic texts in English. These were defined according to type of processing required, ranging from higher-level to lower-level processing, and ranging from more implicit (e.g., making inferences and applying information) to more explicit (e.g., grasping basic syntactic and lexical relationships). Because of the range of types of processing required, the reading construct was treated as consisting of a number of aspects or components. These were grouped into higher-level processing, which engages the areas of language ability required to process implicitly marked information in the text, and lower-level processing, which involves areas of language ability that are required to process explicitly marked information in the text. These components are listed in Table 11.1, along with the associated task formats (see Carr, 2011b) used to assess them.

Lexical knowledge was not explicitly targeted by the test. However, test takers' ability to acquire lexical knowledge by using knowledge of syntax and cohesion to infer the meaning of lexical items was assessed through the "vocabulary in context" items. Furthermore, the test as a whole required a certain minimum overall level of lexical knowledge in order to comprehend the passages. Similarly, the test did not assess knowledge of syntax directly, but rather presupposed and required the ability to process syntax in order to derive meaning accurately from the passages.

Table 11.1 Summary of Reading Construct Components and Their Associated Task Formats

Higher-level processing		Lower-level processing	
Components	Task formats used to assess	Components	Task formats used to assess
• Reading for specific details • Making inferences • Inferring the meaning of unfamiliar vocabulary from the context • Applying concepts from the text • Identifying causality • Evaluating information and arguments • Identifying point of view • Separating fact from opinion	• Limited production items • Selected-response items	• Knowledge of/sensitivity to syntax • Knowledge of/sensitivity to cohesion	• Rational-deletion gap-fill passages • Limited-production items • Selected-response items
• Knowledge of/sensitivity to rhetorical organization	• Incomplete outline tasks		

Web-Based Testing

Web-based testing (WBT) is perhaps the most promising form of computer-based testing (CBT), offering advantages in terms of logistics, design, cost, and convenience (Roever, 2001). Furthermore, like other forms of CBT, it facilitates the use of multimedia (Carr, 2011a; Chalhoub-Deville & Deville, 1999; Ockey, 2007), as well as the use of task formats going beyond simple multiple-choice questions (Huff & Sireci, 2001; Ockey, 2009; Sawaki, 2001). In particular, by transmitting responses to a central computer, WBT facilitates automated scoring, which makes limited production tasks more feasible (Carr, 2008; Carr & Xi, 2010). Such tasks are presumably stronger indicators of test takers' true levels of communicative language ability. This is not a criticism of selected response tasks, but it does seem likely that including additional task formats might yield better results.

Research on Computer-Automated Scoring

It is worth noting that a great deal of the research in the area of computer-automated scoring (CAS) has been done outside the field of language assessment. In language assessment, however, CAS research has focused on three areas (see Carr, 2008, 2014; Carr & Xi, 2010; Chapelle & Chung, 2010; Leacock & Chodorow, 2003; Xi, 2008, 2010): automated essay scoring, speech recognition, and limited production tasks, with automated essay scoring receiving the most attention thus far. CAS for limited production tasks seems to have received much less attention than the other areas. This is somewhat surprising. The technical requirements for limited-production CAS are far simpler than for the other two approaches, particularly if regular expression or key word matching is used, and it is possible to develop a system without the costs associated with developing AES or speech recognition systems, and without having to license commercially developed systems. As noted previously, limited-production tasks are quite desirable in comprehension testing, since they provide an alternative to multiple-choice questions. It seems clear that they would also be useful in some cases for assessing grammar or vocabulary knowledge.

Most previous studies of computer-automated scoring (CAS) have focused on the comparability of human- and computer-produced scores (Clauser, Kane, & Swanson, 2002; Williamson, 2009), but without examining the dependability of scores yielded by different algorithms. A few studies have gone beyond this by not only comparing scores from CAS systems to those from human raters, but also investigating the accuracy of scoring and/or feedback offered by CAS systems (e.g., Bennett, Steffen, Singley, Morley, & Jacquemin, 1997; Hoang & Kunnan, 2016; Liu & Kunnan, 2016), or by comparing CAS scores with other variables (Weigle, 2010).

Clauser (2000), however, notes concerns over the relationship between the particular experts used in deriving scoring criteria and the resulting criteria themselves.

Cizek and Page (2003) echo these concerns, coining the term "interalgorithm" reliability. Similarly, Bennett and Bejar (1998) and Baker, Chung, and Delacruz (2008) note the potential negative consequences of faulty human judgment for establishing and refining CAS algorithms and scoring models. Several studies (Clauser, Margolis, Clyman, & Ross, 1997a; Harik, Clauser, Murray, Artman, Veneziano, & Margolis, 2013; Phillips, 2007; Williamson, Bejar, & Sax, 2004) provide empirical justification for these concerns, reporting that judgments by different scoring committees or groups of experts can produce varying CAS algorithms or regression weights, often leading to meaningful differences in scores.

Several articles by Clauser and his colleagues (Clauser, Harik, & Clyman, 2000a; Clauser, Swanson, & Clyman, 2000b; Clauser, Margolis, & Clauser, 2018; Clauser, Ross, Clyman, Rose, Margolis, & Nungester, 1997b; Harik et al., 2013) further note important concerns over how representative the raters used in such comparability studies might be, and how representative the scoring criteria or algorithms used for CAS might be, including the effect that different groups of raters or experts might have on the algorithms resulting from their scoring decisions.

In human scoring of constructed responses, the most common way of addressing the lack of perfect comparability in the scores awarded by different raters is to use multiple ratings. As a counter to these problems, therefore, Williamson, Bejar, and Hone (1999) propose using multiple human judgments to average out the errors from human scoring (thus approximating a human "true score") when assembling training sets and evaluating the output of CAS systems. How effective this procedure will be must, of course, be empirically evaluated in any given situation.

Examining the interplay of human judgment and item-based assessment, Jafarpur (2003) reports inadvertent variation in the types of items constructed by different test writers. Addressing a different set of scoring-based concerns, Harding & Ryan (2009) and Harding, Pill, and Ryan (2011) discuss ways in which assessors score open-ended items differently while using the same marking guide.

To date, however, no studies appear to have been published that examine the generalizability of machine scores resulting from different scoring decisions—algorithms, regression weights, scoring keys, scores used in training sets, etc.—in the context of language assessment. In other words, no language assessment studies have examined scoring decisions as a random facet of the measurement process, estimating the extent to which such decisions contribute to variations in scores. Rather, existing research has typically involved the ratings, weights, keys, or other scoring decisions of a single set of experts, neglecting the point that a different panel might produce different decisions, resulting in different scores. Only two studies (Clauser et al., 2000a, b) appear to have done so outside of language assessment, both in the context of performance assessments of medical skills. Furthermore, there appears to have been no inquiry at all into the question of generalizability of scoring keys for CAS of limited-production tasks, whether in language testing or in any other area. That is, when various authors or committees of authors create scoring keys for the same test, to what extent do those keys yield different scores? This is an important issue for CAS with limited-production tasks, as the generalizability of scoring keys is a crucial prerequisite for a test's construct validity.

In Bachman's assessment use argument (AUA; Bachman, 2005; Bachman & Palmer, 2010; Bachman & Damböck, 2017) framework, this issue relates to AUA Claim 4, that assessment records are consistent. Specifically, it addresses Warrants 2 and 6: Procedures for producing the assessment records are well specified and are adhered to, and ratings of different raters are consistent.

Generalizability Theory

Generalizability theory (Brennan, 1983, 2001a, b; Shavelson & Webb, 1991) is a statistical approach that allows the estimation of score consistency in both norm- and criterion-referenced frameworks. Even more importantly, it allows for total score variance to be decomposed, showing how much comes from various facets of the measurement process and interactions among them. This is quite useful in helping improve the consistency of assessments, as test developers can use these results to show them where to concentrate their efforts to improve reliability or dependability. As a result, test developers can determine how many raters, items, etc. are needed in order to meet a particular level of reliability or dependability.

The Present Study

This study involves the automated scoring of limited-production reading comprehension questions. It endeavors to answer the following research questions regarding the comparability of scoring keys written by different authors and teams of authors:

1. How consistent are the scores that result when a test is scored using CAS keys written by different authors?
2. How consistent are the scores that result when a test is scored using CAS keys written by different teams of authors?
3. When training teachers to write scoring keys, what issues need to be addressed in order to obtain more generalizable results?

The study addresses these issues by comparing the dependability of scores resulting from each key, examining the proportion of test score variance accounted for by the author (or team) facet, and comparing test scores across individual key authors and authoring teams.

Methods

This study uses scoring keys written by 7 pre- and in-service ESOL teachers in the graduate TESOL program at California State University, Fullerton, and 253 student responses to an academic reading comprehension test developed at the University of California, Los Angeles under the direction of Bachman. The key authors wrote and edited their keys independently, and subsequently worked together in small teams to arrive at consensus versions of their scoring keys.

Instrument

As mentioned above, the test used in the present study was the UCLA web-based ESL Placement Examination (ESLPE) test of academic reading. The test also included listening comprehension and writing sections, which are not included in the present study. The ESLPE was used to place matriculated non-native English-speaking students into the appropriate ESL course, or to exempt them from ESL support courses.

The test form used in this study included two passages. The first passage was taken from a textbook used in a lower-division general education anthropology course, and was about life in ancient South America. It was accompanied by an incomplete outline task with 11 items, and a set of 10 comprehension questions. Of the 10 comprehension questions, 9 were open-ended (i.e., short-answer) items, and 1 was a multiple-choice vocabulary in context question. The incomplete outline and open-ended items all had expected responses ranging from one word to one short sentence in length. The second passage was a gapfill, or rational-deletion cloze, passage about the development of learning theory. It included 30 deletions, and was taken from a textbook used in a lower-division general education psychology course.

Participants

The test takers were 351 students pilot testing an advanced version of the Web-Based UCLA ESL Placement Examination in September, 2005. Background information such as gender, first language, and academic major was not available for this sample.

The key authors were seven pre- and in-service ESOL teachers enrolled in their third or later semester in the TESOL master's degree program at California State University, Fullerton. The keys were written and revised in December of 2009, and the key authors were all close to finishing an introductory course in language assessment.

Automated Scoring of Responses

Scoring was done using the PoorMan scoring engine (see Carr, 2008 for a detailed description of this scoring engine). The purpose of the PoorMan engine is to provide a low- or no-cost system (i.e., a poor man's scoring engine) for automated scoring that can process response data contained in a spreadsheet or other delimited file. The engine itself is a large Microsoft Excel macro—essentially, a Visual BASIC program that uses the Excel interface for data input and output. It searches each test taker's response for key chunks and awards points accordingly.

Key Authoring

The key authoring process included two phases. The phases used in this study were explained to the authors during a meeting, and emailed to them as a reminder or in case they lost the hard copy instructions. The authors were given the passages and items, and the key writing process was modeled using a hypothetical item based on the passage used for the incomplete outline and open-ended tasks. Authors were instructed to write a model answer for each item. After writing a model answer, they identified the key "chunks" (i.e., regular expressions, or keywords or key phrases; these four terms will be used interchangeably henceforth) that were essential to that answer, and which would consequently demonstrate comprehension of the information being queried by that item. The key authors then assigned points to the item as a whole, and to various permutations of the regular expressions, including partial credit for incomplete responses.

When specifying the key chunks of information, the authors were told to use wildcards. The use of wildcards is an essential component of the limited-production CAS key authoring process. Authors were instructed to specify how much of each chunk was necessary in order for an answer to receive credit. They were given examples of wildcards to help clarify procedures, as most of them were unfamiliar with or lacked experience using wildcards. In particular, because the reading construct definition did not include grammatical accuracy in the responses, it was important not to penalize test takers for having missing or incorrect suffixes or other word endings, so long as the meaning expressed was correct.

Following this, the key authors were instructed to think of synonyms where possible for the key chunks, and to specify the points to be awarded for each synonym. Some synonyms might be given full credit, while others might only count for partial credit. Wildcards were to be used with the synonyms as well.

As an illustration—not an actual item, but one using information from the passage—the model answer for an item might be *Scholars dispute every aspect of this developmental pattern, from its chronology to its economic basis*. The author might specify that there were two key chunks, or regular expressions: *dispute* and *every aspect*. The author would write these as (*disput**) + (*every aspect**). The key author might then decide to accept as synonyms *disagree*/not agree*/argu** for *disput**, and *every/everything/all/each* for *every aspect**. The resulting key for that item would be (*disput*/disagree*/not agree*/argu**) + (*every aspect*/every/everything/all/each*). The author would then consider whether to make any changes to the key chunks of information; to continue the illustration, the second regular expression might be simplified to (*every*/all*/each**). The author would then also specify any undesirable responses that seemed appropriate. Undesirable responses are ones that contain key chunks, and which would therefore normally receive full or partial credit, but which are incorrect. The PoorMan scoring engine searches for these responses first, gives them 0 points, and then begins the regular scoring process for a given response. Continuing the previous example, the response *dispute nothing* would normally receive half credit, but it is clearly an incorrect answer. Therefore, *disput* + nothing* would need to be added to the key as an undesirable response, or more precisely, (*disput*/disagree*/not agree*/argu**) + *nothing*.

Finally, the author would decide whether to give one point for the whole item, or one point for each of the regular expressions. The result of this process was the Phase 1 scoring key for a given key author.

In Phase 2, the key authors were randomly placed in two teams. Individual authors were instructed to consult a thesaurus to find additional synonyms for all key chunks in their keys. Following this, each team met and discussed their keys, arriving at a consensus scoring key. Finally, the Phase 2 keys were slightly revised by the researcher by improving the use of wildcards, but without any other modifications (Phase 2wc). The scoring keys from both phases were then subsequently input into Excel using a key generation program, and each was used individually to score the responses to the 51 items.

While the keys were being input into PoorMan, detailed notes were kept, identifying and describing all issues found. These problems were then grouped into categories, as a way of identifying the issues that should be addressed when training teachers to write scoring keys (Research Question 3).

Analyses

Section means and other descriptive statistics for the incomplete outline, open-ended, and gapfill tasks, and for total test score were computed for each scoring run. There were seven sets of scores each for Phase 1 (one set of scores per key author). For Phase 2 and Phase 2wc, there were two sets of scores apiece, one per key authoring team, for a total of 11 scoring runs.

Reliability and dependability were computed individually for all 11 sets of scores $(7+2+2)$ using mGENOVA (Brennan, 2001b). Calculating both the generalizability coefficients ($E\rho^2$) and dependability coefficients (Φ) allowed for examination of the consistency of CAS in both NRT and CRT contexts. The two coefficients were calculated for all three sections (incomplete outline, open-ended questions, and gapfill) and for composite (i.e., total) scores using a multivariate $p^\bullet \times i^\circ$ design (following Brennan, 2001b). In Brennan's notation, the solid circle superscript indicates that every person (i.e., test taker) received scores in all three content categories (i.e., constructs, or test sections). The hollow circle superscript indicates that each item was only associated with one test section—in other words, it was only scored for one construct, not all three. The "x" indicates that every test taker was scored on every item. Although the mGENOVA output included variance components for all of the individual analyses, they are not reported here due to space constraints.

Subsequently, a $p^\bullet \times i^\circ \times h^\bullet$ design was used following Brennan (2001b) to determine first the generalizability of scoring keys written by different authors, and then of keys written by different authoring teams. The solid circle superscript for h indicates that each key author or authoring team was associated with all three content categories (i.e., constructs, or test sections); in other words, since each author or team wrote a key for each item (as indicated by the "$x\ h^\bullet$" notation), they had scores for items assessing all three constructs. As in the earlier design, all test takers received scores for all three test sections, and for every item, and each item was contained within a single test section. The Phase 1, Phase 2, and Phase 2wc scores were reanalyzed using this model. Variance components were calculated as well as both generalizability and dependability coefficients.

Results

In this section, descriptive statistics for the scores produced by using the various scoring keys are presented, followed by generalizability study results for the individual keys, and then generalizability study results examining authors and authoring teams as facets of the measurement process. The section concludes by detailing the types of problems found with the scoring keys written by the authors and authoring teams.

Descriptive Statistics

Descriptive statistics are provided for incomplete outline scores, open-ended question scores, gapfill, and total test score. Percentage-correct scores are used, because individual scoring keys varied in the number of points per item, and therefore in the total number of points possible on the test. The keys are identified by key author's first initial: A, H, N, P, S, V, and X, followed by a 1 to indicate Phase 1. Phase 2 keys are identified by combinations of initials, AHPV and NSX, with *wc* added (AHPVwc and NSXwc) to indicate the versions with improved wildcards. Table 11.2 presents the descriptive statistics for the scores resulting from the Phase 1 scoring keys. The score means are also presented in graphical format in Fig. 11.1. Table 11.3 and Fig. 11.2 present the results for both Phase 2 and Phase 2wc.

When teams of authors, taking their individual scoring keys as a starting point, produced keys in Phase 2, mean scores increased by about 9%. Improving wildcards raised mean scores by an additional 2.5% on average.

Table 11.2 Descriptive Statistics for Results Using Phase 1 Scoring Keys

	A1				H1				N1			
	IO	OE	Gap	Total	IO	OE	Gap	Total	IO	OE	Gap	Total
Mean	72.6%	51.7%	38.8%	51.2%	56.2%	46.8%	35.5%	44.5%	50.4%	42.4%	36.8%	40.8%
Median	76.5%	55.6%	40.0%	52.3%	60.0%	46.7%	36.7%	46.2%	54.5%	45.5%	36.7%	42.3%
SD	17.0%	17.2%	16.7%	13.6%	13.0%	14.9%	16.0%	11.4%	14.1%	14.4%	16.6%	13.0%
Q	8.8%	13.9%	11.7%	8.8%	7.5%	6.7%	11.7%	6.9%	9.1%	9.1%	13.3%	8.7%
Skewness	-1.8	-0.4	-0.2	-0.8	-1.6	-0.4	-0.1	-0.7	-1.3	-0.4	-0.1	-0.4
Kurtosis	3.7	-0.1	-0.5	0.7	3.4	0.7	-0.5	0.7	1.2	0.3	-0.5	-0.1

	P1				S1				V1			
	IO	OE	Gap	Total	IO	OE	Gap	Total	IO	OE	Gap	Total
Mean	48.8%	40.2%	7.1%	24.3%	75.0%	45.7%	32.0%	46.2%	53.8%	17.9%	32.9%	34.9%
Median	50.0%	36.4%	6.7%	25.5%	80.0%	43.8%	33.3%	47.5%	57.1%	16.7%	33.3%	35.7%
SD	13.1%	15.8%	4.7%	6.7%	18.4%	14.4%	15.1%	12.3%	15.1%	8.2%	14.7%	10.5%
Q	7.1%	13.6%	3.3%	4.5%	10.0%	9.4%	11.7%	7.4%	7.1%	4.2%	10.0%	6.3%
Skewness	-1.5	-0.4	0.5	-0.7	-1.6	-0.5	0.0	-0.7	-1.4	0.3	-0.1	-0.5
Kurtosis	2.7	0.0	0.0	1.1	2.6	0.4	-0.4	0.6	2.2	1.1	-0.6	0.3

	X1				Phase 1 Mean			
	IO	OE	Gap	Total	IO	OE	Gap	Total
Mean	54.8%	24.1%	32.7%	34.9%	58.8%	38.4%	30.8%	39.6%
Median	55.6%	22.2%	33.3%	36.0%	62.0%	38.1%	31.4%	40.8%
SD	16.4%	9.8%	15.6%	10.3%	15.3%	13.5%	14.2%	11.1%
Q	11.1%	5.6%	11.7%	7.3%	8.7%	8.9%	10.5%	7.1%
Skewness	-1.0	0.2	0.1	-0.6	-1.5	-0.2	0.0	-0.6
Kurtosis	1.2	0.4	-0.5	0.3	2.4	0.4	-0.4	0.5

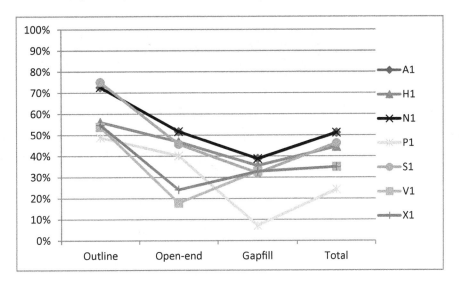

Fig. 11.1   Phase 1

Generalizability Theory Results

As noted above, the generalizability theory results are reported in two groupings: First, those from the 11 scoring runs, each computed individually, and second, the analyses looking at key authors or key authoring teams as a facet of the measurement process.

Generalizability and dependability coefficients for individual scoring keys. The generalizability and dependability coefficients for Phase 1 are reported by key author in Table 11.4. The generalizability and dependability coefficients are also provided in graphical format in Figs. 11.3 and 11.4, respectively, to facilitate the identification of patterns.

Table 11.5 details the generalizability and dependability coefficients for Phases 2 and 2wc. Figures 11.5 and 11.6 provide these values in graphical form. From Phase 1 to Phase 2, there was a clear increase in generalizability, and dependability increased even more markedly. In Phase 2, the use of improved wildcards in the keys in Phase 2wc improved both norm- and criterion-referenced scoring consistency, with the exception of the open-ended questions task for the NSX team. Both generalizability and dependability indices decreased for this section (by 0.17 for $E\rho^2$, and by 0.02 for Φ), although they improved for the other sections and the test overall. The decreases in scoring consistency for this test section appear to be due to very small reductions in the proportions of variance accounted for by persons and the residual, and a very small increase in the proportion of variance attributable to items. In a generalizability study with a $p^{\bullet} \times i^{\circ}$ design, a decrease in person variance will reduce both generalizability and dependability, as will an increase in residual variance. In contrast, a change in item variance will not affect generalizability, only dependability.

Table 11.3 Descriptive Statistics for Results Using Phase 2 and Phase 2wc Scoring Keys

	AHPV				NSX				Phase 2 Mean			
	IO	OE	Gap	Total	IO	OE	Gap	Total	IO	OE	Gap	Total
Mean	71.0%	52.4%	37.1%	49.3%	69.2%	50.8%	42.2%	51.4%	70.1%	51.6%	39.6%	50.4%
Median	73.3%	53.8%	36.7%	51.7%	75.0%	50.0%	43.3%	53.4%	74.2%	51.9%	40.0%	52.6%
SD	17.6%	17.3%	17.1%	14.0%	16.2%	16.7%	18.0%	14.1%	16.9%	17.0%	17.6%	14.0%
Q	10.0%	7.7%	13.3%	9.5%	9.4%	8.3%	12.5%	8.6%	9.7%	8.0%	12.9%	9.1%
Skewness	−1.5	−0.4	0.0	−0.6	−1.6	−0.4	−0.2	−0.7	−1.5	−0.4	−0.1	−0.6
Kurtosis	2.6	0.4	−0.5	0.4	3.1	0.3	−0.5	0.5	2.8	0.3	−0.5	0.4

	AHPVwc				NSXwc				Phase 2wc Mean			
	IO	OE	Gap	Total	IO	OE	Gap	Total	IO	OE	Gap	Total
Mean	77.1%	51.5%	40.7%	52.5%	75.1%	52.1%	42.2%	53.3%	76.1%	51.8%	41.4%	52.9%
Median	80.0%	53.8%	43.3%	55.2%	81.3%	50.0%	43.3%	55.2%	80.6%	51.9%	43.3%	55.2%
SD	18.6%	17.7%	18.1%	14.8%	17.1%	17.1%	18.0%	14.3%	17.9%	17.4%	18.1%	14.5%
Q	8.3%	11.5%	11.7%	9.5%	9.4%	12.5%	13.3%	8.6%	8.9%	12.0%	12.5%	9.1%
Skewness	−1.6	−0.3	−0.1	−0.6	−1.7	−0.4	−0.2	−0.7	−1.7	−0.4	−0.2	−0.7
Kurtosis	3.1	0.2	−0.5	0.4	3.7	0.2	−0.5	0.7	3.4	0.2	0.6	0.6

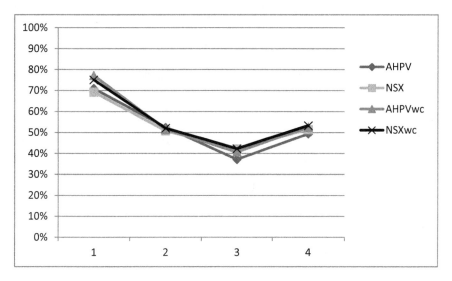

Fig. 11.2 Phase 2 and Phase 2wc mean scores, by team

Table 11.4 Phase 1 generalizability and dependability coefficients, by key author

	$E\rho^2$				Φ			
Author	Out	Open	Gap	Comp	Out	Open	Gap	Comp
A1	0.75	0.61	0.81	0.86	0.55	0.47	0.76	0.79
H1	0.61	0.39	0.80	0.81	0.39	0.20	0.74	0.68
N1	0.60	0.35	0.81	0.84	0.34	0.22	0.76	0.76
P1	0.65	0.36	0.33	0.67	0.43	0.18	0.26	0.48
S1	0.71	0.45	0.78	0.83	0.53	0.25	0.72	0.72
V1	0.70	0.26	0.76	0.81	0.56	0.12	0.71	0.73
X1	0.44	0.38	0.79	0.77	0.22	0.27	0.74	0.63

Note A1 = Phase 1 key written by Author A, etc.

Generalizability of scoring keys across authors and across authoring teams. The subsequent reanalysis of the data from the two phases using a $p^\bullet \times i^\circ \times h^\bullet$ model is reported in this section. The breakdown of the variance components and proportions of variance accounted for by each facet are reported in Table 11.6 for Phase 1, and in Table 11.7 for Phases 2 and 2wc. The variance attributable to differences in item difficulty was relatively large in both phases. The person-item interaction effect in Phase 1, showing the extent to which different test takers found individual items more or less difficult, was generally similar in size to the item main effect, and nearly triple in size for the gapfill section. The key author facet (h) accounted for a little more than 5% of score variance in most cases in Phase 1, indicating that overall, the keys from particular authors did not result in scores that were particularly higher

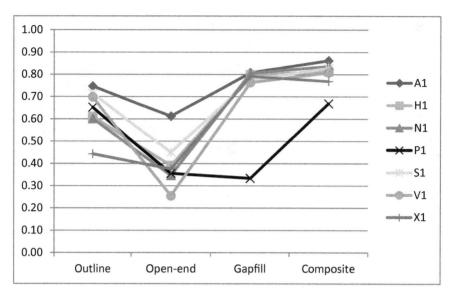

Fig. 11.3 Phase 1 generalizability coefficients, by key author

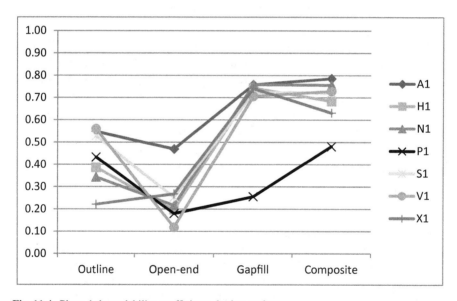

Fig. 11.4 Phase 1 dependability coefficients, by key author

or lower than each other. The person-author interaction effect was nearly zero across the board, indicating that the keys from various authors did not impact individual test takers differentially. The Phase 1 author-item interaction effect was very large for

Table 11.5 Phase 2 and Phase 2wc generalizability and dependability coefficients, by key authoring team

		Phase 3					Phase 3wc			
		Out	Open	Gap	Comp		Out	Open	Gap	Comp
AHPV	$E\rho^2$	0.67	0.51	0.81	0.85	$E\rho^2$	0.71	0.55	0.82	0.87
	Φ	0.51	0.45	0.77	0.80	Φ	0.62	0.49	0.79	0.83
NSX	$E\rho^2$	0.68	0.68	0.83	0.86	$E\rho^2$	0.71	0.51	0.83	0.86
	Φ	0.42	0.43	0.79	0.79	Φ	0.51	0.42	0.79	0.80

Note Team AHPV was composed of key authors A, H, P, and V. Team NSX was composed of key authors N, S, and X

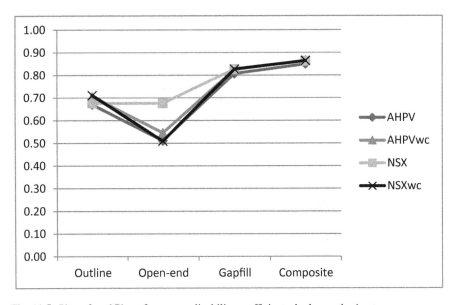

Fig. 11.5 Phase 2 and Phase 2wc generalizability coefficients, by key authoring team

the incomplete outline and open-ended item tasks, and noticeable but much smaller for the gapfill task.

The use of scoring teams to develop keys resulted in variance attributable to differences in item difficulty increasing slightly for open-ended and gapfill items, and remaining moderate, but becoming quite large for incomplete outline items. The authoring team facet accounted for almost no variance. The person-item interaction effect increased markedly from Phase 1, accounting for about half of all score variance in the gapfill section, and substantial portions in the other sections. The item-authoring team interaction effect was small for the gapfill, quite large for the incomplete outline, and relatively small for the open-ended items.

Table 11.8 presents the generalizability and dependability coefficients for the $p^{\bullet} \times i^{\circ} \times h^{\bullet}$ analyses. The generalizability coefficients for a single author are moderately

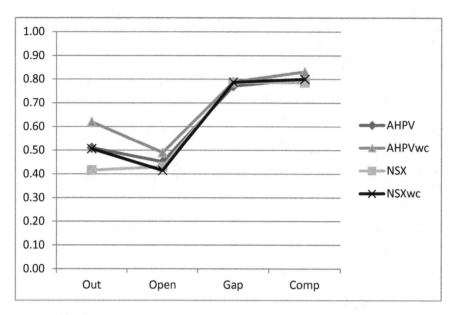

Fig. 11.6 Phase 2 and Phase 2wc dependability coefficients, by key authoring team

Table 11.6 Phase 1 Variance Components, $p^{\bullet} \times i^{\circ} \times h^{\bullet}$ design

	Variance components			Proportions of variance		
	Out	Open	Gap	Out (%)	Open (%)	Gap (%)
p	0.03024	0.01817	0.01506	5.4	3.0	7.0
i	0.04126	0.07302	0.03013	7.4	12.0	14.0
h	0.03228	0.03322	0.01097	5.8	5.5	5.1
pi	0.08639	0.06462	0.08908	15.4	10.6	41.3
ph	0.00093	0.00331	0.00199	0.2	0.5	0.9
ih	0.25714	0.21828	0.01744	45.9	35.9	8.1
pih,e	0.11171	0.19766	0.05126	19.9	32.5	23.7
Total	0.55995	0.60828	0.21593	100.0	100.0	100.0

low, while the dependability coefficients are extremely low. In Phase 2 and Phase 2wc, however, with the implementation of a team-authored scoring key, particularly with the appropriate use of wildcards, both generalizability and dependability reach levels appropriate for a high-stakes test, even with a single authoring team.

Table 11.7 Phase 2 and Phase 2wc Variance Components, $p^\bullet \times i^\circ \times h^\bullet$ design

	Phase 2					
	Variance components			Proportions of variance		
	Out	Open	Gap	Out (%)	Open (%)	Gap (%)
p	0.03924	0.02309	0.02510	7.4	7.2	10.4
i	0.18074	0.05279	0.03946	33.9	16.5	16.4
h	*0.00000*	0.00027	0.00108	0.0	0.1	0.4
pi	0.16462	0.12942	0.12576	30.9	40.4	52.1
ph	*0.00000*	0.00039	0.00017	0.0	0.1	0.1
ih	0.10957	0.02321	0.00612	20.5	7.2	2.5
pih,e	0.03928	0.09151	0.04364	7.4	28.5	18.1
Total	0.53345	0.32068	0.24133	100.0	100.0	100.0
	Phase 2**wc**					
	Variance components			Proportions of variance		
	Out	Open	Gap	Out (%)	Open (%)	Gap (%)
p	0.04265	0.02432	0.02561	9.8	7.5	10.2
i	0.07593	0.04086	0.03767	17.4	12.6	15.1
h	*0.00000*	*0.00000*	*0.00000*	0.0	0.0	0.0
pi	0.16730	0.12992	0.13165	38.4	40.0	52.7
ph	*0.00000*	0.00005	0.00002	0.0	0.0	0.0
ih	0.11147	0.03541	0.00854	25.6	10.9	3.4
pih,e	0.03883	0.09398	0.04651	8.9	29.0	18.6
Total	0.43618	0.32454	0.25000	100.0	100.0	100.0

Note Variance components *in italics* were small negative values which were set to 0 in computing the proportions of variance, following Shavelson & Webb (1991)

Table 11.8 Generalizability and Dependability Coefficients for Phases 1, 2, and 2wc—One Key Author or Key Authoring Team ($n'_k = 1$)

	Phase 1			
	Out	Open	Gap	Comp
$E\rho^2$	0.62	0.38	0.69	0.76
Φ	0.28	0.17	0.44	0.39
	Phase 2			
	Out	Open	Gap	Comp
$E\rho^2$	0.68	0.51	0.81	0.86
Φ	0.47	0.43	0.75	0.79
	Phase 2wc			
	Out	Open	Gap	Comp
$E\rho^2$	0.69	0.52	0.81	0.85
Φ	0.54	0.45	0.77	0.81

Issues in the Scoring Keys

A review of the scoring keys, both reading through them and also reexamining the ones with lower mean scores and lower generalizability and dependability coefficients revealed eight areas that proved problematic. These have been grouped into three categories.

Key authoring quality issues. The first of these was including undesirable responses in the key. Keys may, by failing to specify undesirable options for a given item, allow incorrect responses. For example, if the model answer is *The people ate more maize and less fish and seafood*, the regular expressions might be listed as *more/increasing amounts + maize/crops/vegeta* + less/decreasing amounts + fish/seafood*. However, without specifying either longer key chunks, or undesirable answers, *less maize and more fish* would receive full credit using the PoorMan engine. Dealing with this issue can be challenging, however, as specifying all the possible undesirable responses is impractical sometimes.

The second key authoring quality issue was apparently arbitrary decisions about partial credit and point allocations. In several cases, key authors made decisions about partial credit and point allocations that seemed difficult to defend. For example, one key gave two points for *they/early settlers + eat/consume/take + fewer/less + seafood*, but awarded no partial credit for anything else. Normally, if a full answer were to be worth two points, at least some partially correct answers should be worth one point. Other examples include two gapfill items—for one, the original gapped text was *fewer*, which was given one point, but the author rejected *less* as an acceptable synonym. Equally problematic was the case of the original gapped text *they*, which referred to *animals* (elsewhere in the passage). The author gave one point for *they*, but none for *animals*.

Another key-authoring quality issue was over-paraphrased, poorly-written, or incorrect model answers. One example of this type of problem involves the question *What evidence suggests that war was an important part of Andean culture in the Initial Period?* The passage itself reads *Carvings and sculpture at Cerro Sechin seem to be scenes of soldiers being killed, trophy heads, and other designs...* However, one key author proposed as a model answer *Carvings and sculptures of soldiers commemorating the old life.* In another example, for the question *In the sentence **people moved inland to take up agriculture**, what does take up probably mean?*, one author proposed as a model answer *People were going to change fishing for agriculture as their life's work.*

The final key authoring quality issue was language errors in the key, and failing to proofread for typographical errors. Several of the key authors were non-native speakers of English, and despite their high levels of language proficiency, they made occasional language errors. Errors included quantifier choices (e.g., *fewer* vs. *less*), verb tenses (e.g., *has undergone* vs. *underwent*), suffix choices (e.g., *containment* vs. *containers*), prepositional collocations (e.g., *excellent in* vs. *excellent at*), and incorrect word choices, particularly semantically related but incorrect words (e.g., *happened in many aspects* vs. *in many areas*). There were also several typographical errors (e.g., *cultivation* → *cultuvation*, *scenes* → *scence*, and *sweet potato* → *wet potato*).

Issues involving synonyms. The first of these issues was insufficient selectivity in accepting synonyms. One of the most common problems, which may have been mostly harmless (viz., it led to greater processing time, but probably had no effect on scores), was selecting weak or odd synonyms, often as a result of blind reliance on a thesaurus. For example, various keys accepted *consociation* for *relationship*; *goober* for *peanut*; *being* for *life*; *science test* for *experiments*; and *militia/brave troops/courageous* for *soldiers*, but not accepting *troops*. Two final examples of such blind acceptance of synonyms were accepting *water*/inundat*/irrigate/sprinkle/damp/rinse/shower/spray* for *irrigation* and *fur/skin*/fleece/coat/llama hair/woof/zephyr/thistledown/plush* for *wool*.

Another selectivity issue involved accepting words that fell outside the intended sense of the term being matched. Examples included accepting *store*/space*/keep*/bin*/closet*/warehouse*/wharfage** for *storage* (in the sense of making ceramic containers for food storage), and for *recall* (noun, in the sense of remembering something), accepting *remembrance/revoke/bring to mind/call up/remind/retain/rouse/waken*.

A final category of synonym selectivity issues involved semantically related words that are *not* synonyms. Examples included accepting *wheat* for *maize*, *crop/cultivation* for *harvesting*, *beachhead* for *coast*, and *nut*/peanut*/peanut butter/almonds** for *peanuts*.

Another type of synonym-related issue was neglecting likely or obvious synonyms, alternative phrasings, or other versions of expected responses. This does *not* include obvious synonyms that were not actually used in the passage or model answer, but rather ignoring synonyms that were used in the passage and/or model answer, or omitting likely alternatives involving different use of spacing or hyphens. As an example of the first category, the reading passage used both *pottery* and *ceramics* in the same sentence, and the model answer in one scoring key was *First wide scale distribution of pottery in South America*; however, that key did not include *ceramics* as an acceptable synonym. In another example, the model answer was *scenes of soldiers being killed, trophy heads, and other designs*, and the key included *view*/panoramic*/sight*/vision*/image*/display**, but not *scenes* or *designs*. Examples of problematic choices in the second category include accepting *sea shore*, but not *seashore*; including *1800 B.C.*, but not *1800 B. C.*, *1800 BC*, or *1800 B C*; and including *wide scale*, but not *wide-scale* (as it was written in the passage).

The final synonym-related issue involved supplying few or no synonyms for most items. In Phase 1, Author P only gave 8 synonyms on the first 21 items, spread across 5 items; the other 16 items had no synonyms at all.

Using wildcards incorrectly. This included eliminating possible correct alternatives, and misspecifying wild cards so that the correct answer was scored as incorrect. It was probably the single largest problem, but is perhaps the simplest to correct as well. In some cases, the wildcards used in keys would exclude different parts of speech, singular/plural forms, and verb tenses (especially irregular forms) of the correct responses. For example, one model answer included *ate*; the key had *eat/have/consume*, but not *ate*. In other cases, words were truncated too late (i.e., too far to the right), as in *farming**, *cultivation** and *impossibl**, which would have been better rendered as *farm**, *cultivat**, and *impossib**. Finally, in some cases a key included both a word and then a subset of the word that would also yield a match for the longer word (e.g., *limitations* and *limit**). This error would not impact scoring, but would add to key complexity and increase processing time.

Discussion

In this section, I interpret the results in terms of the three research questions that this study addresses.

Research Question 1

Research Question 1 addressed the issue of how consistent the scores are that result when a test is scored using CAS keys written by different authors. There was considerable variation in the quality of individual scoring keys, as indicated by marked differences in generalizability and dependability coefficients, and in mean test scores yielded by the keys from different authors, with a range in mean composite scores of slightly over 25%. Despite this variation, composite scores from individual key authors *appeared* to be adequately reliable for high stakes decisions in most cases, and nearly dependable enough in most cases. However, when key author was added to the scoring model, it became clear that the high generalizability and dependability coefficients had originally been inflated by ignoring an important component of the measurement process. Differences in the severity and leniency of the scoring across authors did not contribute much to total score variance, but the author-item interaction effect was quite large—much larger for tasks with longer expected responses, and much lower for one-word responses, at least, in the context of comprehension tasks. The qualitative problems with individual scoring keys described above did not apply to every item on a given author's key, which no doubt contributed to the size of the author-item interaction.

Taken together, this indicates that key author recruitment and retention decisions, and author training, are important factors when individual authors are to be used for scoring keys. However, scoring keys written by a single author comparable to the ones in this study are unlikely to yield scores with sufficient reliability or dependability for high-stakes decisions. When authors have better expertise and/or training, though, a single author might suffice.

Research Question 2

Research Question 2 addressed the issue of how consistent the scores are that result when a test is scored using CAS keys written by different teams of authors. A team's meeting together to discuss the scoring key led to generally adequate levels of composite reliability and dependability. This remained true when authoring team was modeled as a facet of the measurement process, even when only a single team was involved. Given the very large author-item interaction effect in Phase 1, it seems likely that the reduction in this effect in Phase 2 was an important contributor to the improvements in consistency, presumably because many of the individual authors' idiosyncratic decisions involving particular items were resolved during the collaborative process. Likewise, the Phase 2 scoring keys contained many fewer questionable choices for synonyms, indicating that as a group, more attention and more "sets of eyes" led to higher quality in the scoring keys.

Overall, improving the wildcards had a negligible effect on scoring consistency, improving dependability by 0.016, and reducing reliability by 0.003. This step did lead to a 2.5% increase in average scores across the two authoring teams, though, indicating that it did help capture a few answers as correct that had been erroneously counted as wrong previously. Since editing the wildcards in a key is a relatively simple task for those with some experience in the matter, this is a step that should be continued, although presumably by the actual scoring teams or at least one of their members.

Scores for individual test sections were not consistent enough to form the basis for making any important decisions, or probably even for providing diagnostic feedback. However, in this particular case, the test was not intended to provide diagnostic feedback regarding the individual sections, much less individual components of the reading construct definition. It is also worth reiterating in this context that the first two sections of the test only had 10 and 11 items, respectively, making reasonable levels of scoring consistency unlikely for either section, regardless of test quality. Based on the results of this study, it appears that any test with a reasonably large number of items can enjoy appropriate levels of scoring consistency using CAS with limited-production tasks, especially if the keys are prepared by an authoring team, not merely a single author. This improvement from using multiple authors working together parallels the improvement in consistency that is seen from using multiple ratings of extended production tasks. In most cases, it is probably best testing practice to have multiple ratings or multiple key authors for high- or medium-stakes tests.

Research Question 3

Research Question 3 investigated what issues need to be addressed when training teachers to write scoring keys, in order to obtain more generalizable results. Eight separate issues were identified, which fell into three categories: key authoring quality issues, issues involving synonyms, and using wildcards incorrectly.

More detailed analysis is needed to determine the extent to which the problems identified in the qualitative results led to differences between individual authors' and authoring teams' keys. It seems clear, though, that explaining to future key authors the findings of this study, especially with examples of where the authors in this study went wrong, would be a useful addition to key author training.

Limitations of the Study

It is a limitation of this study that no cut scores were used in this study; as a result, classification dependability could not be addressed.

Another limitation is that guidance on what to consider in making decisions about partial credit may not have been clear or explicit enough. Similarly, key authors did not demonstrate as strong a grasp of wild cards as might have been expected. This may have had negative consequences on the scoring, in terms of both mean scores and scoring consistency.

It should also be noted that the improvements in wildcards between Phases 2 and 2wc were relatively minor, and did not include the inclusion of additional words, no matter how obvious (e.g., *are*, *was*, *were*, *be*, and *been* were not added as an alternative to *is*). Therefore, more expansive revision of the wildcards and related issues (e.g., irregular verb forms) should be kept as a step in the key authoring and revision process.

Finally, the key authors were volunteers working for extra credit; this may have resulted in some of them not putting forth their best efforts.

Conclusions, Implications, and Future Directions

In conclusion, this study has found that scoring key author is a source of construct-irrelevant variance, and needs to be controlled for. Neglecting this facet can result in more satisfactory generalizability or dependability coefficients, but only because the model is glossing over an important component of total score variance. That being said, keys produced by individuals or teams of authors can be consistent, but still vary appreciably from each other, particularly those written by individual authors. Such variation can perhaps be reduced by providing more explicit guidance on procedures for writing the keys.

It is also apparent from these results that key author assessment expertise and training are important, particularly in the areas of writing keys, choosing synonyms, and using wildcards. Likewise, attention to detail, and care in editing the key and wildcards are important considerations. Careful recruitment is therefore important, after which proper training and experience will probably prove adequate to achieve satisfactory results. Thus, future studies should address recruiting, the effectiveness of training, constraints and guidance on authoring, and other steps in improving consistency across key authors. Such studies should consider the effect on the rater and rater team facet of changes in these variables, and might also look at other indicators of test quality, such as how these variables affect model fit in confirmatory factor analysis.

Based on the results of this study, it appears that a comprehension-based test with a reasonable number of items can enjoy appropriate levels of scoring consistency using CAS with limited-production tasks, particularly if the keys are prepared by an authoring team, not merely a single author. Proper recruitment and training of the authors will help improve the usefulness of keys even further. The resulting product should then yield scores that will provide stakeholders with consistent information about the ability to be assessed, enabling them to make appropriate decisions.

References

Bachman, L. F. (1990). *Fundamental considerations in language testing.* Oxford: Oxford University Press.

Bachman, L. F. (2004). *Statistical analyses for language assessment.* Cambridge: Cambridge University Press.

Bachman, L. F. (2005). Building and supporting a case for test use. *Language Assessment Quarterly, 2*(1), 1–34.

Bachman, L. F., Carr, N. T., Kamei, G., Kim, M., Llosa, L., Sawaki, Y., et al. (2000, March). *Developing a Web-based language placement examination system.* Poster session presented at the 22nd Annual Language Testing Research Colloquium, Vancouver, BC.

Bachman, L. F., Carr, N. T., Kamei, G., Kim, M., Pan, M. J., Salvador, C. et al. (2002). A reliable approach to automatic assessment of short answer free responses. In *COLING '02: Proceedings of the 19th International Conference on Computational Linguistics—Volume 2* (pp. 1–4). Stroudsburg, PA: Association for Computational Linguistics. Retrieved from https://dl.acm.org/citation.cfm?id=1071907.

Bachman, L. F., & Damböck, B. (2017). *Language assessment for classroom teachers.* Oxford: Oxford University Press.

Bachman, L. F., Davidson, F., & Milanovic, M. (1996). The use of test method characteristics in the content analysis and design of EFL proficiency tests. *Language Testing, 13,* 125–150.

Bachman, L. F., Davidson, F., Ryan, K., & Choi, I.-C. (1995a). *An investigation into the comparability of two tests of English as a foreign language: The Cambridge-TOEFL comparability study.* Cambridge: University of Cambridge Local Examinations Syndicate.

Bachman, L. F., Lynch, B. K., & Mason, M. (1995b). Investigating variability in tasks and rater judgments in a performance test of foreign language speaking. *Language Testing, 12*(2), 239–257.

Bachman, L. F., & Palmer, A. S. (1996). *Language testing in practice.* Oxford: Oxford University Press.

Bachman, L. F., & Palmer, A. S. (2010). *Language assessment in practice.* Oxford: Oxford University Press.

Baker, E. L., Chung, G. K. W. K., & Delacruz, G. C. (2008). Design and validation of technology-based performance assessments. In J. M Spector, M. D. Merrill, J. van Merriënboer & M. P. Driscoll (Eds.), *Handbook of Research on Educational Communications and Technology* (3rd ed., pp. 595–604). New York: Lawrence Earlbaum Associates, Taylor & Francis Group.

Bennett, R. E., & Bejar, I. I. (1998). Validity and automated scoring: It's not only the scoring. *Educational Measurement: Issues and Practice, 17*(4), 9–17.

Bennett, R. E., Steffen, M., Singley, M. K., Morley, M., & Jacquemin, D. (1997). Evaluating an automatically scorable, open-ended response type for measuring mathematical reasoning in computer-adaptive tests. *Journal of Educational Measurement, 34*(2), 162–176.

Brennan, R. L. (1983). *Elements of generalizability theory*. Iowa City, IA: The American College Testing Program.

Brennan, R. L. (2001a). *Generalizability theory*. New York: Springer.

Brennan, R. L. (2001b). *Manual for mGENOVA version 2.1*. Retrieved from https://education. uiowa.edu/centers/centeradvanced-studies-measurement-andassessment/computer-programs# GENOVA.

Carr, N. (2008). Decisions about automated scoring: What they mean for our constructs. In C. A. Chapelle, Y.-R. Chung, & J. Xu (Eds.), *Towards adaptive CALL: Natural language processing for diagnostic language assessment* (pp. 82–101). Ames, IA: Iowa State University.

Carr, N. T. (2011a). Computer-based language assessment: Prospects for innovative assessment. In N. Arnold & L. Ducate (Eds.), *Present and future promises of CALL: From theory and research to new directions in language teaching* (2nd ed., pp. 337–373). San Marcos, TX: Computer Assisted Language Instruction Consortium (CALICO).

Carr, N. T. (2011b). *Designing and analyzing language tests*. Oxford: Oxford University Press.

Carr, N. T. (2014). Computer-automated scoring of written responses. In A. J. Kunnan (Ed.), *The companion to language assessment*. Wiley. Retrieved from https://doi.org/10.1002/978111841 1360.wbcla124.

Carr, N. T., & Xi, X. (2010). Automated scoring of short-answer reading items: Implications for constructs. *Language Assessment Quarterly, 7*(3), 205–218.

Chalhoub-Deville, M., & Deville, C. (1999). Computer-adaptive testing in second language contexts. *Annual Review of Applied Linguistics, 19,* 273–299.

Chapelle, C. A., & Chung, Y.-R. (2010). The promise of NLP and speech processing technologies in language assessment. *Language Testing, 27*(3), 301–315.

Cizek, G. B., & Page, B. A. (2003). The concept of reliability in the context of automated essay scoring. In M. S. Shermis & J. Burstein (Eds.), *Automated essay scoring: A cross-disciplinary perspective* (pp. 125–145).

Clauser, B. E. (2000). Recurrent issues and recent advances in scoring performance assessments. *Applied Psychological Measurement, 24*(4), 310–324.

Clauser, B. E., Harik, P., & Clyman, S. G. (2000a). The generalizability of scores for a performance assessment scored with a computer-automated scoring system. *Journal of Educational Measurement, 37*(3), 245–261.

Clauser, B. E., Kane, M. T., & Swanson, D. B. (2002). Validity issues for performance-based tests scored with computer-automated scoring systems. *Applied Measurement in Education, 15*(4), 413–432.

Clauser, B. E., Margolis, M. J., & Clauser, J. C. (2018). Validity issues for technology-enhanced innovative assessment. In H. Jiao & R. W. Lissitz (Eds.), *Technology enhanced innovative assessment: Development, modeling, and scoring from an interdisciplinary perspective* (pp. 139–162).

Clauser, B. E., Margolis, M. J., Clyman, S. G., & Ross, L. P. (1997a). Development of automated scoring algorithms for complex performance assessments: A comparison of two approaches. *Journal of Educational Measurement 34*(2), 141–161.

Clauser, B. E., Ross, L. P., Clyman, S. G., Rose, K. M., Margolis, M. J., & Nungester, R. J. (1997b). Development of a scoring algorithm to replace expert rating for scoring a complex performance-based assessment. *Applied Measurement in Education, 10*(4), 345–358.

Clauser, B. E., Swanson, D. B., & Clyman, S. G. (2000b). A comparison of the generalizability of scores produced by expert raters and automated scoring systems. *Applied Measurement in Education, 12*(3), 281–299.

Harding, L., Pill, J., & Ryan, K. (2011). Assessor decision making while marking a note-taking listening test: The case of the OET. *Language Assessment Quarterly, 8*(2), 108–126.

Harding, L., & Ryan, K. (2009). Decision making in marking open-ended listening test items: The case of the OET. *Spaan Fellow Working Papers in Second or Foreign Language Assessment, 7,* 99–114.

Harik, P., Clauser, B. E., Murray, C., Artman, C., Veneziano, A., & Margolis, M. (2013, April). *Comparison of automated scores derived from independent groups of content experts.* Paper presented at the annual meeting of the National Council on Measurement in Education, San Francisco, CA.

Hoang, G. T. L., & Kunnan, A. J. (2016). Automated essay evaluation for English language learners: A case study of *MY Access. Language Assessment Quarterly, 13*(4), 359–376.

Huff, K. L., & Sireci, S. G. (2001). Validity issues in computer-based testing. *Educational Measurement: Issues and Practice, 20*(3), 16–25.

Jafarpur, A. (2003). Is the test constructor a facet? *Language Testing, 20*(1), 57–87.

Leacock, C., & Chodorow, M. (2003). C-rater: Automated scoring of short answer questions. *Computers and the Humanities, 37,* 389–405.

Liu, S., & Kunnan, A. J. (2016). Investigating the application of automated writing evaluation to Chinese undergraduate English majors: A case study of "WriteToLearn". *CALICO Journal, 33*(1), 71–91.

Messick, S. A. (1989). Validity. In R. L. Linn (Ed.), *Educational measurement* (3rd ed., pp. 13–103). New York: American Council on Education/Macmillan.

Ockey, G. J. (2007). Construct implications of including still image or video in computer-based listening tests. *Language Testing, 24*(4), 517–537.

Ockey, G. J. (2009). Developments and challenges in the use of computer-based testing for assessing second language ability. *The Modern Language Journal, 93*(Focus Issue), 836–847.

Pardo-Ballester, C. (2010). The validity argument of a web-based Spanish listening exam: Test usefulness evaluation. *Language Assessment Quarterly, 7,* 137–159.

Phillips, S. M. (2007). *Automated essay scoring: A literature review* (SAEE Research Series #30). Kelowna, BC, Canada: Society for the Advancement of Excellence in Education (SAEE).

Roever, C. (2001). Web-based language testing. *Language Learning and Technology, 5*(2), 84–94. Available at http://llt.msu.edu/vol5num2/roever/default.html.

Sawaki, Y. (2001). Comparability of conventional and computerized tests of reading in a second language. *Language Learning and Technology, 5*(2), 38–59.

Shavelson, R. J., & Webb, N. M. (1991). *Generalizability theory: A primer.* Newbury Park, CA: SAGE Publications.

Weigle, S. C. (2010). Validation of automated scores of TOEFL iBT tasks against non-test indicators of writing ability. *Language Testing, 27*(3), 335–353.

Williamson, D. M. (2009, April). *A framework for implementing automated scoring.* Paper presented at the annual meeting of the American Educational Research Association and the National Council on Measurement in Education, San Diego, CA.

Williamson, D. M., Bejar, I. I., & Hone, A. S. (1999). "Mental model" comparison of automated and human scoring. *Journal of Educational Measurement, 36*(2), 158–184.

Williamson, D. M., Bejar, I. I., & Sax, A. (2004). Automated tools for subject matter expert evaluation of automated scoring. *Applied Measurement in Education, 17*(4), 323–357.

Xi, X. (2008). What and how much evidence do we need? Critical considerations in validating an automated scoring system. In C. A. Chapelle, Y.-R. Chung, & J. Xu (Eds.), *Towards adaptive CALL: Natural language processing for diagnostic language assessment* (pp. 102–114). Ames, IA: Iowa State University.

Xi, X. (2010). Automated scoring and feedback systems: Where are we and where are we heading? *Language Testing, 27*(3), 291–300.

Chapter 12
Distinguishing Language Ability from the Context in an EFL Speaking Test

Hongwen Cai

Abstract This study attempts to provide empirical evidence for understanding the relationship between ability and context in light of Bachman's conceptualization of the target construct in task-based language assessment. The study was situated in an EFL speaking test in China, Test for English Majors, Band 4, Oral Test (TEM4-Oral), which consists of three tasks: retelling, topic-based talk, and discussion. Each test taker gets a distinct score on each of the three tasks, a fourth score for pronunciation on all three tasks, and a fifth score for grammar–vocabulary on all three tasks. Confirmatory Factor Analyses were conducted on the scores of 23,793 test takers across three years. Interpretation of the best-fitting bifactor model suggests that (1) the contribution of language ability and contextual factors to test scores can be separately assessed and (2) task performance is a multidimensional construct involving both language ability and topical knowledge. This highlights the need for a clear definition of both constructs in practice.

Introduction

In Bachman's writings, the word "context" typically refers to the target language use (TLU) domain and its projection in the test tasks, including such factors as the setting, test rubrics, input, expected response, and the relationship between input and response. Bachman believes that the dialectic of language abilities and contexts lies at the heart of construct definition in language assessment (Bachman, 1990; Bachman & Palmer, 2010). In fact, he described the "fundamental dilemma" of language testing as the difficulty "to distinguish the language abilities we want to measure from the method factors used to elicit language" (Bachman, 1990, p. 288). In his review of earlier literature, Bachman (2007) identified three general ways of defining the construct in language assessment, with different underlying assumptions about the relationship between language abilities and contexts. The first of these is an ability-focused approach, which defines the construct as the language abilities

H. Cai (✉)
Guangdong University of Foreign Studies, Guangzhou, People's Republic of China
e-mail: hwcai@gdufs.edu.cn

© Springer Nature Singapore Pte Ltd. 2020
G. J. Ockey and B. A. Green (eds.), *Another Generation of Fundamental Considerations in Language Assessment*, https://doi.org/10.1007/978-981-15-8952-2_12

underlying performance; the second, a task-focused approach, aims at measuring language performance itself, and predicting future performance on real-world tasks; the third approach, an interaction-focused approach, defines the construct as interactional competence, and sees it as the result of co-construction by all participants in the interaction.

In effect, however, various ways of defining the language ability construct converge on the first two general approaches. As Bachman (2007) noted, proponents of the interaction-focused approach are divided among themselves such that some of them essentially sided with the ability-focused approach while others were in favor of the task-focused approach. The same can be said of task-based language performance assessment, where proponents are also divided as to whether they aim at providing inferences about language abilities that test takers have, or at making predictions about future performance.

Citing Skehen (1998), Bachman (2007) contended that neither the ability-focused nor the task-focused approach can solve the "fundamental dilemma" in distinguishing language abilities from the contexts in and of itself, as it is all too easy to ignore performances or contexts when focusing on abilities, and vice versa. Focusing on topical knowledge, Bachman and Palmer (2010) discussed three options for determining its role in the construct definition: (1) language ability being the sole construct, (2) language ability and topical knowledge incorporated as a single construct, and (3) language ability and topical knowledge as separate constructs. While topical knowledge is a personal attribute, the topical characteristic of the input and expected response is a key contextual factor in Bachman's writings (Bachman, 1990; Bachman & Palmer, 1996, 2010). The nature of topical knowledge, therefore, depends on how the construct is defined. Unless it is clearly included in the construct definition (Option 2), it is of a contextual nature (Option 1). Bachman's approach is essentially Option 3, to define the construct of communicative language ability (CLA) as an underlying trait of the language user while allowing for generalization across contexts (such as topics) by comparing the characteristics of the assessment tasks to those of the TLU tasks (Bachman, 1990; Bachman & Palmer, 1996, 2010). The assumption underlying this option is that language ability can be distinguished "from the method factors used to elicit language" (Bachman, 1990) and the contribution of language ability and contextual factors to test scores can be separately assessed. In contrast, neither Option 1 nor Option 2 makes a clear distinction between language ability and context. In operational testing, Option 1 may resort to random sampling of the contexts to control for their contribution, whereas Option 2 simply subsumes language ability as a component of task performance. Neither option commits itself to distinguishing language ability from context and thus addressing the "fundamental dilemma" outlined above. This reasoning may be generalized to the distinction between language abilities and contexts by extending topical knowledge to other contextual factors, such as the setting, rubrics, other features of the input and expected response, and the relationship between input and response.

In a recent review, Norris (2016) noted that different approaches to task-based language assessment have seldom been implemented in operational testing. In particular, attempts at addressing the "fundamental dilemma" and distinguishing language abilities from the contexts have seldom been made. It is the purpose of this paper to make such an attempt, in the context of English as a Foreign Language (EFL) speaking test.

Literature Review

The Nature of the "Fundamental Dilemma"

Construct confounding. The recent years have witnessed Option 2 gaining much ground in practice, with task performance as the overarching construct, typically in a form of task-based language assessment. In a recent review, Norris (2016) categorized relevant practices into four different levels—tasks as standards, tasks in proficiency assessment, tasks for employment certification, tasks for language educational assessment. Norris noted that the commonality across the categories is "functional language use for the meaningful conveyance of ideas within a clearly defined communicative setting" (p. 239). However, with the exception of proficiency assessment, the other levels focus more on the particular requirements of a given task and language use situation.

Bachman has been implicitly or explicitly critical of Option 2 for construct definition in language assessment (Bachman, 2002, 2007; Bachman & Palmer, 2010). In particular, he has warned against defining the constructs in language assessment as "performance on tasks" or "skills." Essentially, the performance on tasks construct is identified with the task-focused approach mentioned in Bachman (2007), while skills are considered as combinations of language ability and language use activities (listening, reading, speaking, and writing), i.e., a combination of language ability and context (Bachman & Palmer, 2010). Thus defined, these constructs are pestered with potential problems in scoring and interpretation. For example, if the test taker fails a certain task, it is unclear whether the failure results from weakness in language ability, topical knowledge, or from other contextual factors.

In practice, the problems confronting the task-focused approach have exhibited themselves saliently in recent efforts to put the Common European Framework of Reference (CEFR, Council of Europe, 2001) into practical use. The CEFR descriptors take the form of "can-do" statements, which essentially identify the construct with the TLU domain. Although communicative language ability is described as part of the construct, it is only regarded as the resources drawn upon in the completion of communicative activities, which results in the lack of a systematic description of communicative language ability (Weir, 2005). To address this problem, the English Profile program under the leadership of Cambridge ESOL and Cambridge University Press sought to specify the *criterial features* of each proficiency level of learner English. These features are "grammatical, lexical and functional exponents derived empirically as criterial for the levels concerned" (Saville & Hawkey, 2010, p. 4). Interpreted from Bachman's perspective, this endeavor emphasizes the importance of the ability-focused approach, as ratings of the test takers' performance on the designated task (or can-do statement in the case of CEFR) is difficult to interpret "without defining the construct in terms of one or more areas of language knowledge and topical knowledge" (Bachman & Palmer, 2010, p. 219). However, even if the criterial features help the test users to relate the can-do statements to the underlying language ability, the relative contribution of language ability and contextual factors is still confounded without a clear delineation of their boundary.

"Skills" as the construct is another approach that has attracted a lot of researchers in recent years, particularly researchers on interactional competence. A special issue on this topic was published in *Language Testing* in 2018. Of particular interest is a paper by Roever and Kasper (2018), who argued for the integration of interactional competence in speaking assessments to support "inferences regarding test takers' ability to use language in social interaction" (p. 332). From a conversation analysis perspective, the authors quoted Mehan (1979) and defined interactional competence as "the competence necessary for effective interaction" and "the competence that is available in the interaction between participants" (p. 333). Quoting Schegloff (2007), they specified this competence in terms of organizational problems such as orderly distribution of turns, coherent sequences of turns and actions, repairs, mutual understanding, smooth progression of the talk, and management of openings, closings and other larger units of interaction. They emphasized the co-constructed nature of these operations and called for a sociolinguistic-interactional perspective in lieu of a psycholinguistic-individualist perspective. This emphasis on co-construction was a step away from the ability-focused approach toward the task-focused approach, as interlocutor contribution was integrated as part of the construct, a test method facet in the ability-focused approach (Bachman & Palmer, 2010; McNamara, 1996).

Another paper in the special issue of *Language Testing* took an even bigger step away from the ability-focused approach by integrating nonverbal behavior (NVB) as part of the speaking construct (Plough, Banerjee, & Iwashita, 2018). Quoting Jenkins and Parra (2003), the authors listed kinetic features, nonverbal turn taking and active listening as examples of nonverbal behavior that may interact with paralinguistic and verbal behaviors to create an impression of interactional competence. They suggested that a "scope of NVB" be developed in speaking assessment, parallel to ranges of linguistic performance. Obviously, these authors regard nonverbal behavior as a separate dimension beyond language ability, and their approach to the speaking construct is a multidimensional one.

A multilayer view. Roever and Kasper (2018) and Plough, Banerjee, and Iwashita (2018) can be seen as two landmark papers in an expanding view on the target construct in language assessment (Bachman, 2007). In particular, the conception of the interactional competence construct and of the more general speaking construct has expanded to such a degree that they remind the reader of the construct of communication skills, including

- Perceiving and understanding others
- Engaging in verbal communication
- Engaging in nonverbal communication

- Listening and responding to others
- Creating and sustaining communication climates
- Adapting communication to cultural contexts (Wood, 2014).

As Wood (2014) sees it, these are basic skills relevant to all contexts of communication. Obviously, the dimensions of interlocutor contribution (Roever & Kasper, 2018) and nonverbal behavior (Plough, Banerjee, & Iwashita, 2018), which extend beyond the conception of CLA, fit neatly into this list, as CLA itself may be subsumed as part of the more general construct of communicative competence.

In fact, if one traces the development of the communicative competence construct, one will discover an ever-expanding trend. For a big picture, Hymes (1972) and Canale and Swain (1980) may be regarded as two milestones in this process, as Fig. 12.1 displays.

As Fig. 12.1 shows, the story started with the construct of linguistic competence (Chomsky, 1965), which excluded sociolinguistic features such as settings, topics, and communicative functions, considering them as the context of language use. To emphasize the insufficiency of linguistic competence for achieving communicative purposes, Hymes (1972) incorporated sociolinguistic competence as part of the communicative competence notion. However, discourse features such as text type and the modes of listening, speaking, reading, and writing were still considered contextual features. The incorporation of discourse competence, as well as strategic competence, as part of the communicative competence construct, were done by Canale and Swain (1980) and Canale (1983).

Viewed from the perspective of an expanding construct, one might interpret the integration of interactional competence, inclusive of interlocutor contribution (Roever & Kasper, 2018) and nonverbal behavior (Plough, Banerjee, & Iwashita, 2018), as further expansion of the communicative competence construct, and the destination seems to be the communicative competence construct in communication studies, as delineated by Wood (2014). In terms of the relationship between abilities and contexts, the expansion seems to be accompanied by the concession of contextual elements to the language ability construct. For example, sociolinguistic features started as contextual factors with reference to linguistic competence, but was integrated with the latter in the initial conceptualization of communicative competence (Hymes, 1972). The same could be said of discourse competence, which also started as contexts of language use (Canale, 1983). Further absorption of contextual elements into the language ability construct will necessarily result in the definition

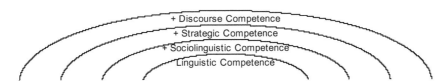

Fig. 12.1 The expanding construct of communicative competence

of constructs as "performance on tasks" or as "skills," which Bachman and Palmer (2010) have criticized.

Thus conceptualized, the distinction between the ability-focused and task-focused approaches to construct definition is essentially the choice between a more restricted "language studies" perspective and a more inclusive "communication studies" perspective. In other words, the ability-focused construct is restricted to the inner layers of the multilayer communicative competence construct, whereas the task-focused construct is inclusive of the outer layers. Depending on the purpose of assessment, the boundary between inner layers and outer layers may be changed, if only the construct is both meaningful and operationalizable.

In practice, delineating the outreach of a construct may be accomplished through confirmatory factor analysis (CFA). Assumptions about the nature of a particular layer in the target construct can be made in accordance with the multilayer view, so that models corresponding to different layer combinations can be fitted and compared. Take, for example, performance on tasks. It can be conceptualized as either a separate layer beyond language competence (Option 3 above) or an integral component of a more inclusive construct (Option 2 above). In factor analytic terms, the former corresponds to a two-factor model while the latter a single-factor model. These models can both be fitted to real data and compared to find out which is better supported. The same idea can be extended to similar situations with more layers in the construct, such as the multiple layers of interactional competence construct advocated by Roever and Kasper (2018) and by Plough, Banerjee, and Iwashita (2018). This endeavor helps one to locate the boundary between language ability and the rich repertoire of contextual factors, fulfilling the purpose of this study.

Research Question

Following the above reasoning, the mission of distinguishing language ability from context may be formulated as the following question: Which option regarding the relationship between abilities and context fits the data best in operational testing?

This can then be operationalized with CFA model-fitting efforts, to identify the best-fitting common factor model and interpret it in terms of the relationship between abilities and context.

Methods

Materials

This study was based on a large-scale speaking test, the *Test for English Majors, Band 4, Oral Exam* (TEM4-Oral, Cai, 2015). The exam is administered annually to

Chinese-native EFL majors toward the end of their second year in university. It is a high-stakes test as its certificate can be used in job-hunting before graduation. The test includes three tasks: story-retelling, talk based on a given topic, and discussion. Story-retelling is an integrated speaking task, where the test takers listen to a three-minute story and retell it in their own words. The topic-based talk is a monolog task that typically requires the test takers to relate and reflect on their personal experience. The discussion task has the nature of a debate, where the test takers are paired up and assigned to conflicting views on a hot topic. They argue for their assigned view and against the opposing view. The test takers are given three minutes to complete each of the first two tasks, but four minutes to jointly complete the third task. They speak into a microphone and have their voices digitally recorded for asynchronous rating.

In rating, the test taker's performance is given five holistic scores, comprising three scores for task completion (one on each task), a pronunciation score, and a grammar–vocabulary score. Both the pronunciation and grammar–vocabulary scores are based on the test takers' performance on all three tasks. The rubric for the retelling task is essentially a checklist of key points retrieved in the reproduced story. The rubric for the topic-based talk is more sophisticated, comprising topic relevance, sufficiency, organization, and fluency. The rubric of the discussion task emphasizes sufficiency, rhetorical structure, and communicative strategies (see Appendix for detail). All five are percentage scores, but the raters are required to give scores that are integer multiples of five, such that the set of possible scores include only 21 categories, such as 0, 5, 10… 95, 100, but never 52 or 64.

Design

TEM4-Oral meets the purpose of this study particularly well in terms of its design. The structure of the five scores makes it possible to interpret them as measures of two different layers, language ability and performance on tasks. While the pronunciation and grammar–vocabulary scores can be straightforwardly interpreted as measures of language ability, the three task-specific scores and their relationship with the pronunciation and grammar–vocabulary scores may be interpreted in three different ways, as illustrated in Fig. 12.2.

Figure 12.2a regards performance on tasks as a single overarching construct, subsuming language ability as a component. In factor analytic terms, the five scores would be explained by a single latent trait, and a single-factor model would fit the data best. If performance on tasks is a different construct from language ability but the two constructs are correlated, then a correlated-factor model would fit the data best, as shown in Fig. 12.2b. However, the observed correlation between task-specific scores and language ability scores may well be due to the confounding of language ability and performance on tasks in the task-specific scores. In the third case, a factor analytic treatment may be to separate the two sources of variation, using the bifactor model (Holzinger & Swineford, 1937), where the task-specific score can

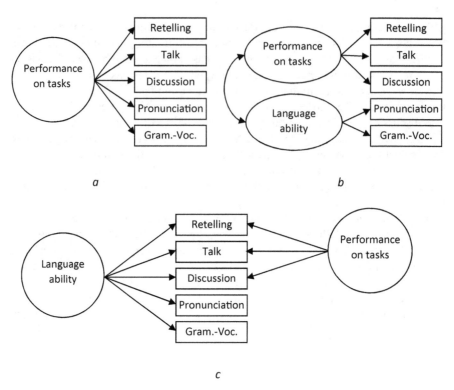

Fig. 12.2 Three hypothetical factor models for TEM4-Oral scores

load on both a language ability factor and a factor reflecting performance on tasks (Fig. 12.2c). These cross-loadings are based on the observation that the task-specific rubrics included criteria related to both factors, such as organization and fluency for language ability, and topic relevance and communication rules for performance on tasks (see Appendix). Furthermore, previous verbal protocol studies found that task-specific scores given by TEM4-Oral raters were affected by their judgment of the language ability of the test takers (Cai, 2015; Xu & Cai, 2019).

In terms of the distinction between language ability and context, the single-factor model subsumes the two layers under the same umbrella and makes no distinction, while the bifactor model makes the clearest distinction, allowing for no correlation between the two layers. The correlated-factor model comes in the middle, distinguishing language ability from context, but allowing for correlation between the two. In terms of the options suggested by Bachman and Palmer (2010), the single-factor model corresponds to Option 2, while the bifactor model is closest to Option 3. The correlated model, however, is ambivalent, so the factor correlation needs to be examined to see which is more tenable between Options 2 and 3. Similarly, the factor loadings of the bifactor model also need to be examined. If all the scores have significant loadings on both factors, then Option 3 is supported; but if the scores do

Table 12.1 Model fitting results and their interpretations

Model	Factor correlation	F1 loadings	F2 loadings	Option
Single-factor	–	Significant	–	2
Correlated-factor	High	Significant	Significant	2
Correlated-factor	Low	Significant	Significant	3
Bifactor	–	Significant	Significant	3
Bifactor	–	Significant	Not significant	1

not have significant loadings on the performance on tasks factor, then Option 1 is more tenable. These possible outcomes can be summarized in Table 12.1.

Thus conceptualized, model fitting and comparison results can be used to evaluate the degree to which language ability and context is distinguishable from each other.

Data and Analysis

The data comprised all the ratings from one of the three rating sites of TEM4-Oral in two consecutive years ($n_1 = 6,466$, and $n_2 = 12,050$ respectively) and part of the ratings from another rating site in the third year ($n_3 = 5,277$). As explained above, five scores were given to each test taker, so that the data matrix was 6,466 by 5 for the first year, 12,050 by 5 for the second year, and 5,277 by 5 for the third year.

EQS6.1 (Bentler & Wu, 2005) was used for model fitting and parameter estimation, using the Maximum Likelihood estimator. Following the suggestion of Hu and Bentler (1999), three indices were examined to evaluate model fit: CFI, RMSEA, and SRMR. For model comparison, AIC (Akaike, 1987) was the principal criterion, as there was no nesting relationship between the correlated-factor model and the bifactor model, thus precluding the possibility of a chi-square difference test between the models. The model with the lowest AIC was considered the best-fitting.

To examine the invariability of the best-fitting model, a multiple-group CFA was conducted, treating the three years as three groups. For the purpose of identifying the relationship between language ability and context, it was considered sufficient to test only the invariance of the overall factor structure, instead of going all the way to test the invariance of parameter estimates.

While multiple-group CFA is typically conducted to check the stability of the scores across similar samples, it was intended in this study to check the stability of the best-fitting model across different administrations of TEM4-Oral, which differed from each other in such contextual features as the topic, input, and language features of the expected response. Invariability across administrations, therefore, can be regarded as cross-validation of the best-fitting model.

Results

Model Comparison

Before model fitting, the reliabilities and descriptive statistics of the scores were examined, together with a key assumption for conducting CFA. The scores used in the CFA were from single raters, but in a more recent administration, the recordings of test takers were assigned to packs of 31 recordings for double marking by a pair of raters, so that interrater reliabilities could be calculated on each scale for each pack. The median of interrater Pearson correlations was 0.954 for Task 1, 0.658 for Task 2, 0.599 for Task 3, 0.695 for pronunciation, and 0.677 for grammar–vocabulary. These provided an indirect indication of the reliabilities of the scores used in this study. The means, standard deviations, skewness, and kurtosis of the five scores, together with the intercorrelations, across the years, are reported in Table 12.2.

As Table 12.2 shows, there were some differences in the means and standard deviations in the different scores across the years, as the specific tasks were different. However, the general patterns were similar. For example, the retelling score was lowest, with the greatest standard deviations, across the years. This was then followed by the topic-based talk score, in both the mean and the standard deviation, while the

Table 12.2 Score distributions and correlations across the years

	M	SD	Skewness	Kurtosis	Talk	Discussion	Pronunciation	Gram.-Voc
Year 1 ($n = 6,466$)								
Retelling	60.03	15.18	−0.848	0.694	0.488	0.453	0.441	0.490
Talk	64.86	11.87	−1.131	2.596		0.545	0.454	0.524
Discussion	69.52	8.19	−0.759	1.852			0.608	0.689
Pronunciation	72.19	7.90	−0.319	0.351				0.786
Gram.-Voc	71.93	7.61	−0.412	0.540				
Year 2 ($n = 12,050$)								
Retelling	60.75	18.64	−0.429	−0.225	0.501	0.461	0.511	0.548
Talk	61.49	14.43	−0.826	0.927		0.591	0.539	0.604
Discussion	66.95	10.17	−1.053	3.161			0.672	0.730
Pronunciation	68.15	10.13	−0.569	1.323				0.848
Gram.-Voc	67.44	10.21	−0.588	1.218				
Year 3 ($n = 5,477$)								
Retelling	57.90	17.39	−0.288	−0.316	0.553	0.550	0.583	0.647
Talk	60.85	10.91	−0.656	1.674		0.655	0.605	0.669
Discussion	64.63	8.33	−0.503	1.456			0.697	0.743
Pronunciation	64.22	9.39	−0.298	0.573				0.812
Gram.-Voc	64.57	9.34	−0.242	0.424				

other three scores were more or less comparable in the mean and the standard deviation, across the years. The pattern of intercorrelations was also comparable across the years, with stronger correlations among the last three scores. The correlation was strongest between pronunciation and grammar–vocabulary, in the range between $r = 0.786$ and $r = 0.848$. As these scores straightforwardly reflected language ability, the high correlation was expected. Otherwise, the correlations between the scores were generally moderate, in the range between $r = 0.441$ and $r = 0.743$.

The key assumption for maximum likelihood estimation in CFA was the distribution of observed variables (Ockey & Choi, 2015). Table 12.2 does show some violations of the univariate normality assumption in the observed variables, particularly in terms of kurtosis. To test for multivariate normality, Mardia's coefficients were examined. This value was estimated at 28.06, 21.89, and 40.87, respectively, for the three data sets, much higher than the values of 3 recommended by Bentler (2006), indicating considerable positive kurtosis. Therefore, the Satorra–Bentler scaled chi-squares (S-Bχ^2) were used in subsequent assessment of model fit following Bentler's (2006) recommendation.

Table 12.3 displays major fit indices for the three models across the three years.

Apart from CFI, SRMR, RMSEA, and AIC discussed above, Table 12.3 also reports the S-Bχ^2 together with the corresponding degree of freedom (*df*) and *p*-value, as well as the 90% confidence interval for the RMSEA. According to the S-Bχ^2 values and their corresponding *p*-values, there was significant misfit between all three models and the real data, as none of the *p*-values was greater than 0.05. Because it is generally believed that the χ^2 test is too sensitive for large samples, evaluation of model fit was based on the other statistics. The CFI was greater than 0.95 for all three models across the years, and SRMR was less than 0.05 except for the single-factor model in the first year. According to these two statistics, all three models fit the data sufficiently. However, the bifactor model fit the data better than

Table 12.3 Fit indices of the three models across years

Model	S-Bχ^2	*p*	CFI	SRMR	RMSEA (90% CI)	AIC
Year 1 ($n = 6,466$)						
Single-factor	777.002 (5)	0.000	0.950	0.052	0.155 (0.146, 0.165)	767.002
Correlated-factor	247.489 (4)	0.000	0.984	0.028	0.098 (0.087, 0.108)	239.489
Bifactor	6.467 (2)	0.039	1.000	0.003	0.019 (0.004, 0.036)	2.467
Year 2 ($n = 12,050$)						
Single-factor	1159.976 (5)	0.000	0.968	0.039	0.139 (0.133, 0.146)	1149.976
Correlated-factor	346.994 (4)	0.000	0.990	0.021	0.085 (0.077, 0.092)	338.994
Bifactor	25.450 (2)	0.000	0.999	0.004	0.031 (0.021, 0.043)	21.450
Year 3 ($n = 5,277$)						
Single-factor	296.973 (5)	0.000	0.984	0.023	0.105 (0.095, 0.115)	286.973
Correlated-factor	131.961 (4)	0.000	0.993	0.015	0.080 (0.069, 0.092)	131.961
Bifactor	22.486 (2)	0.000	0.999	0.005	0.044 (0.029, 0.061)	18.486

the other two models did according to all statistics, particularly RMSEA, as it was the only model that had an estimate less than 0.05, across the years. Comparatively, AIC was also lowest for the bifactor model across the years, considerably less than the other two models, by one or two digits. Taken together, this means that the bifactor model is the best-fitting across the years and across the rating sites.

Cross-Validation

As explained above, the invariability of the best-fitting model across years served to cross-validate the best-fitting model. This was examined through the multiple-group CFA treating the years as the groups. As was the case in each year, S-Bχ^2 test showed a significant misfit between the model and the data, S-B$\chi^2 = 54.404$, $df = 6$, $p = 0.000$. However, the other statistics were encouraging, CFI $= 0.999$, RMSR $= 0.004$, RMSEA $= 0.032$ with 90% CI (0.024, 0.040). Taken together, there was insufficient evidence that the bifactor model was variable across the years.

Further information about invariability can be gleaned from the loadings of the five scores on the two factors. These are reported in Table 12.4.

All the factor loadings reported in Table 12.4 were significantly greater than 0, $p < 0.05$, indicating a significant link between the indicators and the two factors. A further discovery was that the size of the loading was incremental in the order of scoring, so that the first score to be given (Task 1) had the lowest loading and the last score to be given (Grammar-Vocabulary) had the highest loading across the years, indicating an order effect. While the order effect was not desirable in itself, it was an indication that the five scores did share something in common, about which the raters grew increasingly confident when they were exposed to increasing evidence of it.

The loading on performance on tasks was highest for Task 2 (Topic-based talk) across the years, indicating that this task was explained more by the second factor than the other tasks. Therefore, a heavier weight should be given to Task 2 in the interpretation of the second factor.

Table 12.4 Factor loadings of the bifactor model across years

	Year 1		Year 2		Year 3	
	Language ability	Performance on tasks	Language ability	Performance on tasks	Language ability	Performance on tasks
Retelling	0.516	0.320	0.570	0.187	0.684	0.114
Talk	0.549	0.640	0.627	0.710	0.725	0.689
Discussion	0.725	0.227	0.763	0.187	0.797	0.132
Pronunciation	0.834		0.874		0.879	
Gram.-Voc	0.942		0.966		0.947	

Discussion

Distinction Between Language Ability and Context

Before the findings are interpreted, it is important to emphasize the changeable nature of certain factors with reference to the multilayer view proposed above. For example, it was explained early in this article that topical knowledge may constitute part of the construct if it is the object of measurement, but may function only as a contextual factor if it is excluded from the inner layers. In Bachman's writings, the inner layers comprise the CLA construct, and topical knowledge is clearly a contextual factor in the task characteristic framework. Earlier literature on test method facets was mainly restricted to task types, such as multiple choices, gapfilling, and short-answer questions, in the discussion of context, but McNamara's (1996) framework of language performance assessment broadened the view to also include the interlocutor, rater, and scale/criteria as contextual factors, all of which can find their places in Bachman's task characteristic framework (Bachman, 1990; Bachman & Palmer, 1996, 2010). This understanding is the guideline of the following interpretations.

The findings of this study show that the bifactor model best explained the covariances among TEM4-Oral scores and that this result is held across years and rating sites. Moreover, the bifactor model was invariable across years and rating sites. In terms of the relationship between language abilities and context, this result is in favor of Option 3. According to this model, the three task scores are best interpreted as the combination of two uncorrelated factors, language ability, and performance on tasks. The language ability component belongs to the same dimension as the pronunciation and grammar–vocabulary scores. This shows that the raters were able to consider two uncorrelated factors simultaneously and derive a single score.

The findings can also be interpreted with reference to the other options for dealing with contextual factors in the construct (Bachman & Palmer, 2010). For people with a mindset to only assess the language ability of the test takers (Option 1), the different tasks may be regarded as different contextual factors, and random sampling of the contexts may be a way out for controlling the contextual factors. As we can see from the above findings, however, contextual factors contributed considerably to the task scores, thwarting the intention to measure language ability alone. On the contrary, treating performance on tasks as the overarching construct (Option 2) is a practical aim, as language ability is subsumed as a component and does not alter the nature of the scores as measures of performance on tasks. However, this interpretation makes only partial use of the scores, neglecting the fact that the two constructs can be assessed separately.

In terms of the multilayer view proposed in this article, the construct of performance on tasks can be regarded as inclusive of language ability and extra layers such as topical knowledge and interlocuter contribution. These extra layers differentiate the performance on tasks construct from the object of measurement in language assessment to such a degree that it is more appropriate to subsume it under the construct of communication skills (Wood, 2014). In other words, when a task-focused construct is defined, the focus is on performance on tasks, and it is more accurate to categorize the test as a test of communicative skills rather than a language test. To the final analysis, language testers need to stop somewhere and exclude extra layers, such as the contextual factors illustrated in this study, from the construct definition if they want to develop something that can still be called a language test rather than a communication test.

Language Ability

To present language ability as the object of measurement in a language test, the construct of language ability needs a clear definition, such as the definition of CLA (Bachman, 1990; Bachman & Palmer, 1996, 2010). An ensuing question is whether this definition was operationalized in the rating process in this study. The simple answer to this question is yes. The major source of evidence is the rating rubrics for TEM4-Oral (Appendix). Here the major concern is the rating scales for the three task scores, as pronunciation and grammar–vocabulary can be interpreted more straightforwardly as components of CLA. Take retelling, for example, the rubric consists of a checklist of key points to be covered in the reproduced story. In one test paper related to this study, the original story was about turning adversity into advantage, and one of the points in the checklist was "Nancy lost her left arm," stating the adversity. The rubric stipulates that dropping the word "left" and substituting the word "arm" with "arms," "hand(s)," or "leg(s)" should all be considered errors, as the meaning is altered. It is clear from this stipulation that a clear distinction between singular and plural nouns, distinction between similar words and attention to details are linguistic prerequisite to correct response. Similarly, the second task, talk based on a given topic, is designed to be an essentially narrative task, where the test takers are required to relate their own experience. In terms of discoursal organization, narration usually involves knowledge of text structure, a component of CLA included in the rubric. Furthermore, narration typically involves the correct use of tenses. Although the latter may be a feature to be considered when rating grammar–vocabulary, confusion in tense use will necessarily sacrifice the coherence of the narration, which is a key criterion in the rubric. These are examples that language ability is the prerequisite for task completion, which explains why the task scores cross-loaded on both language ability and performance on tasks in the best-fitting bifactor model.

Performance on Tasks

The factor loadings of the bifactor models also showed that all three task scores were significantly influenced by the performance on tasks factor. As this factor was specified to be uncorrelated with language ability, it could be interpreted as a contextual factor. However, the exact meaning of this contextual factor is unclear. A tentative interpretation may be based on the common criteria in the rubrics of the three tasks, as all three task scores have significant loadings on this factor. It was reported earlier that the loading of the second task score on this factor was considerably higher than the loadings of the first and third task scores, in all three administrations (Table 12.4), which makes it reasonable to start the search for common criteria from the rubrics of the second task. As the Appendix shows, topic relevance, sufficiency, organization, and fluency were four criteria used in the second task. Topic relevance is the degree to which the given topics are followed by the test takers in the three tasks, while sufficiency is essentially the amount of message given by the test takers. Both depend on how well the test takers are informed on the given topics, and may therefore be subsumed under topical knowledge (Bachman & Palmer, 1996, 2010). These criteria were also adopted in the other two tasks. More specifically, the first task was rated against a checklist of key messages reproduced in the reproduced story. The more messages are reproduced, the higher the score that is awarded. This is both a relevance issue and a sufficiency issue. As for the third task, the specific criteria used in the three administrations included the number and quality of the warrants given in support of the test taker's arguments, which are also concerned with relevance and sufficiency. In contrast, organization and fluency may be interpreted as a component of CLA, and associated with the language ability factor.

This interpretation poses some problem with regard to the discussion task, as the rubrics for discussion could have depended more on the co-construction with interlocutors. However, a very interesting thing happened to TEM4-Oral several years ago—the raters requested that the test developer turn down the volume of the interlocutor, so that they could focus more on the target test taker's performance, and this request has been implemented since then. It seems that these raters generally regarded speaking competence as a personal trait rather than a co-constructed construct. In effect, turning down the interlocutor's voice muted the contribution of interlocutor performance—and consequently the contribution of communication strategies—to the score. What was left of the rubrics for the discussion task was essentially the same as the other tasks and could be interpreted as topical knowledge in general.

The TEM4-Oral raters' request for turning down the interlocutor voice is suggestive of an important issue in interpreting and using language standards. Alderson (1991) discussed three different functions of language scales, and one of them is providing guidance for assessors who are rating the performances. From the users' point of view, a construct definition should best satisfy the need of the raters. Through the lens of the TEM4-Oral raters, one obviously sees a tendency toward the ability-focused approach to construct definition. In other words, these raters have chosen to regard interactional competence as a personal trait rather than a co-constructed reality.

This need of the TEM4-Oral raters is not dissimilar to the need of textbook writers and test developers, for whom linguistic features of the materials to be included in teaching materials and test input materials are among the top concerns. It is also reminiscent of the English Profile program that aims to specify the CEFR levels by deriving *criterial features* in English as a second language (Hawkins & Filipović,

2012). In sum, although a measure of performance on tasks looks promising for people aiming to predict the performance of test takers in real-life communication, language teachers, textbook writers, test developers, and examiners may benefit more from a more ability-focused approach to construct definition.

Conclusions, Implications, and Future Directions

Thus far, I have sided with Bachman's view on the "fundamental dilemma" of language assessment, arguing that language testers need to delineate the outreach of the language ability construct and treat extra layers as contexts. Much more investigation, both theoretical and practical, is yet to be conducted. First, the nature of some "contextual" factors deserves more in-depth exploration. For example, should interlocutor contribution and nonverbal behavior be integrated into the communicative competence construct or left as contextual features? And how should we balance psychometric properties and practical use when deciding on the nature of a certain factor? Second, the advantages and disadvantages of different approaches to the relationship between language abilities and contexts may need to be examined in operational testing. Theoretically, Bachman's approach, which comprises the CLA construct and the task characteristics framework, serves the need of the practitioners reasonably well, but few studies have been reported on how this approach works in practice. The same could be said of other options. Oftentimes, the merits of a particular approach are taken for granted by its advocates and practitioners alike, before sufficient empirical evidence is collected. Further evidence from operational testing will certainly shed more light on the "fundamental dilemma" of language assessment.

Appendix A: The Brief Rubrics for TEM4-Oral (Translated from Chinese)

The following are general guidelines that apply to test papers across the years. More specific rubrics, e.g., the checklist for messages covered in Task 1, are developed for each paper to accommodate topic variation. These are not presented here due to space restriction.

Task 1

- Excellent (≥90): Can retell the details of the source material in an organized manner.
- Proficient (80/85): Can retell the key messages of the source material in an organized manner.

- Pass (60/65/70/75): Can retell the key messages of the source material in a relatively organized manner.
- Fail (<60): Misses key messages or displays major deviations from the source material.

Task 2

- Excellent (≥90): Can give a well-organized talk closely related to the given topic, with sufficient messages, displaying sufficient fluency and freedom from unnecessary pauses.
- Proficient (80/85): Can give an organized talk closely related to the topic, with relatively sufficient messages, displaying a few hesitations and stutters that do not hinder communication.
- Pass (60/65/70/75): Can give an organized talk related to the given topic, with insufficient messages or some irrelevant messages, displaying frequent hesitations and stutters that hinder communication from time to time.
- Fail (<60): Can give a talk based on the given topic, but displays disorganization, insufficient messages or digression, frequent hesitations or stutters that seriously hinder communication.

Task 3

- Excellent (≥90): Can engage in free and flexible conversation in the assigned role and the given situation, observing communication rules sufficiently.
- Proficient (80/85): Can engage in conversation in the assigned role and the given situation, observing communication rules, but displaying some lack of flexibility and freedom.
- Pass (60/65/70/75): Displays some difficulty engaging in conversations, with out-of-touch content.
- Fail (<60): Displays obvious difficulty engaging in conversations and observing communication rules.

The prononciation scale

- Excellent (≥90): Near-native clear, accurate pronunciation and natural intonation.
- Proficient (80/85): Clear pronunciation and natural intonation, with a slight accent but no obvious errors.
- Pass (60/65/70/75): Obvious accent and some inaccurate pronunciations that do not affect the conveyance of meaning.
- Fail (<60): Unclear, inaccurate pronunciation and unnatural intonation.

The grammar-vocabulary scale

- Excellent (≥90): Generally grammatical with few obvious errors, proper use of words.
- Proficient (80/85): A few obvious but not serious errors in grammar, mostly proper use of words.

- Pass (60/65/70/75): A few major errors in grammar that do not affect the conveyance of meaning, roughly proper use of words.
- Fail (<60): Major errors in grammar that affect the conveyance of meaning, many errors in the use of words.

References

Akaike, H. (1987). Factor analysis and AIC. *Psychometrika, 52*(3), 317–332.

Alderson, J. C. (1991). Bands and scores. In J. C. Alderson & B. North (Eds.), *Language testing in the 1990s* (pp. 71–86). London: Modern English Publications & The British Council.

Bachman, L. F. (1990). *Fundamental considerations in language testing.* Oxford: Oxford University Press.

Bachman, L. F. (2002). Some reflections on task-based language performance assessment. *Language Testing, 19*(4), 453–476.

Bachman, L. F. (2007). What is the construct? The dialectic of abilities and contexts in defining constructs in language assessment. In J. Fox, M. Wesche, D. Bayliss, L. Cheng, C. Turner, & C. Doe (Eds.), *Language testing reconsidered* (pp. 41–71). Ottawa: University of Ottawa Press.

Bachman, L. F., & Palmer, A. S. (1996). *Language testing in practice.* Oxford: Oxford University Press.

Bachman, L. F., & Palmer, A. S. (2010). *Language assessment in practice.* Oxford: Oxford University Press.

Bentler, P. M. (2006). *EQS 6 structural equations program manual.* Encino, CA: Multivariate Software Inc.

Bentler, P. M., & Wu, E. J. C. (2005). *EQS 6.1-structural equation modeling software for windows.* Encino, CA: Multivariate Software, Inc.

Cai, H. (2015). Weight-based classification of raters and rater cognition in an EFL speaking test. *Language Assessment Quarterly, 12*(3), 262–282.

Canale, M. (1983). On some dimensions of language proficiency. In J. W. Oller, Jr. (Ed.), *Issues in language testing research* (pp. 333–342). Rowley, MA: Newbury House.

Canale, M., & Swain, M. (1980). Theoretical bases of communicative approaches to second language teaching and testing. *Applied Linguistics, 1*(1), 1–47.

Chomsky, N. (1965). *Aspects of the theory of syntax.* Cambridge, MA: MIT Press.

Council of Europe. (2001). *Common European Framework of Reference for Languages: Learning, Teaching, Assessment (CEFR).* Strasbourg: Council of Europe.

Hawkins, J. A., & Filipović, L. (2012). *Criterial features in L2 English: Specifying the reference levels of the Common European Framework.* Cambridge: Cambridge University Press.

Holzinger, K. J., & Swineford, F. (1937). The bi-factor method. *Psychometrika, 2*(1), 41–54.

Hu, L., & Bentler, P. M. (1999). Cutoff criteria for fit indexes in covariance structure analysis: Conventional criteria versus new alternatives. *Structural Equation Modeling, 6*(1), 1–55.

Hymes, D. (1972). On communicative competence. In J. Pride & J. Holmes (Eds.), *Sociolinguistics: Selected readings* (pp. 269–293). Harmondsworth: Penguin.

Jenkins, S., & Parra, I. (2003). Multiple layers of meaning in an oral proficiency test: The complementary roles of nonverbal, paralinguistic, and verbal behaviors in assessment decisions. *The Modern Language Journal, 87*(1), 90–107.

McNamara, T. F. (1996). *Measuring second language performance.* London: Addison Wesley Longman.

Mehan, H. (1979). *Learning lessons.* Cambridge, MA: Harvard University Press.

Norris, J. M. (2016). Current uses for task-based language assessment. *Annual Review of Applied Linguistics, 36,* 230–244.

Ockey, G. J., & Choi, I. (2015). Structural equation modeling reporting practices for language assessment. *Language Assessment Quarterly, 12*(3), 305–319.

Plough, I., Banerjee, J., & Iwashita, N. (2018). Interactional competence: Genie out of the bottle. *Language Testing, 35*(3), 427–445.

Roever, C., & Kasper, G. (2018). Speaking in turns and sequences: Interactional competence as a target construct in testing speaking. *Language Testing, 35*(3), 331–355.

Saville, N., & Hawkey, R. (2010). The English Profile Programme–the first three years. *English Profile Journal, 1,* e7. https://doi.org/10.1017/S2041536210000061

Schegloff, E. A. (2007). *Sequence organization in interaction.* Cambridge: Cambridge University Press.

Skehen, P. (1998). *A cognitive approach to language learning.* Oxford: Oxford University Press.

Weir, C. J. (2005). Limitations of the Common European Framework for developing comparable examinations and tests. *Language Testing, 22*(3), 281–300.

Wood, J. T. (2014). *Communication mosaics: An introduction to the field of communication* (7th ed.). Boston, MA: Wadsworth.

Xu, L., & Cai, H. (2019). The effect of task characteristics on raters' use of criteria in an EFL speaking test. *Modern Foreign Languages, 42*(4), 540–551.

Chapter 13
The Effects of Proficiency Differences in Pairs on Korean Learners' Speaking Performance

Sun-Young Shin

Abstract This study aims to identify the effects of the test task type (individual and paired speaking test) on the scores obtained in the two groups (Heritage Language [HL] and Non-Heritage Language [NHL] Learners of Korean) using a univariate and a multivariate G-study. The results of this study show that HL students performed similarly across different test tasks regardless of heritage backgrounds of their partners. Likewise, NHL students did not perform differently between two test tasks when they were paired with the NHL students. On the contrary, when NHL students were paired with HL students whose level of Korean oral proficiency was higher, they tended to gain higher scores in the paired speaking test task than in the monologic one, particularly in their fluency subscores. The findings of this study help us better understand the relationships between test constructs and contextual features in paired oral assessment.

Introduction

The understanding of the relationships among language constructs, test takers' characteristics, raters, and tasks in classroom assessment contexts is one of the major research agendas in Lyle Bachman's work (e.g., Bachman, 1990, 2000; Bachman, Lynch, & Mason, 1995; Bachman & Damböck, 2018). Among the various psychometric tools employed to explore this fundamental issue in language assessment, Bachman and his colleagues used Generalizability theory (G-theory) (see Shavelson & Webb, 1991) which enables us to estimate the effects of multiple sources of measurement errors including raters and tasks in a speaking assessment context (Bachman et al., 1995). This chapter furthers one of Bachman's main research parts of investigating variability among test takers' traits, raters, and tasks by exploring the effects of various factors on test takers' performance in a paired speaking test using a G-study.

S.-Y. Shin (✉)
Indiana University, Bloomington, IN, USA
e-mail: shin36@indiana.edu

© Springer Nature Singapore Pte Ltd. 2020
G. J. Ockey and B. A. Green (eds.), *Another Generation of Fundamental Considerations in Language Assessment*, https://doi.org/10.1007/978-981-15-8952-2_13

Having students perform tasks in pairs or groups has been one of the most common teaching activities in communicative-based second/foreign (L2) language class-rooms; it promotes participation among students, increases opportunities for nego-tiation of meaning, and creates a social learning environment facilitating language learning (Richards & Rodgers, 2014). Such pair or small group activities have also been increasingly accepted as popular L2 speaking assessments since they allow students to interact as active participants in assessment, thus enhancing test authen-ticity and learner autonomy (Katz, 2013; Ockey, Koyama, & Setoguchi, 2013). However, due to the nature of co-constructed interaction in a paired speaking test context (May, 2009), students are likely to be awarded scores differently depending on who they are paired or grouped with (Taylor & Wigglesworth, 2009). From an assessment perspective, this makes it difficult for test users to interpret and use test scores obtained from a paired or group speaking assessment because raters usually assign individual oral ability scores to each participant (Bonk & Ockey, 2003; Ockey, 2009; van Moere, 2006). The degree of separability of each student's contribution and performance in a paired speaking test is, thus, a matter of great concern to many language teachers and testers particularly when they have a mix of students with different language learning abilities and linguistic profiles as in many postsecondary foreign language programs (Brinton, Kagan, & Bauckus, 2008; Carreira & Kagan, 2011).

Literature Review

Heritage Versus Non-heritage Language Learners

In a large number of foreign language classes in American universities, heritage language (HL) learners and non-heritage language (NHL) learners are often mixed together in the same classroom either from the beginning or at the later stages (Carreira & Kagan, 2011; Kondo-Brown, 2010). However, HL learners differ from NHL learners in many aspects including cultural background, motivation for learning the target language, and oral proficiency (Carreira, 2004; Kondo-Brown, 2003; Montrul, 2010b). Such differences between two groups pose pedagogical challenges for many foreign language teachers when they have both HL and NHL learners in the same classroom because they tend to have different linguistic profiles and instructional needs (Montrul, 2010a; Montrul & Perpiñán, 2011). In particular, many HL learners have better pronunciation and higher oral fluency than NHL learners (Kagan & Friedman, 2003) despite their relatively weak literacy skills in the target language. These notable differences in spoken language abilities between two groups of learners (Kondo-Brown, 2003; Montrul, 2010a; Sohn & Shin, 2007) could be a concern for foreign language teachers and testers especially when they attempt to design and implement pair- or group-oriented classroom assessment. Language profi-ciency differences among interlocutors in pair or group work might unfairly affect a learner's speaking performance leading to biased scores (Davis, 2009). Although the effect of interlocutor proficiency on speaking test performance has been extensively investigated (Csépes, 2002; Davis, 2009; Iwashita, 1998; Nakatsuhara, 2011; Norton, 2005), to date, there has been no prior research in exploring the effect of variability of interlocutor proficiency on scores in a paired speaking testing context in which both HL and NHL learners of Korean participate. This study thus aims to investigate the extent to which HL and NHL learners perform differently across individual and paired speaking tests and on the different pairing types on heritage language background.

The term "heritage language (HL)" can be defined in multiple ways, but in the U.S., HL is often used to refer to indigenous, colonial, or immigrant languages other than English (Fishman, 2006). The definition of the term "heritage language learner" in the U.S. tends to vary as well (Wiley, 2001). Although there is no single definition of this term embracing all heritage language learners in the various immigrant communities in the U.S., the following categories are regarded as key factors of HL learner status: heritage language learners can be defined as students who are raised in a home where a language other than the majority language is spoken, who speak or understand the heritage language and are to some degree bilingual in the majority language and in the heritage language (Valdés, 2000). Thus, in this study, heritage speakers of Korean are defined as learners who are exposed to Korean by their Korean parents outside of Korea. The present study explores such learners in the context of a university-level Korean language classroom.

Note that HL students' Korean language ability may not be fluent enough to be called balanced bilingual and they are usually more proficient in spoken than written language skills (Bae & Bachman, 1998; Lee & Kim, 2008). Although they were raised in a Korean-speaking household or community, their Korean language development lags (Sohn & Merrill, 2004) because of their lack of formal Korean instruction prior to taking Korean classes at the university (Sohn, 1995). Several studies have observed HL learners' relatively higher oral proficiency. In particular, Kagan and Friedman (2003) found that most Russian HL learners used more extensive vocabularies and spoke much faster than NHL counterparts in their performance on the Oral Proficiency Interview (OPI). Similarly, Ilieva (2012) reported that Hindi HL learners produced native-like pronunciation and fluency in their practice OPIs.

However, HL learners do not necessarily perform better in untimed written tasks that utilize metalinguistic and explicit linguistic knowledge which might favor instructed and literate NHL learners (Bowles, 2011; Montrul, 2010a; Montrul, Davidson, de la Fuente, & Foote, 2014). This might be due to the fact that HL learners were more exposed to aural input in a naturalistic environment, whereas NHLs have received more written input in an instructed setting. Such unbalanced development of spoken and written language of HL learners poses challenges for instructors and testers. Due to the differences between HL and NHL learners in their diverse learning strategies and linguistic needs, foreign language instructors and testers might as well provide each group of learners with different levels and sequencing of classroom practice and tasks (Kondo-Brown, 2010). These issues are, however, quite complicated as a two-track curriculum system for postsecondary HL and NHL learners is not readily available in many university foreign language programs in the U.S. (Yu, 2008).

The sizable intergroup differences in oral abilities observed in the same class-room cause concern for language teachers and testers, especially when pair or group speaking tests are used to assess the oral proficiency of each individual student. Differences in a learner's performance might be observed across speaking tasks, particularly when learners of differing speaking abilities are grouped together in pair or group oral tests. From a measurement perspective, this could be problematic for interpreting learners' individual speaking ability, which could be generalizable across different tasks, raters, and partners' characteristics. It is thus important to further investigate the extent to which HL and NHL learners perform differentially across varying tasks and partners in order to deepen our understanding of the potential biases in scores obtained from paired speaking tests.

Paired Speaking Tests

The need to understand the influence of speaking test task type on student scores is becoming more and more important, as the use of paired and group assessment has recently begun to increase. The paired speaking test has become a more frequent component of language teaching as it aligns the communicative practice of pair and group work in the classroom to encourage more interaction between learners (Taylor, 2000). Using a paired speaking test of oral proficiency has thus led to positive wash-back (Saville & Hargreaves, 1999; Norton, 2005). In a traditional oral proficiency interview, an unequal power relationship between a test taker and interviewer tends to exist (van Lier, 1989; Lazaraton, 1992), since the interviewer usually initiates all sequences of talk and asks the questions, whereas the test taker simply responds to such questions (Ross & Berwick, 1992; Young & Milanovic, 1992). This imbal-ance between the interviewer's and the interviewee's control over the interaction inevitably elicits limited discourse on the part of the test taker (Zuengler, 1993). However, the power relationship in paired speaking tests is more balanced than in a traditional interview, since both interlocutors are participating as examinees, and, thus, the paired test task induces different types of interactions and a richer language sample (Taylor, 2000; Swain, 2001).

Regardless of the advantages of paired oral tasks, there are still a number of chal-lenges that need to be addressed. The major concern is who is paired with whom, since the test taker's performance can be influenced by various characteristics of the other test taker (Taylor & Wigglesworth, 2009). Research in second language acquisition (SLA) (e.g., Gass & Varonis, 1985; Pica, Holliday, Lewis, & Morgen-thaler, 1989) has shown that interlocutor variables including gender, proficiency, ethnicity, and native/non-native speaker status are related to the linguistic production of interlocutors.

Among such interlocutor variables, the effect of partner proficiency on test takers' performance in a paired or group speaking test has also been widely examined. Some studies (Iwashita, 1998; Norton, 2005) suggested that lower level test takers might benefit from their higher level partners in a paired speaking test. Specifically, Iwashita (1998) observed that lower proficiency test takers talked more and received higher scores when they were paired with higher level partners. Nonetheless, it was not clear how they gained higher speaking scores because she found that the production of more language did not always result in higher scores. Indeed, other studies such as Csépes (2002) and Davis (2009) similarly found that lower level students produced more language with higher level partners; however, these studies found no significant effect of proficiency level on individual test takers' speaking scores.

Among many factors that might affect test takers' performance in a paired or group oral testing context, the effect of L2 proficiency differences in pairs or groups is of particular concern to language testers and instructors when they have mixed-ability level classes. Varying learners' proficiency is an important factor to be considered when organizing them into pairs and small groups (Hess, 2001) because this is closely related to the amount of potential mediation each student may receive during the pair or group work in the actual classroom context (Leeser, 2004).

In paired speaking test contexts, such proficiency disparities between the partners will also affect raters in either holistic or analytic scoring protocols, although possibly differentially. Among the most commonly measured analytic speaking criteria, which are pronunciation, fluency, grammatical accuracy, and vocabulary, fluency is most likely to be influenced by interlocutor effects; speakers tend to speak more and faster when they are in pairs than when they are alone, and thus, their fluency ratings tend to be higher on dialogic oral tasks where they interact with each other than on monologic ones (Ejzenberg, 2000). This might be related to the fact that the flow of the interaction is co-constructed by both participants in a conversation (McCarthy, 2010). However, in the context of paired or small group assessment, the effect of interlocutor proficiency level on scores given based on an analytic rubric remains to be understood. Investigating this issue contributes to a deeper understanding of interlocutor effects on the resulting oral scores in a paired speaking test.

A Generalizability (G) Study

A G-study (Shavelson & Webb, 1991) has often been conducted to estimate the amount of variance contributing to speaking test scores obtained by different speaking tasks (Kenyon & Tschirner, 2000; Stansfield & Kenyon, 1992). G-theory is based on analysis of variance (ANOVA) approaches and has been used as an appropriate conceptual framework and methodology for examining the impact of various measurement facets including tasks, raters, and learners themselves on the total score variance (Brennan, 1999; Shavelson & Webb, 1991). G-theory thus allows the researcher to decompose the total amount of variance into component parts via the estimated components (Shavelson & Webb, 1991). This effectively captures the relative contribution of diverse sources of variation to the test takers' speaking performance. Due to these advantages, G-theory has been widely applied to various language testing situations (Brown, 1999; Kunnan, 1992; Schoonen, 2005; Shin &

Ewert, 2015), and to a number of previous studies in a speaking test context (Bachman et al., 1995; Kenyon and Tschirner, 2000; Lynch and McNamara, 1998; van Moere, 2006). In this present study, G-theory was applied so that the relative contribution of speaking test tasks (monologic and paired) and raters to score variance in different groups (heritage and non-heritage learners of Korean) could be examined.

Research Questions

The present study thus undertakes the issue of whether heritage and non-heritage learners of Korean perform differently on monologic and dialogic speaking tasks when they are paired with partners of the same or different language backgrounds in Korean. In order to address this issue, the following research questions were raised by this study:

(1) Do HL students obtain higher scores than NHL students on both speaking tests tasks (monologic vs. paired)?
(2) Are there any differential effects of speaking test tasks and raters on HL and NHL students' speaking performance?
(3) If a speaking test task effect exists, to what extent does the pairing type by heritage backgrounds (HL-HL, HL-NHL, and NHL-NHL) affect students' oral performances as reflected in their overall scores and subscores (Pronunciation, Grammar, Vocabulary, and Fluency)?

Methods

Participants

Participants for this study consisted of a group of 78 students who were enrolled in the post-secondary Korean language program (Korean I) at a west coast college in the U.S. Their ages ranged from 19 to 25. Forty-two female (F) and 36 male (M) students participated in this study. They had received approximately 50 h of formal Korean instruction when the data were collected. These students self-identified into two groups: the heritage learners of Korean consisted of 46 students (F = 22; M = 24) who were raised in homes in the U.S. where Korean was spoken although English was the dominant language, while non-heritage learners of Korean was composed of 32 students (F = 20; M = 12) who had not learned any Korean before they began taking Korean in this program. Among the NHL group, students' first language backgrounds varied as follows: English ($n = 11$), Japanese ($n = 11$), Mandarin ($n = 5$), Spanish ($n = 3$), and Mongolian ($n = 2$).

Instruments

The tests used in this study were administered in both monologic and paired test tasks. All 78 students took both speaking tests. In the monologic speaking task, participants responded to the three different tasks and recorded their responses on a computer. In the first task, participants were asked to describe the location of three different items in a picture. In the second task, students described various daily activities provided in multiple pictures. In the third task, they were asked to narrate in detail what they did over the weekend (for the first administration) or Thanksgiving holiday (for the second administration). All instructions were given both in English and Korean. The tasks are widely used as production tasks in interaction-based research (Gass & Mackey, 2007), and they were familiar to the participating students because similar tasks had been used as classroom activities. In the paired speaking test task, they interacted with another student to answer the three other comparable task questions. Their interactions in the paired task were video recorded. Participants were provided with similar pictures as in the monologic task, but they were also asked to draw the items that their partners described and to write down the times for each daily activity in the second task. In the final open-ended task, they asked each partner about what they had done during the weekend or Thanksgiving holiday.

Procedures

Test administration procedures. Each participant completed the monologic speaking test individually in a language lab with a proctor present. Participants were handed a question sheet and were then allowed 30 s to organize their thoughts before recording. They stated their names first and then responded to the questions listed on the sheet. Their responses to the individual oral test were recorded in the lab using a Wimba Voice 6.0 (2009), a web-based audio recording and playback application, installed on the lab computer.

For the paired speaking test task, participants were randomly assigned into one of three possible pairings: HL–HL, NHL–NHL, and HL–NHL. In order to control for possible gender effects, each participant was paired with a partner of the same gender. The make-up of the pairs and formats is illustrated in Table 13.1. There were three possible pairings: two with partners of the same heritage language background (HL–HL and NHL–NHL) and one with partners of a different heritage language background (HL-NHL). Each individual received his or her own oral score for each task. Thirty HL students were paired with each other, and the other sixteen HL students were paired with sixteen NHL students whose L1s were English ($n = 6$), Japanese ($n = 6$), Mandarin ($n = 2$), Spanish ($n = 1$), and Mongolian ($n = 1$). The other sixteen NHL students were paired with each other, and their L1s were English ($n = 5$), Japanese ($n = 5$), Mandarin ($n = 3$), Spanish ($n = 2$), and Mongolian ($n = 1$). To minimize a possible ordering effect, half of the students

Table 13.1 Pairing types observed in this study

	First administration		Second administration	
Group 1	Monologic speaking test		Paired speaking test	
			HL-students ($n =$ 22)	NHL-students ($n =$ 16)
			• With HL-students ($n = 14$) • With NHL-students ($n = 8$)	• With HL-students ($n = 8$) • With NHL-students ($n = 8$)
Group 2	Paired speaking test		Monologic speaking test	
	HL-students ($n =$ 24)	NHL-students ($n =$ 16)		
	• With HL-students ($n = 16$) • With NHL-students ($n = 8$)	• With HL-students ($n = 8$) • With NHL-students ($n = 8$)		

Note **HL** and **NHL** denote heritage and non-heritage language learners, respectively

(Group 1 in Table 13.1) took the monologic task first and the other half (Group 2 in Table 13.1) took the dialogic task first, with two weeks between the tests. Each pair sat down on a chair facing each other in a classroom. They were presented with a question sheet for the paired speaking test. They were also given 30-s of pre-task planning time, just as they had in the monologic speaking test.

Scoring methods. The responses were rated by the two trained raters, who were native speakers of Korean with extensive experience teaching Korean in the U.S. Participants' responses were rated based on a six-point scale for each of four oral communication subscales. The six-point scale was adapted from Bonk and Ockey (2003)'s oral rating scale, which contains pronunciation, grammar, vocabulary, and fluency subscales, and is attached in the Appendix. Although Bonk and Ockey (2003)'s oral rating scales were developed and used in the Japanese context, they were generic enough to be applied to other contexts. The pronunciation subscale mostly referred to the degree of intelligibility and foreign accentedness ratings in Korean. The grammar subscale was related to complexity and accuracy of syntactic structures, and the vocabulary subscale referred to richness and accuracy of lexical features of speakers' oral performance. Lastly, the fluency subscale reflected temporal features of speech and disfluency markers including unfilled pauses, frequency of filled pauses, length of pauses, and repetitions. It should be noted that "communication strategies" from Bonk and Ockey's original rating scales was omitted since it could not be applied to the monologic speaking test performances. Participants were given the average of the raters' scores for each component score. Raters participated in a rater training session consisting of an orientation to the test, a discussion of the rating scales, as well as listening to, rating, and discussing their ratings of speaking samples from the two different speaking tasks. During the rater training session, raters first reviewed the benchmark for each subscale, and they listened to anchor samples for each scale along with comments on salient features of each speech sample provided by the researcher. Practice samples were then played for them to score independently. Their scores were checked and discussed with the researcher. After a discussion of their ratings on the practice set, another set of speech samples was given for calibration, and they all agreed on scores on each sample. It is important to note that they were not informed of the goals of the research during or after the rater training session.

Data Analysis

The data in this study were analyzed using SPSS 20 (2011), GENOVA (Crick & Brennan, 1984), and mGENOVA (Brennan, 1999). Descriptive statistics were calculated and assumptions regarding the analysis of variance were checked. In order to examine the effects of the test tasks and raters on performances across the two groups of students, a series of univariate G-study persons ×raters × tasks ($p \times r \times t$) designs, where task is individual vs. paired, were conducted for each pairing type (i.e., HL–HL, HL–NHL, NHL–HL, NHL–NHL). The HL–NHL group represents the heritage students who are paired with the non-heritage students, whereas the NHL–HL group denotes the non-heritage students paired with heritage students. After the univariate G-studies were conducted, multivariate G-studies were carried out to detect the effects of those factors on the four subscores of the speaking tests.

Results

Descriptive Statistics

The mean component and composite scores for the 78 participants for the monologic speaking test task averaged by two different raters are reported in Table 13.2.

As can be seen in Table 13.2, the results reveal a tendency for the HL students to score higher than the NHL counterparts in each score category and total scores from the monologic speaking test (Pronunciation: $t_{(76)} = 8.30$, $p < 0.001$, $d = 1.80$;

Table 13.2 Means and standard deviations for monologic speaking test scores of both groups

Group	Pronunciation	Grammar	Vocabulary	Fluency	Total
Heritage	3.91 (0.75)	3.98 (0.87)	3.87 (0.86)	3.95 (0.99)	15.71 (3.03)
Non-heritage	2.56 (0.75)	2.83 (0.75)	2.55 (0.84)	2.64 (0.85)	10.58 (2.67)

Grammar: $t_{(76)} = 6.38$, $p < 0.001$, $d = 1.42$; Vocabulary: $t_{(76)} = 7.60$, $p < 0.001$, $d = 1.55$; Fluency: $t_{(76)} = 6.70$, $p < 0.001$, $d = 1.42$; Total scores: $t_{(76)} = 7.71$, $p < 0.001$, $d = 1.80$), supporting the fact that HL learners of Korean outperform NHL learners of Korean in overall oral proficiency (Sohn & Shin, 2007).

Variance Components

In order to estimate the effects of the different types of test tasks and different raters altogether,[1] variance components and standard errors of estimated variance components for each facet were computed using GENOVA. Tables 13.3, 13.4, 13.5 and 13.6 show the variance components for the individual students' composite test scores given by the two raters on both the individual and paired speaking test tasks under different pairing conditions (i.e., HL–HL, HL–NHL, NHL–HL, NHL–NHL), respectively, as estimated by GENOVA.

Table 13.3 shows variance components and standard errors for the individual total test scores given by the two raters for the HL students paired with other HL students in

Table 13.3 G-study results for HL students paired with HL students

Effect	df	Variance component	Standard error	Percent of variance (%)
Persons (*p*)	29	7.95	2.13	83
Raters (*r*)	1	0.09	0.08	1
Tasks (*t*)	1	0.48	0.41	5
pr	29	0.18	0.13	2
pt	29	0.36	0.17	4
rt	1	0.00	0.01	0
prt,e	29	0.53	0.13	6
Total	119	9.59		100

Table 13.4 G-study results for HL students paired with NHL students

Effect	df	Variance component	Standard error	Percent of variance (%)
Persons (*p*)	15	9.23	3.35	84
Raters (*r*)	1	0.00	0.04	0
Tasks (*t*)	1	0.00	0.05	0
pr	15	0.28	0.38	3
pt	15	0.17	0.35	2
rt	1	0.00	0.06	0
prt,e	15	1.27	0.43	12
Total		10.95		100

Table 13.5 G-study results for NHL students paired with HL students

Effect	df	Variance component	Standard error	Percent of variance (%)
Persons (p)	15	6.32	2.20	86
Raters (r)	1	0.00	0.01	0
Tasks (t)	1	0.74	0.61	10
pr	15	0.02	0.06	0
pt	15	0.05	0.06	1
rt	1	0.00	0.01	0
prt,e	15	0.21	0.07	3
Total		7.34		100

Table 13.6 G-study results for NHL students paired with NHL students

Effect	df	Variance component	Standard error	Percent of variance (%)
Persons (p)	15	6.42	2.33	85
Raters (r)	1	0.08	0.08	1
Tasks (t)	1	0.01	0.03	0
pr	15	0.20	0.18	3
pt	15	0.33	0.22	4
rt	1	0.00	0.01	0
prt,e	15	0.50	0.17	7
Total		7.54		100

the paired speaking test task. This table shows that the person (p) effect accounted for the majority of the total variance ($\sigma_p^2 = 7.95; 83\%$ of the total variance). The variance component associated with raters ($\sigma_r^2 = 0.09; 1\%$) was negligible, indicating that the raters were quite consistent in their scoring of students' speaking performances. However, there was some task effect ($\sigma_t^2 = 0.48; 5\%$), indicating that when HL students were paired with other HL students, they tended to get slightly higher scores in the paired than in the individual test task.

As with the HL–HL group, in the HL–NHL (see Table 13.4), the variance component for the persons (p) effect accounted for the largest percentage of the total variance ($\sigma_p^2 = 9.23; 84\%$). On the other hand, the variance components for other facets (rater, task, and interaction between facets) were mostly negligible (less than 3%) suggesting that the relative standing of HL students paired with NHL students did not differ across the two tasks. It should, however, be noted that the variance component associated with the error terms ($\sigma_{prt,e}^2 = 1.27; 12\%$) was relatively large; the HL students' speaking scores were affected by the interaction among persons, raters, and tasks, or other unaccounted sources of variances.

As with the other paired groups, in the NHL–HL group (see Table 13.5), the person (p) effect accounted for a fairly large percentage of the total variance ($\sigma_p^2 = $

6.32; 86% of the total variance). However, there was also substantial variability due to task (t) for the NHL–HL group ($\sigma_t^2 = 0.74$; 10% of the total variance). As can be seen in Table 13.9, NHL students obtained higher scores in pairs than individually.

Table 13.6 shows that the person (p) effect in the NHL–NHL group accounted for 85% ($\sigma_p^2 = 6.42$) of the total score variance, indicating that differences among the NHL students were responsible for the vast amount of variance. In the NHL–NHL group, the main effects of the raters and tasks were negligible ($\sigma_t^2 = 0.08$; 1%). However, the relatively large variance component for prt,e ($\sigma_{prt,e}^2 = 0.50$; 7%) shows that there was a larger effect of person-by-rater-by-task interaction plus undifferentiated error on the total score variance in this group of students.

From these analyses, we can see substantial variance components for persons (p), which indicates that the largest amount of variation in student scores was accounted for by differences in speaking ability. This result was expected, given that students' speaking proficiency was what we intended to measure. The small variance component for the rater effect indicates that the two sets of ratings were relatively consistent. For the group whose partners were HL students, the task (t) effect was fairly large, showing that students, particularly NHL students in the NHL–HL group, tended to perform better in the paired task than in the individual one.

We can also see that NHL students paired with HL students were most influenced by the task effects. In other words, both their speaking scores and their relative standing differed across the two task types. Since students' speaking scores were the composite of four different speaking dimensions (pronunciation, grammar, vocabulary, and fluency), it was of interest to look at the task effects on each dimension of rating.

Tables 13.7, 13.8, 13.9, and 13.10 show the descriptive results of the oral test scores averaged over two raters for the four different speaking dimensions in each group. Results suggest that both HL and NHL students performed quite similarly across two tasks. However, it is important to note that NHL students gained higher

Table 13.7 Mean component scores for HL students in the HL–HL group in the two test tasks

Components	Monologic speaking test				Paired speaking test			
	*P	G	V	F	P	G	V	F
Mean	3.88	3.92	3.87	3.97	3.98	3.88	3.88	4.05
SD	0.67	0.77	0.93	1.09	0.71	0.91	0.86	0.76

* P, G, V, and F stand for pronunciation, grammar, vocabulary, and fluency subscores, respectively

Table 13.8 Mean component scores for HL students in the HL–NHL group in the two test tasks

Components	Monologic speaking test				Paired speaking test			
	P	G	V	F	P	G	V	F
Mean	3.97	4.09	3.88	3.91	4.00	3.91	3.69	4.00
SD	0.90	1.05	0.74	0.80	0.97	0.88	0.77	0.80

Table 13.9 Mean component scores for NHL students in the NHL–HL group in the two test tasks

	Monologic speaking test				Paired speaking test			
Components	P	G	V	F	P	G	V	F
Mean	2.53	2.75	2.56	2.81	2.47	2.69	2.75	3.97
SD	0.70	0.64	0.70	0.81	0.70	0.56	0.79	0.62

Table 13.10 Mean component scores for NHL students in the NHL–NHL group in the two test tasks

	Monologic speaking test				Paired speaking test			
Components	P	G	V	F	P	G	V	F
Mean	2.59	2.91	2.53	2.47	2.47	2.72	2.63	2.44
SD	0.80	0.84	0.96	0.87	0.74	0.82	0.74	0.91

scores in the paired test task than in the individual speaking test task. It also reveals that differences between individual and paired speaking test tasks were quite large for the fluency subscores compared to the task differences for the other subscores.

Multivariate G-theory

Unlike univariate methods, multivariate G-theory allows the investigator to examine sources of covariation among multiple scores (Webb & Shavelson, 1981). Since a multivariate G-study can decompose both variances and covariances into components, it provides us with useful information about consistency in speaking performances across four different speaking subscores. A multivariate G-study person-by-rater-by-task ($p \times r \times t$) design for each subtest was carried out for the NHL–HL group (see Table 13.11).

In Table 13.11, the diagonal elements are variances, the lower diagonal elements are covariances, and the upper diagonal elements are correlations among the four speaking dimensions. The person facet accounted for most of the variances in scores of NHL students paired with HL students. The small estimated variance components for the rater (r) (less than 0.01 for all categories) indicate that raters were consistent in their scoring of all speaking components. The effect of task facet was negligible for pronunciation, grammar, and vocabulary, suggesting that students performed similarly across the two different speaking test tasks. However, the variance component for the task facet (t) for fluency was quite large ($\sigma_{t4}^2 = 0.66$), which indicates that the test takers tended to perform better in fluency in the paired speaking test task than in the individual task, as can be seen from the mean score differences in Table 13.7. It is noteworthy that the variance components for task effect (t) for fluency rating were larger than the person (p) effect ($\sigma_p^2 = 0.50$), indicating that task-to-task differences for the *fluency* ratings were larger than average differences between persons. It should

Table 13.11 Estimated G-study Variance and covariance components for NH students in NH–H pairs

Effect		Pronunciation (1)	Grammar (2)	Vocabulary (3)	Fluency (4)
Persons (p)	(1)	0.47	0.74	0.81	0.91
	(2)	0.28	0.32	0.81	0.88
	(3)	0.40	0.33	0.52	0.93
	(4)	0.44	0.35	0.47	0.50
Raters (r)	(1)	0.01			
	(2)	0.01	0.00		
	(3)	0.02	0.00	0.00	
	(4)	0.00	0.00	0.00	0.00
Tasks (t)	(1)	0.01			
	(2)	0.00	0.00		
	(3)	0.00	0.00	0.01	
	(4)	0.00	0.00	0.11	0.66
pr	(1)	0.00			
	(2)	0.00	0.03		
	(3)	0.00	0.00	0.00	
	(4)	0.01	0.00	0.00	0.00
pt	(1)	0.00			
	(2)	0.01	0.00		
	(3)	0.00	0.00	0.06	
	(4)	0.00	0.00	0.01	0.03
rt	(1)	0.00			
	(2)	0.00	0.00		
	(3)	0.00	0.00	0.03	
	(4)	0.00	0.01	0.01	0.01
prt,e	(1)	0.10			
	(2)	0.00	0.10		
	(3)	0.03	0.00	0.05	
	(4)	0.00	0.01	0.00	0.07

also be noted that there were some non-negligible estimated covariance components for task ($\sigma^2_{t3t4} = 0.11$) between fluency and vocabulary subscores. This suggests that some NHL students who scored higher in the fluency rating in the paired task than in the individual one were also likely to score higher in the vocabulary rating when paired with HL students in the paired task. In order to check if there are any serious outliers affecting these results and how NHL students scored differently across two speaking tasks, a breakdown of the number of scores in each score category for this group is provided as in Table 13.12. It shows that NHL students scored similarly

Table 13.12 Breakdown of the number of scores in each category for NH students in NH–H pairs in both monologic and paired speaking tasks

Monologic task	Pronunciation	Grammar	Vocabulary	Fluency
Score 6	0	0	0	0
Score 5	0	0	0	0
Score 4	1	2	2	4
Score 3	7	7	5	5
Score 2	7	7	9	7
Score 1	1	0	0	0
Paired task	Pronunciation	Grammar	Vocabulary	Fluency
Score 6	0	0	0	0
Score 5	0	0	0	3
Score 4	0	1	4	7
Score 3	7	6	2	6
Score 2	7	9	10	0
Score 1	2	0	0	0

in pronunciation, grammar, and vocabulary categories across two tasks, but most of them moved up to higher ratings in fluency when they were paired with HL students.

Discussion

In foreign language teaching contexts in the U.S., HL and NHL students are often mixed in one class. From a measurement perspective, this hybrid nature of student populations in foreign language classes could be a cause for concern in paired speaking tests given that HL students typically have higher oral/aural proficiency than NHL students. Such discrepancies in proficiency may result in biased scores for students completing paired speaking tests.

The findings of this study show that HL students performed similarly across different test tasks (monologic and dialogic tasks) regardless of the heritage background of their partners. Likewise, NHL students did not perform differently between two test tasks when they were paired with the NHL students. As had been expected, however, when NHL students were paired with HL students whose level of Korean oral proficiency was higher, they tended to perform better. The follow-up multivariate G-study results reveal that the large differences in *fluency* subscores across the two tasks contribute to the large variance components for task effects (t) in the composite speaking scores of NHL students paired with HL students. Fluency subscores were significantly higher when NHL students were paired with HL students than with other NHL students.

These findings support previous studies (e.g., Iwashita, 1998; Norton, 2005) that observed differences in test takers' scores when paired with students of a different proficiency level. The results are also in line with prior research showing that low-proficiency learners tend to obtain higher scores when they are paired with higher proficiency learners in the paired speaking test. Low-proficiency second language learners seem to benefit more when they interact with more orally proficient interlocutors like heritage students.

However, this study further reveals that the partners' proficiency effect was not consistent across all components of speaking ability. The effect of proficiency differences in pairs stands out more on fluency ratings. This result might be related to the vulnerability of one speaker's fluency to the influence of the partner's higher oral proficiency. As opposed to pronunciation, grammar, and vocabulary subscores, which are relatively consistent across the monologue and dialogue task types, paired assessment can easily affect a test taker's fluency because the flow and speed of conversation could be controlled by the more fluent interlocutors.

It should be noted that in this study, fluency subscores were defined and operationalized in terms of temporal variables, such as speech rate and length and frequency of pauses and hesitations, as is common in oral rating scales used for L2 group oral tests (Bonk & Ockey, 2003; van Moere, 2006; Leaper & Riazi, 2014; Ockey, 2009). As Chambers (1998) suggested, this concept of fluency may lead to multiple interpretations in different speaking test tasks. It is possible that heritage students often felt uncomfortable when their non-heritage interlocutor paused at the inappropriate junctures. They may have sometimes jumped into the NHL students' turns, rephrased their questions, or added some lexical fillers in Korean to avoid unnatural silences during the test. This kind of conversational act could actually reduce non-heritage students' pausing time, which is not possible in the individual speaking test setting. It is also plausible that HL students' successful strategic skills in conversation could have contributed to NHL-students' fluency scores. Thus, a careful discourse analysis of the speech data is needed to fully understand the results of the present study.

It may not be appropriate to directly compare the present study to some previous research exploring the influence of partners' differing proficiency levels on test takers' performances (e.g., Davis, 2009; Iwashita, 1998). One reason for this is that the notations "high-level" and "low-level" in these studies refer to groups of students whose proficiency levels were not strikingly different. By contrast, in this study, the discrepancy in oral proficiency between two HL and NHL students was large, as can be seen in their monologic speaking test scores. In addition, there are some differences between HL and NHL students that may not exist between "high-" and "low-proficiency" groups in other studies. Specifically, many HL students have more experience with informal oral exchange than NHL students do, which may allow them to provide some scaffolding support to NHL partners in their paired speaking test. Thus, while it is useful to compare the results of studies observing high- and low-proficiency students, it is reasonable to expect some discrepancies in the findings based on the difference in student backgrounds.

Limitations

In a similar vein to the issues discussed above, note that the findings of the present study cannot be generalized to other foreign language learning contexts where heritage and non-heritage learners coexist, but their oral proficiency levels are comparable. In this study, oral proficiency differences between heritage and non-heritage language learners are only determined by the monologic task. In future research, a more solid oral proficiency measure should be used to demonstrate that heritage language learners are significantly more proficient than non-heritage language learners. Additionally, participants' other characteristics such as communication style and personality were not controlled in the present study. These uncontrolled factors may also affect student performance. Although it might not be feasible to control all these potential factors, the results of this study suggest that scores from paired interactions must be interpreted with care and that different pairings should be tried to examine the possible effects of these factors on the speaking test scores. The small number of raters and tasks ($n = 2$) also limits the generalizability of findings about the effects of raters, tasks, and rater-by-task interactions to other contexts. Finally, due to small enrollment in a Korean program, the sample size of this study is relatively small for G-studies, which may reduce the generalizability and stability of the results.

Conclusions, Implications, and Future Directions

Overall, the results of the present study reveal that HL students performed similarly across different test tasks regardless of heritage background of their partners. Likewise, NHL students did not perform differently between two test tasks when they were paired with the NHL students. On the other hand, when NHL students were paired with HL students whose level of Korean oral proficiency was higher, they tended to gain higher scores in the paired speaking test task than in the monologic one, particularly in their fluency subscores. This suggests that perceptions of fluency in monologic discourse may be different from those of fluency in dialogic discourse. As McCarthy (2010) argued, the former is mainly related to temporal features, such as speaking speed and pausing, whereas the latter is more relevant to the addition of lexical fillers and smooth turn-taking, which maintain the flow of the interaction. Such a view of fluency as "the joint production of flow by more than one speaker" (McCarthy, 2010, p. 1) may explain why L2 raters were not always able to translate differences in temporal measures of breakdown fluency into test takers' score differences (Leaper & Riazi, 2014).

This notion of co-constructed fluency in dialogic discourse provides important implications for rubric development and rater training in paired and group oral assessment. It would be unwise to directly apply fluency rating descriptors designed for monologic speaking tasks to the paired or group tasks. A focus on interactive and turn-taking skills is needed to define and operationalize the concept of fluency in dialogic oral tests. Such approaches echo Bachman's recommendation of using more broad and inclusive language assessment theory and methodology which will deepen our understanding of the role of language abilities, contexts, and the interactions between them in the way we design, develop, and use language assessments (Bachman, 2007).

Note
1. For information about how to calculate variance components and standard errors of estimated variance components for two-facet, crossed G-study design, refer to Moore (2010, p. 17 and p. 107, respectively).

Appendix A: Analytic Oral Rating Rubrics

Pronunciation

1. Pronunciation is almost unintelligible.
2. Frequently mispronounces words with a very heavy accent in Korean.
3. Frequently mispronounces words, and accent often impedes comprehension. Difficult to understand even with concentrated listening.
4. Pronunciation is not native-like but understandable. Speaker may not have mastered some vowel or consonant sounds.
5. No conspicuous mispronunciations. Accent may sound foreign but does not interfere with comprehension.
6. Native-like pronunciation with no trace of foreign accent.

Grammar

1. Grammar is almost entirely inaccurate except in stock phrases.
2. Produces constant grammatical errors showing control of very few major structures.
3. Uses simple inaccurate sentences and fragmented phrases, causing occasional misunderstanding.
4. Relies mostly on simple (but generally accurate) sentences. Complex sentences are used but often inaccurately.
5. Shows ability to use full range of grammatical structures but still makes some errors, which do not impede comprehension.
6. Uses high-level discourse structures with near native-like grammatical accuracy.

Vocabulary

1. Vocabulary is inadequate for even simple expressions.
2. Vocabulary is limited to basic personal and survival areas.

3. Choice of words is sometimes inaccurate; limitations of vocabulary prevent task completion.
4. Vocabulary is generally adequate for tasks but often used inaccurately.
5. Vocabulary is sufficient for tasks although not always precisely used.
6. Vocabulary is both accurate and extensive with near native-like use.

Fluency

1. Speech is so halting and fragmentary that conversation is virtually impossible.
2. Speech is very slow and uneven except for short or routine sentences.
3. Speech is frequently hesitant and jerky; sentences may be left uncompleted.
4. Speech is occasionally hesitant, with some unevenness caused by rephrasing and groping for words.
5. Speech is effortless and smooth, but perceptibly non-native in speed.
6. Speech shows near native-like fluency, effortless, smooth, and natural rhythm.

References

Bachman, L. F. (1990). *Fundamental considerations in language testing.* Oxford, UK: Oxford University Press.
Bachman, L. F. (2000). Modern language testing at the turn of the century: Assuring that what we count counts. *Language Testing, 17*(1), 1–42.
Bachman, L. F. (2007). What is the construct? The dialectic of abilities and context in defining constructs in language assessment. In J. Fox, M. Wesche, & D. Bayless (Eds.), *Language testing reconsidered* (pp. 41–72). Ottawa, Canada: University of Ottawa Press.
Bachman, L., & Damböck, B. (2018). *Language assessment for classroom teachers.* Oxford, UK: Oxford University Press.
Bachman, L. F., Lynch, B. K., & Mason, M. (1995). Investigating variability in tasks and rater judgments in a performance test of foreign language speaking. *Language Testing, 12*(2), 238–257.
Bae, J., & Bachman, L. F. (1998). A latent variable approach to listening and reading: Testing factorial invariance across two groups of children in the Korean/English Two-Way Immersion Program. *Language Testing, 15*(3), 380–414.
Bonk, W. J., & Ockey, G. (2003). A many-facet Rasch analysis of the second language group oral discussion task. *Language Testing, 20*(1), 89–110.
Bowles, M. (2011). Measuring implicit and explicit knowledge. What can heritage language learners contribute? *Studies in Second Language Acquisition, 33*(2), 247–271.
Brennan, R. L. (1999). *Manual for mGENOVA version 2.0.* Iowa City, IA: The University of Iowa.
Brinton, D., Kagan, O., & Bauckus, S. (Eds.). (2008). *Heritage language education: A new field emerging.* Mahwah, NJ: Lawrence Erlbaum.
Brown, J. D. (1999). The relative importance of persons, items, subtests and languages to TOEFL test variance. *Language Testing, 16*(2), 217–238.
Carreira, M. (2004). Seeking explanatory adequacy: A dual approach to understanding the term "Heritage Language Learner". *Heritage Language Journal, 2*(1), Retrieved November 11, 2019, from https://www.heritagelanguages.org.
Carreira, M., & Kagan, O. (2011). The results of the National Heritage Language Survey: Implications for teaching, curriculum design, and professional development. *Foreign Language Annals, 44*(1), 40–64.
Chambers, F. (1998). What do we mean by fluency? *System, 25*(4), 535–544.

Crick, J. E., & Brennan, R. L. (1984). *GENOVA: A general purpose analysis of variance system. Version 2.2.* Iowa City, IA: American College Testing Program.

Csépes, I. (2002). Is testing speaking in pairs disadvantageous for students? A quantitative study of partner effects on oral test scores. *novELTy, 9*(1), 22–45.

Davis, L. (2009). The influence of interlocutor proficiency in a paired oral assessment. *Language Testing, 26*(3), 367–396.

Ejzenberg, R. (2000). The juggling act of oral fluency: A psycho-sociolinguistic metaphor. In H. Riggenbach (Ed.), *Perspectives on Fluency* (pp. 287–313). Ann Arbor, MI: The University of Michigan Press.

Fishman, J. A. (2006). Three hundred-plus years of heritage language education in the United States. In G. Valdés, J. A. Fishman, R. Chávez, & W. Pérez (Eds.), *Developing minority language resources: The case of Spanish in California* (pp. 12–23). Clevedon, UK: Multilingual Matters.

Gass, S., & Mackey, A. (2007). *Data elicitation for second and foreign language research.* Mahwah, NJ: Lawrence Erlbaum Associates.

Gass, S., & Varonis, E. (1985). Variation in native speaker speech modification to non-native speakers. *Studies in Second Language Acquisition, 7*(1), 37–57.

Hess, N. (2001). *Teaching large multilevel classes.* Cambridge, UK: Cambridge University Press.

Ilieva, G. N. (2012). Hindi heritage language learners' performance during OPIs: Characteristics and pedagogical implications. *Heritage Language Journal, 9*(1), 18–36.

Iwashita, N. (1998). The validity of the paired interview in oral performance assessment. *Melbourne Papers in Language Testing, 5,* 51–65.

Kagan, O., & Friedman, D. (2003). Using the OPI to place heritage speakers of Russian. *Foreign Language Annals, 36,* 536–545.

Katz, A. (2013). Assessment in second language classrooms. In M. Celce-Murcia, D. M. Brinton, & M. A. Snow (Eds.), *Teaching English as a Second or Foreign Language* (pp. 320–337). Boston, MA: National Geographic Learning.

Kenyon, D. M., & Tschirner, E. (2000). The rating of direct and semi-direct oral proficiency interviews: Comparing performance at lower proficiency levels. *The Modern Language Journal, 84*(1), 85–101.

Kondo-Brown, K. (2003). Heritage language instruction for post-secondary students from immigrant backgrounds. *Heritage Language Journal, 1.* Retrieved November 11, 2019, from https://www.heritagelanguages.org.

Kondo-Brown, K. (2010). Curriculum development for advancing heritage language competence: Recent research, current practices, and a future agenda. *Annual Review of Applied Linguistics, 30,* 24–41.

Kunnan, A. J. (1992). An investigation of a criterion-referenced test using G-theory, and factor analysis. *Language Testing, 9*(1), 30–49.

Lazaraton, A. (1992). The structural organization of a language interview: A conversation analytic perspective. *System, 20,* 373–386.

Leaper, D. A., & Riazi, M. (2014). The influence of prompt on group oral tests. *Language Testing, 31*(2), 177–204.

Lee, J. S., & Kim, H. Y. (2008). Heritage language learners' attitudes, motivations and instructional needs: The case of postsecondary Korean language learners. In K. Kondo-Brown & J. D. Brown (Eds.), *Teaching Chinese, Japanese and Korean heritage language students: Curriculum needs, materials, and assessment* (pp. 159–186). New York, NY: Erlbaum.

Leeser, M. J. (2004). Learner proficiency and focus on form during collaborative dialogue. *Language Teaching Research, 8*(1), 55–82.

Lynch, B. K., & McNamara, T. F. (1998). Using G-theory and many-facet Rasch measurement in the development of performance assessments of ESL speaking skills of immigrants. *Language Testing, 15*(2), 158–180.

May, L. (2009). Co-constructed interaction in a paired speaking test: The rater's perspective. *Language Testing, 26*(3), 397–421.

McCarthy, M. (2010). Spoken fluency revisited. *English Profile Journal, 1,* 1–15.

Montrul, S. (2010a). Current issues in heritage language acquisition. *Annual Review of Applied Linguistics, 30*, 3–23.

Montrul, S. (2010b). How similar are L2 learners and heritage speakers? Spanish clitics and word order. *Applied Psycholinguistics, 31*(1), 167–207.

Montrul, S., Davidson, J., de la Fuente, I., & Foote, R. (2014). Early language experience facilitates gender agreement processing in Spanish heritage speakers. *Bilingualism: Language and Cognition, 17*(1), 118–138.

Montrul, S., & Perpiñán, S. (2011). Assessing differences and similarities between instructed L2 learners and heritage language learners in their knowledge of Spanish Tense-Aspect and Mood (TAM) morphology. *Heritage Language Journal, 8*(1), 90–133.

Moore, J. L. (2010). *Estimating standard errors of estimated variance components in generalizability theory using bootstrap procedures.* Unpublished doctoral dissertation. University of Iowa, Iowa City, IA.

Nakatsuhara, F. (2011). Effects of test-taker characteristics and the number of participants in group oral tests. *Language Testing, 28*(4), 483–508.

Norton, J. (2005). The paired format in the Cambridge Speaking Tests. *ELT Journal, 59*(4), 287–297.

Ockey, G. J. (2009). The effects of group members' personalities on a test taker's L2 group oral discussion test scores. *Language Testing, 26*(2), 161–186.

Ockey, G. J., Koyama, D., & Setoguchi, E. (2013). Stakeholder input and test design: A case study on changing the interlocutor familiarity facet of the group oral discussion test. *Language Assessment Quarterly, 10*(3), 292–308.

Pica, T., Holliday, L., Lewis, N., & Morgenthaler, L. (1989). Comprehensible input as an outcome of linguistic demands on the learner. *Studies in Second Language Acquisition, 11*(1), 63–90.

Richards, J. C., & Rodgers, T. S. (2014). *Approaches and methods in language teaching* (3rd ed.). Cambridge, UK: Cambridge University Press.

Ross, S., & Berwick, R. (1992). The discourse of accommodation in oral proficiency interviews. *Studies in Second Language Acquisition, 14*(2), 159–176.

Saville, N., & Hargreaves, P. (1999). Assessing speaking in the revised FCE. *ELT Journal, 53*(1), 42–51.

Schoonen, R. (2005). Generalizability of writing scores: An application of structural equation modeling. *Language Testing, 22*(1), 1–30.

Shavelson, R. J., & Webb, N. M. (1991). *Generalizability theory: A primer.* Newbury Park, CA: Sage.

Shin, S.-Y., & Ewert, D. (2015). What accounts for integrated reading-to-write task scores? *Language Testing, 32*(2), 259–281.

Sohn, S. (1995). The design of curriculum for teaching Korean as a heritage language. In *The Korean language in America 1: Papers from the first national conference on Korean language education* (pp. 19–35).

Sohn, S., & Merrill, C. (2004). The Korean/English dual language program in the Los Angeles Unified School District. In D. Brinton & O. Kagan (Eds.), *Heritage language acquisition: A new field emerging* (pp. 269–287). Mahwah, NJ: Lawrence Erlbaum.

Sohn, S., & Shin, S.-K. (2007). True beginners, false beginners, and fake beginners: Placement strategies for Korean heritage speakers. *Foreign Language Annals, 40*(3), 407–418.

SPSS Ins. (2011). *PASW Statistics for Windows, Version 20.0.* Chicago, IL: SPSS Inc.

Stansfield, C. W., & Kenyon, D. M. (1992). The development and validation of a simulated oral proficiency interview. *Modern Language Journal, 76*(2), 129–141.

Swain, M. (2001). Examining dialogue: Another approach to content specification and to validating inferences drawn from scores. *Language Testing, 18*(3), 275–302.

Taylor, L. (2000). Investigating the paired speaking test format. *University of Cambridge Local Examinations Syndicate Research Notes, 2*, 14–15.

Taylor, L., & Wigglesworth, G. (2009). Are two heads better than one? Pair work in L2 assessment contexts. *Language Testing, 26*(3), 325–339.

Valdés, G. (2000). *Introduction. Spanish for native speakers, Volume 1. AATSP professional development series handbook for teachers K-16.* New York, NY: Harcourt College Publishers.

van Lier, L. (1989). Reeling, writhing, drawling, stretching, and fainting in coils: Oral Proficiency Interviews as conversation. *TESOL Quarterly, 23*(3), 489–508.

van Moere, A. (2006). Validity evidence in a university group oral test. *Language Testing, 23*(4), 411–440.

Webb, N. M., & Shavelson, R. J. (1981). Multivariate generalizability of general educational development ratings. *Journal of Educational Measurement, 18*(1), 13–22.

Wimba Voice. (2009). *Wimba Voice Version 6.0.* New York, NY: Wimba, Inc.

Wiley, T. (2001). On defining heritage languages and their speakers. In J. K. Peyton, D. A. Ranard, & S. McGinnis (Eds.), *Heritage languages in America* (pp. 29–36). Washington, DC & McHenry, IL: Center for Applied Linguistics & Delta Systems.

Young, S., & Milanovic, M. (1992). Discourse variation in oral proficiency interviews. *Studies in Second Language Acquisition, 14*(4), 403–424.

Yu, W. H. (2008). Developing a "compromise curriculum" for Korean heritage and non-heritage learners. Issues and future agenda for teaching Chinese, Japanese, and Korean heritage students. In K. Kondo-Brown & J. D. Brown (Eds.), *Teaching Chinese, Japanese and Korean heritage language students: Curriculum needs, materials, and assessment* (pp. 187–210). New York, NY: Erlbaum.

Zuengler, J. (1993). Encouraging learners' conversational participation: The effect of content knowledge. *Language Learning, 43*(3), 403–432.

Chapter 14
Conclusion

Gary J. Ockey and Brent A. Green

It is clear from reading the papers in this Festschrift that Professor Lyle Bachman's contribution to the field of language assessment continues through the graduate students that he has helped to educate. Moreover, based on many of the citations in this book, readers of his publications who never took a class from him have also been inspired by his work and are playing a role in moving the field forward. As pointed out in Adrian Palmer's *Foreword*, Bachman's influence on the field of language assessment may be second to no one else's. We believe that the papers in this book provide further evidence of this view.

In this conclusion, we provide directions for future research. We revisit chapters in the book to provide context for this endeavor. We hope these directions for future research will inspire a next generation of language assessment researchers to continue with Bachman's legacy of aiding in the development, analyses, and interpretation of effective language assessments. We finish the conclusion with a few comments about our experiences working with Lyle and how he has impacted our professional lives.

Summaries and Directions for Future Research

The papers under Part I, *Assessment of evolving language ability constructs*, discuss some of the innovative constructs that have evolved in the twenty-teens. These developing conceptualizations move the field closer to better language assessments, ones which not only more effectively assess real-world language abilities but that lead to

G. J. Ockey (✉)
Iowa State University, Ames, IA, USA
e-mail: gockey@iastate.edu

B. A. Green
Brigham Young University–Hawaii, Laie, HI, USA
e-mail: Brent.Green@byuh.edu

© Springer Nature Singapore Pte Ltd. 2020   243
G. J. Ockey and B. A. Green (eds.), *Another Generation of Fundamental Considerations in Language Assessment*, https://doi.org/10.1007/978-981-15-8952-2_14

positive impacts on second language teaching and learning. This part follows with much of Bachman's writings. He emphasized the importance of identifying, articulating, and measuring language ability as it is found in the real world (e.g., Bachman, 1990; Bachman & Damböck, 2018; Bachman & Palmer, 1996; Bachman & Palmer, 2010).

In the first chapter of Part I, *A step toward the assessment of English as a lingua franca*, Ockey and Hirch provide a framework, which can be used to determine the degree to which an assessment can be considered to be measuring ELF. They use their framework to evaluate a university placement test of oral communication, which was developed with ELF as a guiding principle. They call for more cooperation between English as a lingua franca researchers and English language assessment researchers and developers. They indicate the importance of these two groups coming to agreement on what constitutes ELF and how it might be best assessed. Their chapter is likely to attract the attention of ELF researchers who have been critical of language assessments and their failure to address ELF concerns. Some particular areas ripe for research include: How much can a test taker be reasonably expected to accommodate to an unfamiliar speech variety? What is the role of prescriptive grammar in the assessment of ELF? What types of test tasks are most conducive to assessing ELF? What are the impacts of using ELF principles to steer language assessment development? What types of language assessments would most benefit from the use of ELF principles in their development? Needless to say this is a fairly new area for language assessment. As Ockey and Hirch point out, language assessments have been evolving to assess ELF, even though there has not been a particular focus to do so.

In the second chapter of Part I, *Revisiting the role of content in language assessment constructs*, Llosa calls for a rethinking of language ability constructs, one that does not attempt to separate language from content. She argues that in certain contexts, particularly in classroom situations, content and language should be assessed together. She believes that this thinking grows from Bachman's model of communicative language use (Bachman, 1990), which recognized the importance of content, or topical knowledge as he called it, in assessing second language ability. Llosa calls for language assessment and content area researchers to work together in exploring novel ways of assessing language and content together. She suggests that future research could examine the way these two constructs overlap in particular contexts. She calls for research that investigates ways that content and language can provide classroom teachers with valuable information that can aid student learning. She believes that rethinking constructs in ways that allow for measuring content and language together can lead to more effective classroom teaching and learning.

In the third chapter of Part I, *What does language testing have to offer to multimodal listening?* Gruba picks up on an important part of Bachman's; language assessment has a lot to offer other disciplines of language learning, and language assessment can benefit from thinking in other areas as well. Gruba discusses some of the ways that systemic functional linguistics (SFL) can be used to help language assessment researchers design assessments, particularly for listening. He suggests that Bachman and Damböck's (2018) assessment use argument structure for classroom learning can be used to guide such an endeavor. Gruba recommends a number of areas for further research as language assessment and SFL learn from each other. He believes that research on the use of SFL to aid in better understanding videotext and how it impacts listening assessments is a fruitful area. He suggests the need for using SFL to develop measures of videotext complexity and believes that research that examines ways SFL can be used to better understand tasks and their meaning will be enlightening. He also calls for research on better ways to understand test taker processes, possibly via eye tracking. Gruba's chapter provides language assessment researchers a glimpse of some of the ways language constructs can be redefined with an SFL lens, one that has had little attention in the language assessment arena.

In the last chapter of Part I, *Learner perceptions of construct-centered feedback on oral proficiency*, Schmidgall discusses the value of using a test-based "construct-centered" approach to giving test takers feedback on their performance on an oral communication assessment. Schmidgall points out that Bachman was a strong proponent of clearly defining a construct to guide test development. Schmidgall extends this thinking about the importance of clear construct definitions to providing clear feedback that focuses on the test takers' strengths and weaknesses in relationship to the operational construct, the rating scale. Schmidgall argues that such construct-centered feedback can lead to positive washback on learning. It makes sense that with such systematic feedback, students would be able to focus on strengthening their weaker language abilities. Research which provides an indication of the extent to which this is actually true would be enlightening. To what extent are students aware of their weaknesses without receiving any feedback? To what degree does construct-centered feedback lead learners to focus on their weaknesses? And, to what extent can students alleviate their weaknesses with effort to overcome them? Future research along these lines may provide not only an indication of the effectiveness of the construct-centered feedback approach, but provide guidance to learners and teachers in structuring learning.

The four papers under the second part of the book, *Validity and validation in language assessment*, address concerns about validity of and approaches to validation of language assessments. They all emphasize the importance of ensuring language assessments are fair for everyone. They provide and/or use frameworks, models, and rationale to steer language assessments toward fair ethical practice, a point found throughout many of Bachman's writings (e.g., Bachman, 1990, Bachman & Palmer, 1996; Bachman & Palmer, 2010; Bachman & Damböck, 2017).

In the first chapter of Part II, *A case for an ethics-based approach to evaluate language assessments*, Kunnan discusses what can be gained from using both Bachman's Standards-based and Argument-based approaches to validation of language assessment and then argues for the importance of expanding these approaches to include principles of fairness and justice, and emphasizing an underlying Ethics-based foundation. He convincingly argues that such attention to these principles provides a more defensible and effective means of articulating a research agenda for evaluating language assessments. Kunnan demonstrates the importance of continuing to consider relevant factors in validation approaches and building on them to aid in making more effective language assessments and directing research on them. Research which compares the Standards-based (Bachman & Palmer, 1996) and Argument-based (Bachman & Palmer, 2010) approaches both with and without Kunnan's Ethics-based approaches would be enlightening. It would seem obvious that focusing attention on the fairness and justice of language assessments in the validation process would improve the quality of language assessments, but this should be empirically examined prior to making any strong claims about this approach. Future research on the useability and effectiveness of Kunnan's Ethics-based approach would certainly be enlightening and may have a profound impact on the way language assessment practitioners and researchers view validation research as the field evolves.

In the second chapter of Part II, *Alignment as a fundamental validity issue in standards-based K-12 English language proficiency assessments*, Wolfe discusses the value of aligning the content of a language assessment with the target language use domain and the effect this alignment has on consequences which stem from the assessment. She argues that given the importance of these consequences in the US K-12 context, language assessment validation and associated research should emphasize the importance of this alignment. She discusses how Bachman and Palmer's (2010) Assessment Use Argument framework aids in highlighting this alignment in creating, implementing, and evaluating a language assessment validation research agenda. As Wolfe points out, many validation frameworks address issues of alignment between test content and the target language use domain. However, the connection to critical test consequences is generally not obvious. Wolfe's approach highlights this critical connection. Moreover, Wolfe's emphasis on consequences provides a further argument against researchers touting discrete-point approaches to assessment on the grounds that test tasks do not need to align with target language use domain tasks to be valid indicators of certain language abilities (Van Moere, 2012). Whether or not unaligned tasks are valid indicators may not be the critical issue; if test tasks are not aligned with the target language use domain, the test consequences are likely to be negative, which is more than reason enough to insist on such alignment. Wolfe suggests research on a clear construct that articulates the types of language expectations included in content and ELP standards, more effective methods and tools to measure the alignment between assessment content, standards, and the target language use domain, and better use of ELP and content student performance data to better understand student needs. We would add that research on the consequences of test content and tasks that do not align with the target language use domain should be further examined. In what ways and to what extent do these consequences negatively impact learning and instruction?

In the third chapter of Part II, *Validating a holistic rubric for scoring short answer reading questions*, Cushing and Tywoniw use Bachman and Palmer's AUA (2010) to frame the validation of "a practical scoring procedure" for sentence length reading comprehension items. Their approach was to use a holistic rating scale to score sets of responses rather than scoring items individually. They found that the holistic section-based scores were associated with fidelity to the source-text item-level scoring but not to item-level ratings for simply writing a sufficient number of words nor to overlap with source text language, that is, copying from the source. Their study demonstrates the effectiveness of Bachman and Palmer's (2010) AUA in helping to frame the evidence in validating the scoring approach for a language assessment. The authors suggest that this short-cut approach to scoring makes it possible to validly assess a rather large number of test takers in a short time with limited human resources. As they point out, an alternative would be machine scoring. It would be enlightening for future research to examine the differences between such an approach and basic machine scoring that could be feasibly implemented in similar contexts. Local placement tests, such as the one the authors discuss, are likely to take on a more important role (Dimova, Yan, & Ginther, 2020) and research that examines practical scoring approaches on them is becoming increasingly valuable.

In the last chapter of Part II, *The curse of explanation: Model selection in language testing research*, Choi reminds us of the challenges associated with statistical modeling. He points out the difficulty of building a model that is similar to the true model based only on theory and previous research and notes that it is common to resort to data-driven model selection to find a model that approximates the data. He provides various examples to demonstrate where we can go wrong with statistical modeling and gives suggestions for how to limit some of these problems. Complex statistical modeling in the field of language testing is fairly new. Areas ripe for research include examinations of multi-dimensional models for better modeling complex language constructs. How effective can such approaches be at modeling these complex models and how useful to better understanding language and developing language assessments can these complex multi-dimensional models be? As Choi infers, it is likely that language theories have been built on statistical models that are not completely accurate. Research that continually evaluates these models and the statistical approaches (and theories) they are built on is critical to helping ensure accurate models and conceptualizations.

In Part III, *Understanding internal structures of language assessments*, the authors use advanced statistical procedures, including generalizability theory and confirmatory factor analysis, to examine the structure of complex language ability constructs. Along with providing insights into conceptualization of complex language ability constructs, they demonstrate some of the advanced quantitative techniques that have been effectively used to better understand the complex nature of language and how to best assess it. These papers also provide insights into the quantitative expertise that Bachman helped to bring to the field of language assessment (e.g., Bachman, 2004; Bachman & Kunnan, 2005).

In the first chapter in Part III, *Developing summary content scoring criteria for university L2 writing instruction in Japan*, Sawaki uses Bachman and Palmer's (2010) AUA framework to steer her investigation of approaches to effectively assessing summary writing. Her study employed multivariate generalizability theory to examine content point scoring and a holistic summary content rating scale for this purpose. She found that the holistic ratings resulted in acceptably dependable scores while the content point scores were less consistent. Sawaki suggests further research on the individual rater behaviors for these approaches in a Many-facet Rasch Measurement framework would be valuable. We would add that think alouds, eye tracking, and rater interviews may all contribute to a better understanding of how raters interact with these approaches and the extent to which they can be used to judge language abilities targeted by the test developers. Sawaki also calls for more research on the approaches' convergent and divergent validity and suggests stakeholder perspectives, particularly teachers' and students' in classroom situations, should be examined to aid in connecting them to learning.

In the second chapter of Part III, *Consistency of computer-automated scoring keys across authors and authoring teams*, Carr uses multivariate generalizability theory to examine the dependability of computer automated scoring of limited production tasks. After empirically showing that scoring keys written by individual writers may not be acceptably dependable, Carr shows that an acceptable level of dependability can be reached by using authoring teams rather than individuals. Carr recommends that future research should investigate the recruiting, training procedures, and constraints and guidance on authoring. What types of background are most useful when recruiting scoring key authoring groups? For instance, is training in coding helpful? Is some level of applied linguistics knowledge needed? If so, what type and to what degree? What approaches to training are most useful? How much training is needed to reach an acceptable level of consistency with a given group of raters for a particular purpose? As automated scoring continues to expand to less restrained tasks, such as spoken discussions, research along these lines will likely gain increased importance.

In the third chapter of Part III, *Distinguishing language ability from the context in an EFL speaking test*, Cai investigates the relationship between language ability and contextual factors, such as topical knowledge when assessing retelling, topic-based talk, and discussion speaking tasks. His use of confirmatory factor analysis with a bifactor model indicates that language ability can be separated from these contextual factors and that task performance includes both language ability and contextual factors such as topical knowledge. Cai calls for further research on whether the interlocutor's contribution to the discourse and nonverbal behavior should be considered contextual factors or a part of communicative competence. This issue of construct definition becomes more complex in a context where oral language assessments are much more commonly being taken at home via computers. Should such tests be video-mediated (Ockey et al., 2019, Nakatsuhara et al., in press), so body language can be part of the construct? Should such tests be delivered via virtual environments where test takers speak synchronously with other interlocutors but see avatars representing the speakers rather than the actual speakers (Ockey et al., 2017)? If spoken dialog systems (Vikram, Evanini, & Tsuprun, 2019), "Systems capable of orally 'interacting' with a human, for aiding in eliciting interactive speech samples," (Ockey & Chukharev-Hudilainen, in press) are used, what should the test taker see? A hologram which shows body language? A still image of a speaker? Something else, and if so, what? Such questions must be answered as the field moves forward?

In the last chapter of Part III, *The effects of proficiency differences in pairs on Korean learners' speaking performance*, Shin uses multivariate generalizability theory to explore the differences of monologic and paired speaking tasks on heritage and non-heritage Korean language learners' test scores. He found that non-heritage language learners, when paired with highly proficient heritage language speakers, scored higher on paired tasks than expected (based on their scores on the individual task), particularly on the subconstruct of fluency. Other pairings between heritage and non-heritage learners did not lead to significant score impacts across the two tasks. Shin's research leads him to question whether fluency can be conceptualized in the same way for the two task types. This suggests a need for research on the use of different rating scales for judging fluency when paired or monologic tasks are used. The use of think alouds when raters are evaluating fluency for these two task types might be one fruitful avenue for untangling these effects. The research also raises questions about whether it is test taker performance or rater perception differences that lead to these score variations and the extent to which rater training could mitigate the effects. Research to explore these effects would also be enlightening.

A Few Final Thoughts

While the influence of Bachman's publications is obvious from the papers in this volume and in other writings, his influential teaching that has positively altered professional lives may not be so clear. We conclude this book with a few of our experiences of taking classes from Lyle and working with him on various research projects. Our aim is to demonstrate the positive impact he has had on our and many others' lives.

I (Gary) am reminded of a time when I was taking one of Lyle's classes. We were asked to go through some papers that discussed trait-based approaches to designing assessments. At that time, I did not see the point of including a construct definition and accompanying operationalized rating scales when rating speaking or writing. To me, it made more sense to simply create assessment tasks that mirrored the tasks in the target language use domain and then provide example performances of test takers who had abilities at each of the score levels of interest to train raters. I felt that having raters constantly referring to rating scales with operationally defined constructs made the rating task unnecessarily more complicated. Having read numerous articles and books that Bachman had written, I knew how he felt about this issue. Therefore, I spent a great deal of time preparing my arguments against a construct-based approach. At what I thought was an appropriate time during class, I raised my hand and offered all of the reasons I felt a construct was unnecessary. Lyle patiently listened to me, and then in less than 15 minutes thoroughly convinced me that I was wrong. This experience not only changed my thinking about constructs, but impressed on me how patiently and articulately adept Lyle is at explaining conceptually challenging information in a lucid manner. I remember thinking that I wanted to be able to explain such concepts to my students in a similar fashion, and I continue to try to emulate his ability to explain opaque ideas in a clear and patient fashion. Of course, this was not a unique experience. Many of us have had our thinking forever altered by Lyle's ability to explain his position in a lucid way.

Like Gary, my (Brent's) experience working with Lyle in the early 2000s was invaluable. Lyle not only espoused the three guiding principles of working with students outlined in his *Preface* to this book but demonstrated them in his actions. The two principles that were most relevant to me were to "always let your students know that they have your support and your respect," and "always let your students know that you care not only about their research, but also about them as individuals, as human beings." Lyle's commitment to these principles became evident to me when I made the decision to return to full-time work after finishing my coursework at UCLA. Lyle counseled me against it; however, he allowed me to make the decision on my own and supported me when I left UCLA. It did not take long for me to realize that working full-time while trying to complete my dissertation was not going to be easy. In fact, I spent three full spring quarters back in LA in the years that followed my departure, working on data analysis, writing a dissertation proposal and defending that, and then writing my dissertation. Throughout that process, Lyle was very supportive. At one point, I really had doubts about being able to finish my dissertation, but all it took was a phone call during which Lyle encouraged me to keep moving my work forward. If Lyle thought I could do it, then I became certain that I could. I was in my seventh year when I decided to return to UCLA and spend my fourth and final spring term working on and hopefully finishing my dissertation. At that point, I had not seen Lyle for over a year and was wondering if he still believed I could finish. When we met outside his office, he greeted me with an embrace and said to me, "Brent, I feel like the father of the prodigal son, welcoming him back home." Through those words and that action, Lyle demonstrated that he cared about me not only as a language testing researcher, but also as a human being.

When I (Gary) was trying to decide where to study for a Ph.D., I spent many hours researching and even traveling thousands of miles to visit schools. While I knew that I wanted to study assessment, I was not sure if I would focus on language assessment or assessment more broadly. I had narrowed my options down to three universities, one of which was UCLA. I went to a conference that was also attended by some of Bachman's doctoral students. I made an effort to speak with each of them about their experience at UCLA. All were very positive about studying there, but one of them told me something that would have a huge impact on my decision. He told me to attend sessions presented by UCLA doctoral students, who were advised by Bachman, and compare their presentations to those of other doctoral students who were presenting at the conference. After attending numerous presentations, some of which were given by UCLA doctoral students, my decision became an easy one. It was obvious to me that I wanted to be like the UCLA students. They appeared to be skilled with both qualitative and quantitative research methodology, able to discuss conceptually challenging information with seeming ease, and on the cutting edge of new conceptualizations of language assessment theory. Before I got on a plane after the conference, I sent an email to my wife asking her if she was okay about moving to Los Angeles. Fortunately, she was. A few years later after I had become a recent graduate of UCLA, I was asked by a highly sought after doctoral applicant if I would recommend studying with Lyle at UCLA. I didn't need to say much; I simply gave him the same advice I had been given. He must have been impressed by Lyle's influence on his students' presentations like I was because he authored one of the chapters in this book.

We have tried to follow much of what we learned from Lyle in our own teaching and advising of undergraduate and graduate students. For example, just as Lyle had weekly language assessment meetings with students to share their research ideas, practice conference presentations, and develop university-wide assessments, we are doing similar things in working with our students. In this way, Lyle's influence continues not only on us, another generation of language assessment researchers, but on the next generation of language assessment researchers as well. Thank you Lyle! We hope this book gives you a flavor of how much you have done to positively impact the profession of language assessment and many of the professionals in it.

References

Bachman, L. F. (1990). *Fundamental considerations in language testing*. Oxford: Oxford University Press.

Bachman, L. F. (2004). *Statistical analyses for language assessment*. Cambridge: Cambridge University Press.

Bachman, L. F., & Kunnan, A. J. (2005). *Statistical analysis for language assessment workbook*. Cambridge: Cambridge University Press.

Bachman, L. F., & Damböck, B. E. (2018). *Language assessment for classroom teachers*. New York, NY: Oxford University Press.

Bachman, L. F., & Palmer, A. S. (1996). *Language testing in practice*. Oxford: Oxford University Press.

Bachman, L. F., & Palmer, A. S. (2010). *Language assessment in practice*. Oxford: Oxford, U.K.

Dimova, S., Yan, X., & Ginther, A. (2020) *Local language testing: Design, implementation and development*. Routledge.

Nakatsuhara, F., Inoue, C., & Taylor, L. (in press). Comparing rating modes. Analysing live, audio, and video ratings of IELTS Speaking Test performances. *Language Assessment Quarterly*.

Ockey, G. J., & Chukharev-Hudilainen, E. (in press). Human vs computer partner in the paired oral discussion test. *Applied Linguistics*.

Ockey, G. J., Gu, L., & Keehner, M. (2017). Web-based virtual environments for facilitating assessment of L2 oral communication ability. *Language Assessment Quarterly, 14*(4), 346–359.

Ockey, G. J., Timpe-Laughlin, V., Davis, L., & Gu, L. (2019). Exploring the Potential of a Video-Mediated Interactive Speaking Assessment: Video-Mediated Interactive Speaking Assessment. *ETS Research Report Series*.

Van Moere, A. (2012). A psycholinguistic approach to oral language assessment. *Language Testing, 29*(3), 325–344.

Vikram R., Evanini, K., & Tsuprun, E. (2019), Beyond monologues: Automated processing of conversational speech. In K. Zechner and K. Evanini, (Eds.). *Automated speaking assessment: Using language technologies to score spontaneous speech*. Routledge-Taylor and Francis.

Index

CPSIA information can be obtained
at www.ICGtesting.com
Printed in the USA
LVHW082337021220
673288LV00001B/3

- get rid of blue lines
- key
- move text to next to bees
- make words clearer
- separate positive + negative
- by Dec 15